FIFTH-DIMENSIONAL
Soul
PSYCHOLOGY

VYWAMUS through DAVID K. MILLER

Other Publications by
David K. Miller

Print Books: Visit Our Online Bookstore www.LightTechnology.com
eBooks Available on Amazon, Apple iTunes, Google Play, and Barnes & Noble

FIFTH-DIMENSIONAL
Soul
PSYCHOLOGY

VYWAMUS THROUGH
DAVID K. MILLER

LIGHT
Technology
PUBLISHING

For more information about special discounts for bulk purchases, please contact Light Technology Publishing Special Sales at 1-800-450-0985 or publishing@LightTechnology.net.

ISBN-13: 978-1-62233-016-4
Published and printed in the United States of America by:

PO Box 3540
Flagstaff, AZ 86003
800-450-0985
www.LightTechnology.com

Contents

Dedication and Acknowledgments

I would like to dedicate this book to my wife, partner, and supporter, Gudrun Miller. Gudrun is also a soul psychologist and has integrated art therapy, life-between-lives therapy, and hypnotherapy into her longstanding psychotherapy practice.

I also want to thank Linda Abell for her editorial assistance in preparing this manuscript.

Preface

*T*have worked in the mental health, psychotherapy, and medical social work fields for more than thirty-five years. I have an extensive background in psychology and psychotherapy practices. Over that thirty-five-year period, I have worked in a psychiatric hospital, two rehabilitation centers, and three mental health clinics, and I've also been in private practice as a clinical social worker. Through these practices, I've gained great knowledge about the Western approach to psychotherapy and the psychological process.

At this point in my career, I am working exclusively in soul psychology work, and I have a practice that is focused on doing personalized readings, phone readings, and group healings, including using a specialized group method called the Talking Circle. This method is based on Native American healing techniques, but I have adapted it for modern Western use.

I've also done a broad range of studies in the psychology and psychotherapy fields. I have studied Gestalt therapy, psychoanalytical-oriented psychotherapy, and cognitive therapy, including a special anxiety disorder study. However, none of these methods seems to work in totality. Each method has great benefits, yet I've found that in many cases, even these highly advanced techniques do not work with patients who have difficult soul issues.

One of the most fascinating personality theorists I have studied is named Abraham Maslow. His work in the early 1950s and 1960s focused on the groundbreaking concept called self-actualization. He developed descriptions of patients who had self-actualization experiences in which they were able to connect with their higher soul energy. Maslow's work in higher consciousness set the basis for my future studies in soul psychology.

As a psychotherapist, I also have worked in the field of hypnotherapy and have been able to integrate the concepts of hypnotic trance work into psychotherapy. In my quest for a higher and more soul-integrated approach, I began my channeling career approximately eighteen years ago. It began with a fascination with trance work and my personal study of the field of Jewish mysticism known as the Kabbalah.

The Kabbalah is a mystical study that emphasizes three levels of self: lower, middle, and higher. The early Kabbalah masters were involved in connecting with their spirit guides and angelic guides using a methodology called automatic speaking. Over the years, I've developed this ability, and now I focus my psychotherapeutic energies in personal or psychic readings. Using this approach, I am able to gather information for my clients in an altered state also known as a light trance. In that light trance, I am able to gather information, ideas, and energies about the patient. This information and healing energy would not normally be available to me in the "regular" state of consciousness.

Since I began channeling, I've been able to put together and publish more than nine books, many of which are focused on different personal healing issues, including personal development, soul psychology, and planetary healing. I now have developed an international soul psychology practice, and I offer seminars and workshops dealing with personal planetary healing methodologies.

While using this channeling approach, I then began to channel a special soul psychologist or guided teacher. His name is Vywamus. This book is devoted to the techniques and information I have channeled over several years using Vywamus. I have divided the presentation of this book into several parts: The introduction was written in normal consciousness and reflects my view as a practicing psychotherapist; Part 1 contains directly channeled lectures from Vywamus, a spirit guide and teacher from the fifth dimension; Part 11 contains relevant lectures from other ascended masters related to the subject of soul psychology, which includes the Arcturians and Archangel Michael; and the final chapter is by Gudrun Miller, a practicing counselor, and discusses her experiences doing past-life and life-between-lives therapy.

David K. Miller
March 2013
Prescott, Arizona

Introduction

David K. Miller

*T*rance work — the state of going into a trance — in modern psychology is described as hypnosis or hypnotherapy. Hypnotherapy is the practice of using hypnosis for therapeutic purposes. Hypnosis has been used in modern psychotherapy, for example, for the treatment of weight loss, cigarette smoking cessation, and many anxiety disorders.

Perhaps one of the most famous and successful modern therapists to explain and use hypnosis and hypnotherapy is Milton Erickson. Erickson was a well-known hypnotherapist who used the trance state for treating anxiety and other cognitive disorders. His theories and practices have made a deep and positive impact on modern psychotherapy. He helped develop the modern psychotherapy movement known as cognitive therapy.

Trance work has a direct relationship to channeling. A person who is channeling goes into an altered state of consciousness or a trance. The word "trance" can be described as a hypnotic state. The trance state has three levels: light, middle, and deep.

Most people do not realize that they often go into a light trance state while watching television, for example — especially sports events such as football. This is exhibited when someone talks to you while you are watching a football game and you may not hear or respond to them. Another example of being in a light trance state is driving on a freeway over long periods of time. Sometimes people don't realize that they've traveled thirty miles, and then they look at the sign to indicate that a great distance has transpired.

Three Trance States

Let's look at these three states — light, middle, and deep — from the aspect of trance and channeling work. The famous American channel Edgar Cayce exhibited the deep trance state. He was known as the Sleeping Prophet because he would actually go to sleep and then begin to channel. He would induce himself into a deep trance that would bring him into a deep sleep, and then he would begin to channel.

I think it is important to mention that Cayce did not remember anything that he channeled. In fact, much of the information that he channeled did not agree with his basic religious beliefs. For example, he did not consciously believe in the existence of the ancient civilization of Atlantis nor did he believe in reincarnation; yet in his deep trance state, he gave a great deal of information about these subjects.

A middle trance state can be described as someone allowing an energy or entity to take over the body and then the person beginning to channel or automatically speak. In the middle trance state, the person who is doing the channeling may or may not remember what is transpiring.

The light trance state is described as allowing an energy in or connecting with a higher energy but still remaining totally conscious. Also a light trance has been described as stepping aside and allowing the higher energy to come through you. This is probably the basis of some great artistic work in which artists feel that they are connecting with a higher energy that allows them new images. It is probably also the basis of the inspiration of musicians and composers and perhaps even scientists, such as Einstein, who received deep insights in a seemingly altered state.

The Trance State in Soul Psychology

In soul psychology, we use the trance state in two ways. The first way is the therapist being willing to go into a trance state to access higher information for the client. This is a novel idea because, in most traditional hypnotherapy sessions, therapists put the clients in the trance state rather than the therapists themselves going into the trance state. There is a concept in soul psychology known as resonance. This states that when the therapist goes into a trance state, sometimes the client will, by complimentary vibrations, also go into a state of altered consciousness.

I want to describe an Ericksonian technique in trance work called anchoring, and I want to describe how this applies to helping the therapist go into a trance state immediately. Milton Erickson described a situation in which one can go into a deep altered state of consciousness in which there are many pleasant things. For example, a patient can visualize a pleasant vacation while sitting in a deep meditation. The patient can experience the remembrance of this vacation visualization and then use a technique known as anchoring. The anchor can be an action such as pinching the cheek, tapping the shoulder, or tapping the forehead.

When a person is in a deep meditation with a positive visualization, during that meditation, the patient can anchor or link the visualization with a kinesthetic feeling through a tapping or pinching type of motion. There are other types of objects or behaviors that can also be used for anchoring. At a later time, the person can recall or re-create the feeling of the meditation through the anchoring.

This technique is especially useful in treating anxiety patients. When patients are facing anxiety-inducing situations, they can anchor — tap the forehead or pinch the cheek. This would remind them of a pleasant sensation or experience that they had earlier when they were not feeling anxiety. This would help them diminish their anxiety immediately.

As a practicing soul therapist, I use anchoring to help me get into a deeper, or more immediate, state of trance with my clients. I often say that it may take thirty minutes to get into a deep meditation in which I can access higher energy and go into a trance state. In working with a patient, this is a long time. So in order to bring myself quickly into an altered state, I use the anchoring technique.

I link my conscious state to an earlier state of deep meditation when I could access higher energies. I use a sound for anchoring: a chime. I strike the chime three times, and afterward I chant the word *Shalom* three times. This helps to trigger, or anchor, the earlier higher state of consciousness that I wish to use in the current therapeutic situation. Anchoring is an important tool to use not only for the patient but also for the therapist — especially the soul psychologist who wants to go into altered states of consciousness. Going into a trance state is helpful when the therapist does psychic readings, past-life readings, or any other type of review of a person's energy fields.

It is clear that soul psychologists are interested in altered states of consciousness and will use tools such as the anchoring technique to put themselves into altered states of consciousness. Soul psychologists are also interested in helping patients go into altered states of consciousness. It is important to note that when a therapist goes into an altered state of consciousness, the therapist's ego is removed or out of the way, allowing more direct communication with the spirit world.

Another important concept of soul psychology has to do with accessing guides and teachers. A soul psychologist wishes to access guides and teachers of the patient. One of the key ideas is that before the actual session or reading begins, the soul psychologist asks the patient to give permission for the soul psychologist's guides to access the guides and teachers of the patient. This suggests that the soul psychologist has the ability to connect with the client's guides and teachers and, furthermore, that the soul psychologist's guides and teachers can then access the guides and teachers of the client with whom he or she is working. The purpose for this is to bring forth higher energy and higher information. I think it is appropriate for the soul psychologist to ask permission from the client to allow his or her guides to contact the patient's guides.

Past-Life Therapy

Another important issue in soul psychology is accessing past lives. As stated previously, Edgar Cayce brought through a great deal of information in altered states of consciousness about past lives and karma. It is clear that he did not believe in past lives or karma in his waking consciousness, but in his altered state he brought through much information about this subject. Soul psychologists can access and use the information from past lives in several ways.

First, the soul psychologist can do what I call a psychic reading in which he or she connects with the guides and the information from the patient and gets information directly about the person's past lives. Cayce described different aspects of and reasons for karma in past lives; for example, sometimes people must come into a life and experience a certain disability or problem due to events and transactions from past lives that were not positive. Another example would be that if someone was critical with a particular race and was prejudiced in a past life, then sometimes that person would come back in a future life exactly as that race of which he or she was critical. Karmic lessons can be complicated to understand.

From my position, I also note that karma can come from what I call "cosmic sources" — that is to say, there are other planets in our galaxy in which some of us have been living, and the karma we are experiencing may be coming from other planetary systems besides Earth.

Other aspects of past-life therapy are called life-between-lives therapy, past-life regressive therapy, or past-life regression. Past-life regression refers to the fact that the therapist will put the patient in a trance state and help that patient remember past lives. Life-between-lives therapy is a technique in which a therapist brings patients to a state of consciousness in which they remember their experiences and conversations with their guides and teachers in between lives.

The theory and belief behind these methods is that there is a council of elders who works with people before they come into this lifetime. The council is composed of higher guides and teachers who discuss how you've done in past lives and what lessons and information you are going to learn in this lifetime. In life-between-lives therapy, it is highly useful for patients to talk to their guides and teachers in order to get information about a better overview of what they are supposed to do in this lifetime, what they are supposed to learn, and how they are doing in their life lessons.

Past-life and life-between-lives therapies are some of the tools for the soul psychologist. Other tools include the ability to go into a light, middle, or deep trance state and to use the concept of altered states of consciousness as well as concepts such as anchoring that are found in modern-day hypnotic therapy techniques.

PART I

LECTURES BY VYWAMUS
ON
SOUL PSYCHOLOGY

Soul Evolution

Vywamus

Vywamus is an ascended spiritual teacher and healer who helps lightworkers awaken their inner power and spiritual gifts, discover their life purposes, and face their shadows as a way of illuminating them. Vywamus also helps with all aspects of emotional, mental, physical, and spiritual healing.

halom, Shalom, Shalom. Greetings. I'm Vywamus. I'm a soul psychologist. In this series of lectures, we will explore the meaning of soul psychology and how it relates to modern psychology. More importantly, we will show how soul psychology as a practice is becoming more popular and is an especially useful technique for starseeds and others who are awakening to the fact that there is reincarnation and that there are soul lessons that must be learned.

The basic essence of soul psychology rests with the idea that the soul is evolving and that part of this evolution is occurring through incarnations on the third dimension. Now, to even speak about the soul evolving is perhaps a controversial subject because we know that the soul is eternal. We know that the soul has been in existence for infinity, and we know that the soul is perfect. So why would the soul have to evolve?

The answer to this question is complex, and we may not be able to totally answer it using third-dimensional terminology. But it is an important question to answer, because the nature of soul evolution is inherently connected to your experiences on the third dimension. The soul, in completing its evolutionary journey, needs these experiences on the third dimension, and it needs to complete the lessons here.

I can tell you that, from my perspective as a soul psychologist, one of the traits, one of the skills, that the perfect soul needs lies in its ability to manifest a third-dimensional incarnation and to complete the lessons in that incarnation. The soul's need to complete the third-dimensional incarnational cycle and learn its lessons can be compared to the Creator, the Creator energy, and the purpose of creation. The Creator has manifested the third dimension, and it is the will and wish of the Creator that this third dimension manifest. It is the wish of the soul that you manifest a third-dimensional incarnational cycle.

So what I'm suggesting is that when you look at the universe, when you look at the world, when you look at life on Earth, you will conclude that life is manifested by the Creator. Now, you might say that the Creator is perfect, which is a logical assumption in most theologies and most philosophies. Yet you could look at the world, at your life, at life on this planet, and at your history, and you might conclude — or you might observe — that there are things that are not perfect.

You might conclude that there are many imperfections in the world. You could point to war, famine, and destruction from volcanoes and storms. You could point to global shifts in temperatures and asteroids striking the planet and destroying it. There are many things you could point to that would indicate that there are many imperfections and many tragedies in this third-dimensional world that the Creator has manifested.

But remember that it is a basic tenet, a basic idea, of soul psychology that you are only experiencing one part of your entire self here on the third dimension. In other words, the self is greater than what you manifest on the third dimension. There is a greater self that includes the supermind, which is to say, there is also a greater soul, and you are only experiencing a section of the whole — although a very important section of your soul — in your third-dimensional existence.

You do not have all the information on your soul history in third-dimensional consciousness. One of the other important ideas of soul psychology is this: Making sense of an Earth lifetime, making sense of the third-dimensional reality, requires more soul information and a higher perspective. And when you obtain a higher perspective, many things that look illogical, contracted, or without purpose actually appear differently from that higher perspective.

The Greater Purpose

An asteroid hitting a planet and causing some destruction may have a greater purpose. For example, the dinosaurs dominated Earth for many millions of years. They had total control and were the rulers of this planet, but their rule ended after a meteor strike that occurred on the Yucatán Peninsula in Mexico.

This "tragic" strike of a meteor on Earth changed the conditions on the planet and allowed for the emergence of other life forms that, eventually, would allow humans to exist and to thrive. But to make that determination or judgment that the asteroid had a greater purpose, you would need to have a longer, higher perspective of the history of Earth. So it is with soul psychology and your incarnations on Earth.

In order to make a definitive evaluation of your life and what is happening, you need to have more information — more actual, historical information about your lifetimes. This is why one of the important aspects of soul psychology is gaining the higher perspective of the self, of the soul. Such tools as past-life regression therapy, life-between-lives therapy, and soul retrieval become important.

In fact, soul retrieval, as we know it in soul psychology, can be defined as obtaining or reintegrating higher parts of your self that were frozen or, for one reason or another, were not carried through from previous lifetimes. So what I'm suggesting is that the soul is perfect and that your perspective determines how easily you can understand that. The higher your perspective, the greater your opportunity to realize the perfection of this experience and your soul journey. I suggest you compare the manifestation of your third-dimensional existence to the fact that the Creator manifested this existence also, and your soul development is in line with the will of the Creator who manifested this third dimension. There is a perfection in your whole soul journey, and you will, as you study soul psychology, understand your own soul issues.

The Cosmic Aspect of Your Soul's History

Some important aspects of soul psychology are understanding the nature of the soul, the soul's perspective, the history of your soul, and your different incarnations. Now, what is particularly important is that there is a cosmic aspect of the soul history. So when we say that we are working with understanding the soul lessons, we understand the soul lessons from the Earth perspective and also from the cosmic perspective. "Cosmic" refers to the experience of having soul incarnations on other planets in the universe.

Remember that not all souls have had cosmic experiences, and some souls have only had Earth experiences. You could say that all the souls were created at the same time and that all the souls are eternal. This is a true statement, but the souls also manifest into different dimensions and different planets at different times. And the only thing I can compare this to is the birth of stars. All the matter for this universe was created at the same moment, yet some stars were born while others waited and are born at a later date. So from this perspective, there are older souls and younger souls. The older souls are those souls who have been on Earth for many lifetimes, but many of the older souls have also been on other planets.

These are exciting times on Earth for a soul psychologist. These are exciting times for those people who wish to explore the nature of their souls. Starseeds can now realize that they have had experiences on another planet, in another part of the galaxy, or even in another galaxy. This is a sure sign that you are an older soul, and there are many older souls — many starseeds — who are now awakening to their soul histories.

Awakening to Your Soul Journey through Psychology

There are several interventions in soul psychology that will help you awaken to your soul history. Soul psychology is based on the self, just like modern psychology. But you know that modern psychology is not able to solve or help everyone. In fact, modern psychology has become sidetracked by the biochemical issues in the body.

People are now coming back and understanding that chemicals and drugs are not the breakthroughs that everybody thought. That's because people incorrectly thought that a lot of the discontent and a lot of the mood issues were related to biochemical problems, but a lot of these biochemical problems are created by environmental pollutants that are distorting cell structure. So modern psychology and psychiatry are now treating problems that are created by pollution.

Soul History and Soul Lessons

I will address some of these mental health issues. I'm only pointing that out at this moment to make it clear that modern psychology is not able to solve many difficulties with people because, for the most part, it doesn't have the soul perspective. Now, there have been some exceptions because a few modern psychologists have looked at the soul. Carl Jung, for example, looked into the nature of the deep unconscious and the soul. But even these approaches, such as Jungian psychology, still have not taken into consideration the soul history for treating mental illness.

When you speak about soul history, you also are speaking directly about soul lessons. The basic hypothesis of soul psychology focuses on your soul lessons. The soul psychologist tries to help the patient understand that he or she is evolving and that there are certain things that he or she needs to do and learn here on the third dimension. This perspective becomes a healing one, and it helps to set up a whole healing energy for the patient that was not previously available.

Now I want to point out that the soul carries imprints of all previous incarnations. Those imprints are carried in the supermind and often will manifest in a lifetime. So the problems, issues, and lessons there that were not completed in a previous existence are carried over through imprints into this lifetime. There are both positive and negative aspects of that, but actually, from the soul perspective, it is all positive.

The best example we like to use is somebody like Mozart, who brought in with his soul the great imprints from his previous lifetimes — especially his previous lifetimes on other planets where he was a great musician — and he was able to achieve fantastic musical accomplishments starting at a very young age. He had the whole musical soul imprint available to him.

There are other examples of people who come into this lifetime and have great genius. They are able to function far beyond their normal Earth experiences. There are examples of soul histories emerging all the time. So it's really not that controversial. It's really not that unknown. But the other side — or the negative side — is that, just as Mozart could come in with all of his knowledge and experiences, another person who has had blocks in other lifetimes could manifest those blocks with the same strength as the positive energies of Mozart.

People will readily admit to having a strong musical background from another lifetime or what can be called the Mozart connection. On the other hand, they might have a hard time admitting their blocks are from other lifetimes. From the soul psychology perspective, those blocks are probably based on past-life experiences. The emergence of the blocks in this lifetime could be considered a positive development from the soul psychology view. Nothing is more important to the soul than removing the blocks that are emerging, especially if they are blocks from other lifetimes.

Therefore, from the perspective of soul psychology, we have a good opportunity for evolution when the blocks emerge. Blocks present very good opportunities for growth and learning. The perspective of soul psychology and working with blocks encourages the study of the nature and the history of the soul and past soul experiences on both this planet and other planets. Having information from these past-life experiences can help you grasp and understand the blocks that are manifesting in this lifetime. You can then more easily and with more understanding take the opportunities to resolve these issues.

A Great Opportunity

I am very fond of saying that many souls line up to come to Earth — even you. Many of you will say that Earth is a hard place to live, but from our perspective, these souls are coming here because there is something special about this opportunity to be here for soul development. This is especially true because Earth is known as a freewill zone. A freewill zone means there are greater choices. When there are greater choices, there are opportunities to make greater advancements.

One favorite example is that we know there have been many women who, in previous lifetimes on Earth, were dominated by men and by a strong male culture. They were not able to pursue their own individuality or their own spirituality. Now, in this lifetime, they are able to manifest great freedom to pursue their spirituality. But at the same time, they may feel confused because they feel as though they don't belong to any one group. They don't feel as though they belong to any group, any religion, or any structure. The soul psychologist will point out to them, "You were dominated and controlled by other groups in previous lifetimes; therefore, in this lifetime, you need to experience the freedom."

What I'm suggesting is that sometimes the soul wants freedom. Yet, paradoxically, when the soul finally gets the freedom, it may have difficulty, discomfort, and anxiety about how to deal with it. Then the soul psychologist points out to this person that he or she needs to experience the confusion, and even emptiness, from having no structure imposed on him or her. Thus, having freedom is exactly what you need to experience, and it's not a fault or weakness that you don't feel like you belong to anyone. You have to look at the freedom and the problems that come with it as a positive opportunity for your soul development.

Sometimes having freedom in choosing relationships can be a soul lesson. Sometimes people need to have freedom. So the perspective of the relationship becomes very important in processing this. Sometimes it's important to learn to accept the freedom. Having freedom to choose who you marry, for example, can be a challenge, but having that freedom of spirit in this lifetime is also wonderful.

There are souls now that are awakening in male-dominated cultures, and they need to have their freedom, but they cannot have it now because of their situation in the male-dominated cultures. However, there still are things they can do in that situation for soul evolvement.

So this is the basic groundwork. This is a basic approach. The soul psychologist then will attempt to help the person obtain past-life information and to develop a soul history. This can help a person identify and learn the soul lessons in this lifetime.

There are various tools that are available to do this, as I have described, including past-life regressions, life-between-lives readings, and direct psychic readings. Some therapists and some soul psychologists are able to perceive the issues in the soul from other lifetimes through psychic readings. They are able to tell the person what these issues are through psychic channeling.

That information and knowledge can help in the healing process. You have to understand that there can be resistance to learning the lessons. Becoming aware of the soul history is part of the healing, but awareness alone does not always solve the problems. Awareness sets the stage for the healing to begin.

I am Vywamus. Good day.

The Nature of the Soul

Vywamus

*S*halom, *Shalom*, *Shalom*. Greetings. This is Vywamus, a soul psychologist. The nature of the soul is infinite. The soul is multidimensional. The soul can have multiple incarnations in a given period of time, which from the third dimension, would seem to be simultaneous.

The soul has a journey. This journey is related directly to the concept of incarnations and reincarnations. Incarnations can be defined as the process whereby the soul manifests itself into the third dimension. This is considered a contraction of its true nature because the soul, by manifesting into a lower dimension, loses some of its inherent abilities.

For example, the soul is infinite and eternal, yet when it manifests in an incarnation of the third dimension, the experience is that of limitation and finiteness. This means the soul is moving its consciousness and its energy into an incarnation in which it is experiencing a limitation. Why would the soul want to experience such a limitation? If the true nature of the soul were infinite and eternal, then what would be the purpose of the experience of an incarnation?

When we look at incarnations, we see (from a higher perspective) that the soul has a progression — that is, the soul has a pattern of incarnations. It is difficult to see that pattern unless you are looking at it from a higher perspective. The pattern of incarnations could be, for example, that you incarnate as a spiritual master or as a spiritual teacher. You could incarnate as a scientist in multiple incarnations. You could incarnate into the realm of music or into the role of a composer.

Why Incarnate?

The reasons why the soul incarnates into a limited third-dimensional body are several. First, the soul exists as part of the group. The soul does not exist individually. However, there are aberrant cases in which souls have been removed from family groups. Some of these souls can be considered lost souls. The lost soul that does incarnate without a connection to the soul group often can be doing dangerous and evil things.

In understanding why the soul incarnates, we have come to the point of understanding that the soul exists in groups. The group helps make decisions about the experiences that are necessary for the group growth, the group expansion, and the group energy.

In fact, the nature of the soul can be described in terms of the group hierarchy. When you look at higher souls and higher spirits, such as Jesus (Sananda), you are actually looking at the soul group that he represents. There was a group of twelve Apostles around Jesus. These were all part of his soul group. There was a greater soul group that was above him that also was working with him.

The soul group has a purpose and a lesson. These are related directly to the third dimension. The soul group, these family groups, have become intensely interested in the third dimension. The third dimension has been manifested for a specific process, for specific learning, and this learning has to do with the energies that are inherent to the third dimension. Those energies are the energies of separateness and a lack of unity.

You might ask, "What is there that the soul would want to learn that could be contained in a dimension in which there is an illusion of separateness?" The answer is that the soul families are intensely curious and intensely expansive. It is clear why, from the analogy that I am going to offer, it would be interesting and necessary for the soul to have this experience on this dimension. The best analogy that I can give to you is the analogy of the fish in water. The fish does not know it is in the water; it doesn't know that it needs the water until it is out of water, and then it realizes that it is missing something that has separated from itself or from its process.

The soul is in a similar environment — especially in the soul group and in the nature of the soul existence; that is, it is experiencing the unity and experiencing oneness. The curiosity of the soul and the expansive energy of the soul "push out" so that it can have the experience of separation to process and understand what it is experiencing continually.

You would not be surprised to learn that when you return to the soul group, for the most part, people there don't want to leave that soul energy. This is only for those who are in the higher evolvement. Many of you have had to be talked into returning to the third dimension. Many of you reluctantly left the comfort of this unity. You can also understand this concept because, in many of the religions and in meditations, you often hear that you are going to return home, that when you leave this body, you are returning to a place of great unity and great connection to your soul family.

I would like to mention that there are experiences and there are times when people have been cut off from their soul families or when they cannot find their soul families, and part of the incarnational process focuses on helping them to rediscover the nature of their soul families and where their soul families are.

There is no question that when you come down to the third dimension and are coming into an experience of separateness and duality, you are faced with the idea of losing your connection and losing the awareness of who you are. You could lose the awareness of the unity that is part of your identity. It is a soul lesson that when you elevate your individuality and elevate yourself on the third dimension, the unity that you can experience increases when you return to your soul family.

When you elevate yourself on the third dimension, you are able to bring a vast experience to your soul family. You can look at your experience on Earth as a journey for the soul group. In other words, your soul group does not (for the most part) manifest at the same time on the planet in one unit.

This is the same concept as the twin flame. As people have been looking for their twin flames in the third dimension, the truth is that the twin flame usually will not manifest at the same time. Your twin flame, which is like your soul brother or sister, will stay on the other side while you are here doing the work, experiencing the duality and the separation.

We want to also speak about the important concept of why people are so eager to incarnate on Earth. What it is about the Earth experience that is so special? And why do the soul groups encourage their family groups to come to Earth? The answer lies in the nature of the Earth experience, and this will become clearer when we speak about Earth as a special planet.

Earth Is a Freewill Zone

The intense soul experiences increase when there is a planetary experience that can be defined as a freewill zone. The freewill zone is a place where there is ultimate freedom. There is freedom of choice. There is freedom from determinism. When there is such freedom, the soul has greater opportunities to experience higher experiences, higher unity, and can bring back more powerful information and lessons to its soul family.

Earth is a freewill zone. The special nature of this freewill zone is quite unique in terms of what is available. Earth has an extremely high population for a planet. Its population is well over 7 billion. Most of the other planetary systems, even in this galaxy, are well below that figure. One planet might have 3–5 million beings, and some planets have 10 million, but it is unusual to find a planet that has so many souls on it as Earth. Because of the number of people on Earth, the opportunity for different experiences and different choices dramatically increases.

The incarnations can be within a planet, but they also can be in a cosmic incarnation. The cosmic incarnation means that the person is able to incarnate on different planets in different places in the galaxy. Therefore, the person is not limited to just Earth.

There are great advantages to incarnating on different planets. It can be helpful in terms of the soul progression and soul lessons that you need to learn. You have to always remember that there are specific optimum circumstances that are necessary for your next incarnation. If you are limited only to Earth, then sometimes you have to wait centuries for the right circumstances to occur. This is especially true when Earth has had periods of highs and lows, such as periods of enlightenment and periods of darkness.

Sometimes is it is necessary to reincarnate with certain soul groups. You want to incarnate with certain energy. I have used the example of the Atlanteans and the scientists there. Many of them are reincarnated here in Western culture. Now on Earth, they have looked for situations in which they can learn similar soul lessons again. Those soul lessons might be what to do with your military and scientific knowledge. One such soul lesson for them is this: Do you use your scientific knowledge for military purposes, and if so, how does that affect you?

I think that the one obvious answer or example lies in the history of some of the famous scientists of this twentieth century, including Einstein. These modern scientists were advanced beings in previous lifetimes. Einstein was also in the Atlantean times. Could a scientist who lived in Atlantis now use his powers and energy for the production of nuclear bombs that ultimately could lead to the destruction of the planet? To find the right incarnational experience in which that lesson could be learned, he had to wait for a time period on Earth when sufficient technological advancements existed to offer the same opportunities and the same lessons.

So if Atlantis existed from 10,000 to 15,000 BC, that means that someone would have to wait many centuries in order to find that similar experience. At the same time, there are thousands of other third-dimensional planets in the galaxy, and some are also offering the same possible experience.

If you could have the same possible experience on another planet outside of Earth, then you would not have to wait, and you might decide to go to a cosmic incarnation. Not everyone has cosmic incarnations, though. To be able to

cross-fertilize yourself on other planets indicates a higher level of soul development. You have called those who have incarnated to other planets "starseeds,"
and this is a good description. That is a good opportunity for people.

The fact is that not all of the planets have the free will or the same number
of opportunities as Earth. Earth has hundreds of religions and hundreds of languages; therefore, there are great opportunities in the Earth experience. Most
other planets only have one or maybe two religions. It is unusual for a planet
to have so many religions as one finds on Earth. Having many religions offers
the expansiveness of free will. You have the opportunity to experience different
religious or spiritual energies.

Reincarnating with Soul Groups

I want to return to the concept of the group and the group family. You see evidence of this continually on Earth because there are examples of soul groups
who have incarnated on Earth and try to bring others into their soul groups.

People try to convert others and get them to commit to joining the soul
group. That commitment carries itself until death. Those who commit agree to
allow their souls to join the soul group in a specific place in the galaxy.

There are examples of teachers or gurus who are trying to increase their
soul group power by bringing people into their soul group energy. The Rev-
erend Moon has sought to do this and has been successful. You might ask, "Is
this good, or is this bad?" I do not really make a judgment on that. I can only
tell you that each group has its own branch. Some people are really lost. As
I said at the beginning of this lecture, there are lost souls, and it is probably
better to be in a soul group than to be lost.

Many people are incarnating on Earth because they believe that they can reat-
tach themselves to a soul group. There would be greater hope that the soul groups
could unify more if there weren't so much separation. You've seen from your experiences on Earth that a lot of these groups believe that they have the only truth, the
only answer. They want to strengthen their energy and soul group.

Cosmic Drama

There is also soul energy leftover from earlier conflicts in the galaxy. You've
heard stories about the Lyrans; you've heard stories about other constellations
that have planetary systems. There were large wars and destruction of some
civilizations. The battles and conflicts that you see on this Earth are remnants
and leftovers from some of the earlier battles in the galaxy. These battles and
energies of conflict have been carried over to Earth, especially as you see conflict among groups.

These conflicts contribute to what I call the cosmic drama. The cosmic drama of Earth is how the differences in the soul groups can be worked out so that there is a greater harmony on Earth. Some of you are watching this drama; some of you are not really becoming attached to it.

There is a core soul group that we call the ascension group. They are seeking to transcend a lot of these differences. They want to move themselves up to higher energies, and they are working for unity.

There are massive karmic events of soul groups that have been transferred as an entire group onto Earth. You may see large groups of people in certain sections of the world, and you may see certain destructions or genocides of these groups. Often, these groups have coalesced and come in as one group to experience that particular energy.

All this may seem confusing, but just remember that when you consider this concept of cosmic karma, you have to understand that there are many different planets and there have been many different experiences over the millennia. Earth is offering such a unique opportunity to work out and experience some of the lessons that have not been resolved on other planets.

This is the reason I speak of cosmic karma. I think that the concept explains some of the unthinkable, unsolvable, and unreasonable events that are occurring on this planet. Even on a planetary basis, sometimes planets or whole groups of planets will reincarnate together on a planet. So there are thousands of soul groups that are now incarnating on to this planet.

I am Vywamus. Good day.

Enlightenment

Vywamus

*S*halom, *Shalom, Shalom*. Greetings. I'm Vywamus. I'm a soul psychologist. Everybody is so worried about soul development. I think that's a good thing to worry about. I think that one of the great missions in this lifetime is to get to know your soul. What a great focus it is to connect and learn about your soul! Your soul has incarnated in so many lifetimes. Your soul is an eternal spiritual being. You can access your soul history through past-life regressions; inner life journeying; between-life, after-life, or before-life regressions; and regressions in this lifetime.

It is a great journey to discover the depth of your soul. The soul is so extensive that it's hard to comprehend in one lifetime who you really are. Yes, you have an inclination of who you are. You have a sense of your soul history, and as each of you grows in this lifetime, you're beginning to have a sense of your soul mission. The greatest thing you can do for your development is integrate your soul, your soul light, and your soul energy into this lifetime and begin to express and share your soul presence.

The more you share your soul presence, the more fifth dimensional you're going to become and the more you'll feel like you're enlightened. I like that word "enlighten" because, to me, it means that you carry more light. The idea of enlightenment might be reserved for those who are able to study meditation for many years. They say, for example, that you can meditate for twenty years and will maybe achieve enlightenment. Sometimes, if you can meditate continually for three weeks, maybe you can become enlightened then. There is no guarantee. That system of attaining enlightenment through meditation has a certain structure.

Your Spiritual Life Quotient

I'm suggesting that connecting with your soul in this time is so powerful that the experience can open you up to a similar experience of enlightenment. I'm suggesting that you have the abilities now to become enlightened. Let us look at the idea of the spiritual life quotient, or the light energy that you carry in your aura. Your spiritual life quotient is accumulative. It's accumulative in the lessons and the spiritual energy that you've gathered in this lifetime. It accumulates from your past lifetimes with the energy and the work that you've done in those past lifetimes. It is accumulative at this point on Earth.

There are points of acceleration for soul dynamics and soul evolution. There are points in a lifetime and in the incarnation cycle when there are great possibilities for accelerated soul work and soul advancement. There are special opportunities for coming into union with your soul and for getting to know who you really are. So when you reach an era of resonance for your soul work, you will incarnate in that time.

I know that you may have a million questions about your soul. You may have numerous doubts about what is going on and whether you have finished with all of your soul lessons. All of the doubts about your soul work usually come from your lower self. Bless your lower self, love your lower self, but don't let it be in the driver's seat. You're looking at a planet that is out of control with lower-self energy, and you do not want to participate in that lack of control. The beauty is that staying connected to your soul energy will protect you and also lead you on the right path for your soul evolution.

Contraction and Expansion

People frequently ask me this question: "Vywamus, why does the soul have to evolve?" The answer is paradoxical. The soul is expanding itself through the interaction with other dimensions. Expansion is the basic law of the universe and of the spirit. You have contraction, and you have expansion. If you expand too fast, then you have to contract until you can grasp and hold the energy, and then you can expand again. So we could define this planet and the energy of the third dimension as both a contraction and an expansion. That is polarity. That is the polarization that you all see.

Now, some people will say that contraction is bad, and to that, I'm just saying *no*. The contraction needs to be understood as part of the process, which includes both expansion and contraction. The idea from the soul level is that you don't stay in the state of contraction but allow it to progress and try to accelerate so that you can move out of the contraction, and then you can continue to expand again. This is the cycle. You are in a cycle here where both contraction and expansion are occurring simultaneously.

You have seen so much contraction on Earth recently. You have seen contraction in the political world. You have seen it in the economic world. There are many places where there is contraction, but unbelievable expansions are also going on. You are part of the spiritual expansion energy, and now it is affecting your personal development.

Now I am asking you this question: How do you feel being part of these spiritual expansions among all the contractions that you see? How are the political and economic contractions affecting you?

I feel gratitude. Gratitude.

I see — gratitude for being here watching the expansion and the contraction and how that is affecting you and your soul development? You're expressing gratitude. I like that. That's a nice answer.

Motivation to do more.

Motivation to do more service?

Yes.

Service is the quickest way to connect to the fifth dimension. The service is golden, and in time, certain periods there are various levels of service, but the highest level is doing the service without expecting any type of reward. Certainly, though, doing service and receiving a reward is still acceptable because, ultimately, the higher energies in the universe and the galaxy are in service to the Creator, and they are helping the starseeds' spirits — such as those on Earth — elevate themselves. This means there are many beings who want to see Earth successfully become elevated. You who are doing service are helping to purify yourselves, and this service is helping to accelerate your karma so that you are closer to completing the graduation of Earth.

Graduation, Ascension, and Grace

Everybody wants to graduate as soon as possible, but some people want to graduate without completing the courses. Some people want to graduate and escape a grade thinking that they can just buy the access. Remember, if you escape or skip a grade (for example, if you skip the eleventh grade and go from tenth to twelfth), then you have to work harder in the top grade. But it's great to skip grades. I think that there is nothing wrong with skipping grades, but just remember that you are here on Earth to graduate. You want to finish your Earth lessons. I know that everyone might not complete the lessons before the ascension, but I also know that there is grace, which grants the right to ascend.

Grace is like a service award, because this ascension process is going to be a unifying spiritual opening for millions, and when you go through the ascension process, you will be offered grace.

How many people feel that they have completed all their Earth lessons? How many people think that they will be able to complete their lessons by the end of this year?

You who raised your hand: Could you tell us about that?

It's a feeling that so much is ready to change. We are learning so much. It seems to be that everything is accelerating by the end of the year.

So you are optimistic that at the end of the year you will be able to learn all of the lessons you came here to learn?

I believe so. Well, I don't know whether I will by the end of the year, but what I mean is that it is time for us to complete our lessons before the planetary ascension.

I think that's beautiful. It's a beautiful thought, a beautiful statement about your faith in yourself, and I think that statement also shows a lot of love for yourself and commitment. That is beautiful.

Dealing with the Ego

I would love not to come back. I am ready. I feel ready, but I'm not sure whether my soul has finished all of my Earth lessons.

Well, you have to make a distinction between the Earth self and the soul, and that's a high distinction because you identify with who you are based on this Earth self. So, generally, people don't usually identify themselves with their souls. It is hard to identify with your soul because you are not trained to do so. You are not trained to expand and adapt your Earth self with your soul. The way you are trained is to identify with your ego, or the self. The self can be beautiful, but the self can also be neurotic.

You are trained to believe that the Earth self is all that you are, but you are also this greater self. You are this beautiful presence, and you have the ability to do great healings. You have the ability to work on fifth-dimensional light, and you have great psychic powers. Try to begin to separate the programmed self — which refers to your ego and Earth self — from the higher soul self. Do you think that you can do that? Do you feel that you are making progress?

Yes.

Good. Would you say you are 50 percent, 60 percent, or 100 percent there?

Seventy percent there.

Seventy percent there. That's pretty encouraging, isn't it? So tell me about yourself.

I believe that my soul self has really chosen hard lessons here, and I've grown a lot, so that's why I think I'm at about 70 percent.
   So how do you deal with your ego?

I keep reaching for more soul knowledge.
   One thing about ego: The ego believes that you never have enough money; you never have enough accomplishments. You never have enough whatever. So if you are going on a path that says you are waiting until the ego tells you that now you have reached a point where you have enough, then you are going to wait for a long time.

I feel myself separating from things that are on Earth, even from my family. I am really reaching for higher consciousness. It makes me feel free. That is the feeling I have. I really have no interest in the news. I do not watch TV; I think that's not important, and I'm not worried about it, either. I think this is a shift in me.
   Good, all that sounds very positive. I congratulate you. As I was listening to you, I was reminded that I want to speak a little bit about what relationship you should have to the programmed self, because we call the ego the programmed self. We want to separate or detach from the Earth self, but what kind of relationship are we going with the Earth self when we separate? Are we going to separate in joy? Are we going to separate in respect? Are we going to separate in mutual understanding? Because your relationship to your ego is still an important part to your ascension process. It may seem surprising when you realize that your relationship with your ego is an important part of your ascension work. What kind of relationship do you think you have to have with the ego to help your ascension?

Continue with your work being in joy. You need to continue working joyfully.
   So working will be joyful, okay. Any other responses?

Another participant: I think a lot of it has to do more with deprogramming.
   You should have the proper perspective on the ego because, honestly, you need the ego to function on this reality. It is almost impossible to be egoless. There are people who have achieved the state of egolessness, and they are special earthly and loving people, but generally, when you are trying to function on this planet, you need some kind of defense. You need some kind of ego. So yes, I agree that you have to have a positive relationship with the ego, but also

the ego can become an enemy if it gets out of control. Look at the emotional age of the people who are running this planet. We would say that many of the leaders on this planet are at a very low age emotionally. There a lot of "babies" running this planet. Many of the world leaders are looking for control and are unhappy when they can't stay in control.

We are all human, and we have to recognize that we are human. What does it mean to be human? Because there are different levels of being human. One level that we are talking about is being on the higher consciousness. This includes the higher consciousness of evolving, the higher consciousness of uniting with the spirit of this Earth, and the higher consciousness of uniting with other dimensions. Many people call higher consciousness an altered state of consciousness.

We can compare the programmed self to the higher self. The higher self is the more natural state. Higher consciousness is more of who you really are. It is the part of you that is connected to your soul. Your job is to connect and let that part of you come through on this planet. When you are able to do that, then you are powerful, you are brilliant, you are beautiful, and you will naturally fulfill your soul mission.

Thank you. Are there other conditions about the ego?

Well, there are many conditions, or states, of the ego. I could write a book about the many conditions of the ego, and you would be fascinated and also shocked at the level of programmable ego actions. The biggest conflict in ego programs emerges from that side of the self that has been invaded through television and advertisements. You have been bombarded with many programs through the media.

It's not so simple to be on this planet. There is a lot of competition for your consciousness. Isn't it interesting how there are so many influences on your level of consciousness? Actually, it is the level of consciousness and the freedom of consciousness that is so attractive to being here on Earth. It's unprecedented to have this level of freedom of consciousness. People say that Earth is a freewill zone, and I speak about that often. But the free will is expressed in how you think and what you choose to maintain in your consciousness. You can choose how to use your consciousness. People will die for that right to experience spiritual consciousness, religious consciousness, or political consciousness. The final frontier of your consciousness, and the next evolutionary step in humanity, is the expansion of consciousness to the fifth dimension. There will come a time in the future when the fifth dimension and mass consciousness will be friends and will be united.

Blessings to you all. I am Vywamus. Good day.

Earth Soul Evolution and
Earth Incarnational Cycles

Vywamus

reetings! I am Vywamus, a soul psychologist. In soul psychology, we understand that the soul is evolving and that part of the evolution of the soul occurs through a third-dimensional manifested existence. We understand that to complete a cycle of soul progress, it is necessary to complete an incarnational cycle on Earth or an incarnational cycle of third-dimensional existence on another planet.

This idea of completing the Earth incarnational cycle also is referred to as graduation from Earth. Graduation from Earth means you will not need to return to the third dimension. Remember that the third dimension is a place of duality and polarization, but it is also a place where you can experience unity. In fact, one of the higher healings that can occur on Earth is the ability to unify dualities. This ability to unify dualities also includes the ability to unify dualities within the self. It involves unifying dualities within the ego and other aspects that manifest in your third-dimensional existence.

Karmic and Cosmic Justice

So let us understand that usually the soul cannot complete all of its lessons in one lifetime. There are examples, some of them extraordinary, of certain high beings who have been able to come to Earth to learn and evolve in one lifetime. But for most people, it usually takes many lifetimes. Sometimes it can take 100 or 200 lifetimes. I think it is also interesting that, if you have to repeat many lifetimes, then that sometimes means you are "a slow learner." At other times, it may mean that there are many opportunities and you really want to study a lesson to make sure you understand all aspects of it.

There is no judgment if you have to repeat lessons. For example, if you are in high school and you fail, then you have to repeat the year, and many look down on that. In soul journeys, sometimes, because of the nature of certain actions, your progress could be thrown back, and you could go back into lower soul manifestations. An example of that might be that somebody who committed a heinous crime on Earth in an incarnation might find him- or herself going backward to a much lower level of existence in another lifetime. For example, the person might come back to experience being a victim of crimes in a follow-up lifetime.

All of these effects imply some interesting rules and regulations that are occurring in the soul history and the soul journey. For example, we need to use new terms such as "karmic justice." In fact, we can even talk about cosmic justice. Karmic justice has to do with what is traditionally known by the phrase "what you reap is what you sow." So if you are hurting people in one lifetime, in another lifetime, you could receive some type of punishment for that. I want to see that the soul is very wise, and the soul will look to manifest the right circumstances for the lessons you need to learn.

Sometimes soul lessons can occur in the same culture that you grew up in or in the same culture that you experienced in a previous lifetime. In other experiences, it may be that you have to wait several lifetimes and go into a different culture. But the soul is multidimensional and multi-wise, and it has the ability to understand an entire lifetime before you even manifest in that lifetime. That is pretty extraordinary. So that means that the soul will know the people, the circumstances, and many of the outcomes of the experiences that you will have. But everything is not totally cast in stone because, remember, there is free will. So there can be differences and intervening variables in each lifetime. The soul often chooses which people you need for your soul lessons.

From a higher perspective, I can say that the soul will reincarnate into situations, into cultures, and into circumstances that will provide you with the right interactions and the right people to learn the necessary lessons. Sometimes those people may seem to be causing you problems, and sometimes they may be acting impolitely or cruelly to you. Sometimes those lessons are based on some very difficult circumstances that those whom you are meeting can provide you. But from the soul psychology perspective, the actions of those around you, as uncomfortable as they may be, are helping to provide you part of the soul lesson. For example, you may need to learn how to free yourself from domineering men, from domineering women, or from abusive relationships. These lessons are important for your soul because they are connected with self-esteem.

So you could find that in a lifetime you are experiencing those types of relationships I have just described, and you would find yourself in a great deal of discomfort and unhappiness. But those circumstances and relationships are most likely part of a learning process. It is difficult because sometimes the lesson is complicated. Sometimes the lesson has to do with learning what it is like to be in an abusive relationship, and that might be because, in a previous lifetime, you were abusive. Sometimes the lesson may be that you've had a series of dominating relationships in many lifetimes, and therefore, you need to figure out how to free yourself from that pattern.

Understanding from a Higher Perspective

It is difficult to totally understand all aspects of the soul lessons without gaining the higher perspective and without relating to the soul history. In one aspect, as I said, it may be that you have to, in one sense, be punished so that you can understand what it is like to receive abuse. On the other hand, you might be in the difficult relationship because you have to learn how to free yourself from it. Or the lessons could be both of those circumstances. Truly, it is amazing that the soul knows how to help you incarnate into the right circumstances so that you will get the right experiences for your soul lesson.

Sometimes it can take many years; sometimes the soul has to wait lifetimes for the right circumstances for the exact lesson. Sometimes the lesson happens right away. Many people ask me, "Vywamus, why did I incarnate with these parents?" or "Why do I have to have this brother?" or "Why am I having these earlier traumas in my lifetime — at the beginning of my lifetime?" Part of the answer is that the soul is unable to find the right circumstances immediately. It is not always a perfect adjustment. It is not always a perfect fit. The reason is that there are many intervening variables, many different souls, many different circumstances, and of course, much free will.

Soul placement is not an exact science, which means that the soul looks for the best possible circumstances to emerge. When those right circumstances emerge that have the highest probability of giving you the soul lessons you need, you take that opportunity. One reason why this time (2013) is such a powerful experience is that the opportunities for intense soul lessons are high.

In 2013, there was a tremendous amount of freedom and interactions because of global communications and also because there are dramatic Earth changes occurring. When there are dramatic Earth changes, there are always great opportunities for soul lessons. When we are talking about the now, we have to talk about the ascension and the possibility that some soul lessons can be accelerated. Now, what do I mean by that?

You know that sometimes it may take three, four, or even ten lifetimes to learn a certain lesson. Sometimes people actually incarnate to do what I call a "glide through" of a lifetime. That means that they don't really want to do a lot of work, and perhaps they have done a lot of work in other lifetimes. So they just want to experience what it's like to be alive, to not have a lot of stress, and to just be unimportant. It could be that one person could have been a king in one lifetime and had a lot of responsibility and didn't have time for himself. Then you might find that in the next lifetime, instead of being the king, that soul wanted to just be unimportant, unnoticed, and have time to be alone and contemplate reality and life.

Setting Up and Resolving the Lessons

So then, how do you experience and resolve lessons your soul set up or that your soul wants to learn? You might think that you come into a lifetime and immediately learn the lesson because all of the circumstances are there — so then you automatically learn all the lessons. But you know, even from your own experience, that it is very difficult to learn and resolve issues. Think of all the psychological problems and all the stress people are having. Think of all the illnesses and all the wars that people are fighting and all the struggles going on. This is not a harmonious planet.

This is not a place where people are being born and living in harmony with everyone. In fact, it is exactly the opposite. This is a planet where there is an unbelievable amount of conflict and an unbelievable amount of struggle. I can tell you that many people now on Earth are going through their life lessons. Some are not resolving their soul issues and so are setting themselves up to repeat the circumstances. Jokingly, I have said, "Well, if it is too difficult for you to resolve your soul lessons now, then would you feel more comfortable coming back another thirty years from now?" I say this because, thirty years from now, Earth isn't going to be as easy to live on as it is right now. "Would you like to come back fifty years from now, or would you like to come back at all?" Many people tell me they don't want to come back to Earth. I say, "Well, okay, if you don't want to come back to Earth, then let's learn your soul lessons."

Then the person will say, "Okay, well, what lessons do I have to learn?"

Then we can do a soul reading, and say, "Well, there are three or four lessons that you have to learn. And if you want to accelerate your progress, you can have all these lessons come forward into three years."

Everybody will say, "Yes, that's great!" But these are difficult lessons, and the people say that it is too much for them. But in an accelerated time, we say that it is a great gift that you can have the opportunity to resolve three or four soul lessons in one lifetime.

Physical Lessons and Problems

I also want to say something about physical illnesses and physical problems because many people are experiencing a great number of physical problems. They are asking, "What is the karmic lesson? Why do I have fibromyalgia?" or "Why did I have a stroke?" or "Why am I suffering from this paralysis?" or "Why do I have physical illness?"

There is no one simple answer. Even Edgar Cayce pointed out that some people experience an illness because, in a previous lifetime, they were critical of other people who had the same illness and now they have to experience it to see what it's like. Or sometimes it is a punishment. You might find that somebody was a warrior in a previous lifetime and caused a great deal of harm, and that person may come back incapacitated. This might be partly karmic because the warrior incapacitated many other people in his or her previous life. Now that person is going to learn about that through his or her own incapacitation or illness.

Unpredicted Lessons

I call some lessons "unpredicted." Remember, I said that the soul is not able to predict 100 percent of the circumstances of all the energies that are going to happen, so sometimes there are unforeseen events — unforeseen circumstances. Sometimes these events can happen accidentally. Sometimes they are not meaningful in terms of the whole soul lesson, and the person just has to say, "Well, this is really not important" and then just adjust to it. Remember that the body is a coat, and you're going to take off that coat — the body — when you leave. This is not your final destination. This is not your final home. Your body is not your final home.

Other times, there are serious lessons with the illnesses. Some have to do with not overly identifying with the body so that you will not accept that you are your body. One lesson is that, if you have illnesses, then you think that your soul is ill — that your higher self is ill. The lesson could be to *not* do that.

Some great, enlightened people on the planet have shared their enlightenment despite experiencing some pretty severe illnesses or difficulties. Stephen Hawking is one name that comes to mind. Here is a physicist who, despite having a severe physical illness that's left him totally paralyzed, is still able to complete his soul mission. It is a demonstration that, in many cases, the soul lessons and the soul work can be accomplished without total physical health.

The Ego and the Defense Systems

I also want to look at the ego and the defense systems because there is resistance to learning soul lessons, and this resistance is important to understand. The third dimension is dense. By "dense" I mean that you don't have easy access to your higher self and the higher soul information. The soul does manifest in the third dimension through the higher self, but the self must have an ego to function.

Now, the ego is developed based on rules and regulations of the culture and society in which you live. This means that such things as self-centeredness, selfishness, and relating to groups are all fashioned by the culture and society you live in. So you may be living in a primitive culture that has lots of group energy, and your sense of self may be totally connected to your soul family, to sharing, and to not having possessions.

But most Western societies are the exact opposite. The people are trained into a culture of having individual identities and possessions. One result of capitalism is that it divides people; it separates them more. There is a necessity for possession and self-worth or success in a society that is based on possessions. Now, I'm not criticizing this, and I'm not suggesting that everyone should become socialists, because there are problems in socialism too. Socialism puts the responsibility on the group, so if there is an imbalance of too much sharing, then it could move the person away from individual responsibility.

Yourself and Society

You can see that how you develop is a result of the society in which you grow up. Also, that society in which you are now growing up often is not spiritually minded. That is, this current Western society is not open to past lives. It is not open to higher soul context. It is not open to the higher dimensions. It is not open to the ascension.

Certainly, people are not trained as children for this. People are not raised to answer the question, "What is my soul lesson in this lifetime?" On other higher planets, soul lessons are an immediate concern. It is a concern of the parents; it is concern of the elders: "What did this person come into this lifetime to learn?" Once that is discovered, in a higher society, they try to provide the right circumstances and direct the person into what is necessary and to train that person for his or her soul lessons.

So, for example, if you knew that one of your soul lessons was to avoid being involved in abusive relationships, then it would be helpful to have this information when you were very young. Then when you are growing up, you could be trained to recognize it and not fall into that pattern. That approach to childhood education would be a sign of an advanced society. Certainly this type of education and preparation is possible. But in this society, and I am speaking generally of the Western society, you do not have that luxury. In fact, it is exactly the opposite because the soul memories are repressed, and the soul information is repressed. Therefore, you often have to experience the negative pattern that is part of your soul lesson. You experience the pattern with the lack of awareness, and you could easily just end up experiencing the pain. Then you must seek some kind of assistance, either from your higher self or from other people, to help you understand that this was your soul lesson. You must find the knowledge and tools to resolve the problem and learn from it.

Working with Resistance and Defenses

I want to say that resistance often is fierce. The defenses are fierce, and people sometimes need to be prodded because you know that when people are resistant, generally they don't want to learn. Some people give up. That is permissible, but just remember that if you avoid your soul problem, then you will have to come back to another lifetime. I know many people just don't want to come back, so then the question is: "How can I learn the soul lesson now?"

We need to develop ways as soul psychologists to get around the resistance, and sometimes we prod people through humor or through a confrontation. For example, we can, with humor, suggest to them that if they choose to avoid the problem, then they may have to experience the same problem in several more future lifetimes. Generally, we also try to be compassionate and let them know that this society and the circumstances in it are not always conducive to soul lessons. The societies are also improving. Witness the overwhelming interest in modern psychology worldwide. This is an indication that people do want to learn and need assistance. In summary, the soul psychologist will use these tools, which include accessing the higher self, discussing soul lessons, trying to help people learn what their soul lessons are in this lifetime, and encouraging them to resolve those through various techniques.

I want to emphasize that the soul knows what the soul lesson is in every lifetime and how to manifest the family that would be the most beneficial. Also, there is a great inclination to incarnate with those people who are going to provide the right circumstances for soul advancement. So sometimes people are reincarnating with the same problematic people again until they learn to break the bonds of abusive relationships.

Now, there are also good sides to this because sometimes you are incarnating with people who are going to help you grow. Sometimes you are incarnating so that you can be with a certain leader or certain spiritual person. So soul lessons are not always defined as negative things that you have to overcome, because the soul lessons can be positive things. And this is clear when you think that sometimes people incarnate to be with a certain spiritual person or to be with a group that will provide them certain spiritual opportunities.

Positive Soul Lessons

One of the hardest things in the third dimension is to live without that unity feeling, to live in separation. But that is the basic mode of how this dimension operates so that you do not experience the unity but you experience yourself as separate. That also is a challenge and can be tormenting. The lack of the unity feeling can lead to lack of faith, doubt of the higher reality, or even doubt of the higher self.

Sometimes people incarnate just to learn that lesson: how to overcome the division, the polarization. But the higher self is set up to unify. One goal from the soul psychology perspective is that you are here to unify yourself and to do so with all past lives and present lives because this could be a unification of your traits and your higher skills.

I want to emphasize that the soul lessons are not always phrased as negative problems, because sometimes the soul lesson is to be the spiritual person you are. Sometimes the soul lesson is to manifest spiritual harmony in other people. Sometimes the soul lesson is to be a planetary healer. Sometimes the soul lesson is to provide great music to people. For some, it is to provide words of wisdom through writing. Please understand that these soul lessons are also couched in very positive dynamics. Believe it or not, sometimes the soul lesson is here just to help other people. Sometimes people have come back just to be of service to other people. We have worked with people who are caregivers, for example, and are coming back mainly to be of service to one or two other people. This is fulfilling a soul promise.

Unifying the Multidimensional Self

I also want to point out the idea of the higher self in soul psychology. I want to compare that to the idea of a pie. Think of the higher self as the center, and there are maybe one hundred slices in the pie. Each slice in the pie represents a different part of your higher self from a different lifetime. In any one lifetime, you could unify yourself. You could say, "Well, I have been a shaman in one lifetime, and I've been a warrior in another lifetime. I've been a rabbi in another lifetime, and I've been a priest. And, you know, I've been a man, and I've been a woman." So there are all these different parts that the soul has manifested in Earth lifetimes because the soul wants to experience all aspects that are possible in the self in the third dimension.

From the soul psychology perspective, we are saying that one of the goals of any lifetime is to unify all of these aspects. You can understand that you are multidimensional, and because of upcoming opportunities, we can say that this pie is also a multidimensional pie. You even have other aspects of your higher self that are in other dimensions and on other planetary systems.

The unity of your higher self is now being expanded. The opportunities for the unity of the self include these other aspects of your higher self in other dimensions. This is one of the main things that starseeds want to experience. It is a great opportunity now on Earth to be able to experience the unities of the higher self on Earth and in Earth incarnations and to help unify the other parts of the higher self that are multidimensional in other areas of the galaxy or the universe.

This awareness of the multidimensional self is a huge evolutionary leap in the consciousness of humanity and in the development of the higher self. It is true that you give up the body when you leave Earth. You take off the coat of the body, but you don't give up the higher self. That is an illusion because the higher self that you have is imprinted and carried with you. So all of the information from this lifetime is processed — including all of the information you are gathering, all of the experiences you are gathering, and all of the people you are meeting. This is all processed and is part of your learning experience. You will experience this through the life review at the moment of your transition from Earth.

The life review is the ability to go through all of your experiences and see what it is that you are here to learn. One of my favorite comments is, "Why not do the life review now? Why do you have to wait until the three seconds before your death to do the life review?" Incidentally, this is another powerful technique that a soul psychologist will use: to encourage people to do their life reviews before they die. You can do the life review before you die and when you are seriously ill, before you face your death. You do not have to wait till that moment when you are facing your death to do the life review. Your soul psychologist can help you do it and let that life review help you answer the questions regarding your soul lessons in this lifetime.

I am Vywamus. Good day.

Soul Psychology and the Ascension

Vywamus

*S*halom, *Shalom, Shalom.* Greetings. This is Vywamus. We will now look at the relationship of soul psychology to the ascension. The idea of ascension focuses on being able to complete your Earth incarnational cycle and move into a higher dimension. In the ascension, you are relieved of all future Earth karma and all third-dimensional Earth karma. You are then able to move into your fifth-dimensional self without having to return for any reason to the third dimension, unless you decide you want to return as an ascended master to provide assistance to Earth.

Moving into your fifth-dimensional self is key to understanding soul psychology and its relationship to the ascension. There is an acceleration of psychological development that is necessary for everyone who wants to ascend. It is a mistake to think that people will just ascend without doing any type of preparation. It is a mistake to say that you could ascend without doing continual work on yourself. In fact, it is exactly the opposite because when you are doing work on yourself, you are accelerating and preparing yourself for the ascension.

What is the nature of the work that you need to do on yourself, and how does that work that you do on yourself relate to soul psychology and the ascension? The work is based on one simple question: What Earth lessons do you have to learn in this lifetime? What lessons do you have to finish in your soul evolution as a third-dimensional being? The reason why you are here on the third dimension is to learn lessons. The only exceptions are the ascended masters who come here and want to provide service. For everyone else, you should understand that you are only here on Earth now because there are certain lessons that you need to learn.

Lessons to Learn

The lessons can be on a variety of different subjects or in different areas. You could have a lesson in relationships, or you could have a lesson in self-esteem. You could have a lesson involving greater expansion of consciousness and how to integrate that consciousness on the third dimension. Certainly, there are varied lessons that people come to Earth to learn.

In relating soul psychology to the ascension, you should ask another simple question: "What other lessons do I have to learn so that I can complete my soul karma on the third dimension?" Once your soul karma is completed on the third dimension, then you are prepared for your ascension. The guides have said, though, that it is not required that everyone be 100 percent cleared or have completed all their lessons. That is to say, you might have certain soul lessons, and maybe in this lifetime, you are doing soul psychology work, but you have only completed 80 percent of the lessons. (I'm using this as an example.) The fact is that your intention and your commitment to continue to work on these lessons counts because the ascension also includes grace.

Grace means that you are given advancement. It's like you are getting a bonus, a promotion. Any lessons or ideas that you were not able to completely integrate will not be held against you if you are working with the intention of completing those lessons before the ascension. This means that intention and commitment to work on your issues do count.

Using the Principles of Soul Psychology

Let us look again at the principles of soul psychology and how they can help you advance yourself. Soul psychology is really based on the idea that you are accessing fifth-dimensional energy and fifth-dimensional parts of yourself to accelerate your development on the third dimension. These various techniques can include past-life regression therapy, talking with your fifth-dimensional guides and teachers, life-between-lives therapy, advanced work in healing chambers (where you connect with your future self), and accessing parts of yourself from the past (which includes the technique of soul retrieval).

In all of these techniques, you seek to connect with a greater part of yourself, and you seek to bring that greater part of yourself into unity with this current self. This implies that you are reaching a point in your development where you can broaden your identity. You can make the statement or the affirmation that *you are more than just this Earth self and this Earth ego.*

It is important to understand that you do not want to reject this Earth ego; rather, we are saying that you are part of a greater self. Soul psychology is going to help you connect with your greater self. By connecting to your greater self, you can gain access to new energies that will help you accelerate your development on Earth. By accelerating your development on Earth, you are closer to completing your soul missions and your soul lessons; therefore, you are putting yourself into an excellent position to ascend.

I am Vywamus. Good day.

Soul Psychology and Planetary Healing

Vywamus

*S*halom, *Shalom, Shalom.* Greetings. I am Vywamus, a soul psychologist. We will be talking about soul psychology and planetary healing. People may be surprised to learn that there is a connection between soul psychology and planetary healing. Actually, the principles of individual psychology and ascension do relate to planetary healing and planetary ascension. One big reason for this is that some lessons that people have reincarnated to learn involve the practice of planetary healing. People have come to Earth with one of their soul lessons to become planetary healers.

Sometimes becoming a planetary healer in this lifetime is related to karmic lessons from the past. I will give you an example: Some starseeds were working on Atlantis, and they were involved in military and scientific development in that advanced civilization. The military and scientific developments that occurred led to the destruction of their civilization. Now people can reincarnate, and they may have highly advanced skills, either scientific skills or other planetary healing skills. They now can revaluate and use those skills for higher development and higher planetary purposes instead of military purposes.

Another example would be someone who was a planetary healer in a past lifetime but was prevented from doing that healing because of domination by a foreign culture. Many Native American Indians were great planetary healers and were helping to hold this planet in a very high vibration. However, they were dominated by Europeans, lost their planetary healing abilities, had to go underground, and weren't able to perform their planetary healing ceremonies.

The basic principle of planetary healing is closely related to personal healing. The idea of advanced personal healing lies in identification with your fifth-dimensional self and your ability to bring your fifth-dimensional self back into the third-dimensional self so that you can advance yourself. In planetary healing, we talk a lot about connecting with the fifth-dimensional Earth. We also talk about bringing the energy from the greater Earth into the third dimension. Planetary balance is also based on the principles of individual balance.

The individual balance comes from some healing techniques that have been described in Chinese medicine. These healing techniques include meridian balancing and keeping meridian pathways open. It is the same with the planet and planetary healing. The planet has pathways. The planet has meridians. The planetary healers want to apply these methodologies of balancing meridians to keep the planet in balance. Soul psychology, on a personal level, looks at individual health and how to keep the balance. Planetary healing uses the same principles of individual healing but applies those principles to a large planet.

I want to talk about planetary healing and the concept of a future self because the future self is an important concept in soul psychology. In soul psychology, we look at the greater self, and we say that the self is not linear. We say that the self is not just past, present, and future, that it is not in a line but rather is circular so that the past interacts with the present and the future interacts with the present.

It is the same with the planet. The planet's past interacts with its present, which you are now seeing in this accelerated time. The future of this planet is interacting in a very obvious way with the present. This is shown in the climate change issues. It is shown in nuclear radiation contamination and many other pollution issues in which the future of the planet is affecting the outcome of the present.

In soul psychology, we look at ways to bring future technology and the future self back into the present. In fact, there is a large group of people who feel that healing techniques and healing energy from the future are available now in the present for the planet. Also, there are future time travelers and future energies for the planet that people are trying to bring back into the present.

From the soul psychology perspective, this is very much in accordance with our principles. The basic principle is that the future self can interact with the present. The future of this planet can be energetically helpful if higher energy and higher connections are made through a more advanced future Earth. In essence, Earth will ascend. We must connect with this fifth-dimensional ascension energy for Earth to bring her into a higher balance.

I am Vywamus. Good day.

Soul Group Psychology

Vywamus

*S*halom, *Shalom, Shalom*. Greetings. I am Vywamus. I am a soul psychologist. We wish to explore in further detail the nature of the individual soul relationships to the group. It is interesting that many people feel that their souls are individual. They may be surprised to learn that their souls are parts of soul groups.

The analogy can be that of a tree: There are different trees that represent different types of souls in the universe. There are branches on the trees, and some of you have soul brothers and sisters who are on the same branch. Some of you relate to people who are part of the same tree.

The Adam Prototype

There are also different soul groups entirely. There are different soul groups representing different planetary systems. The main soul group name for Earth is the Adam soul group, the soul of Adam. This is the primary organizer and prototype for the incarnating spirits who have come and are coming to this planet.

The prototype of Adam is a fascinating and complex prototype. The soul prototype is able to receive incarnations from other planetary systems. It is a very flexible soul type. It is able to work with multiple incarnations — some of them even on a multidimensional basis. The Adam prototype has the inherent ability to ascend, meaning that it can bypass the death experience and elevate itself into the fifth dimension.

There are other prototypes that receive souls for incarnations throughout this galaxy. If I were to call the name of the tree of the predominant souls on Earth, I would call it the tree of Adam. There are also other trees that have come to Earth and other soul groups that have come to Earth, but the tree of Adam is the largest and accommodates the most variations.

Soul Groups and Packs

All souls belong to groups. This is similar to animals. I will use the example of the dog. Dogs have soul groups, which people generally find refreshing and comforting. They know that when the animal, their pet, moves on, it returns to its soul group. Dogs often have a high-vibrational existence with their owners, and then they return to their soul groups and share that information with the hope of raising the vibration of their soul families. Often you will hear the discussion of dogs being on this Earth and being part of a pack, for example. This is a reflection of their soul groups, their soul families, and their love and comfort in being part of their soul families. Of course, a dog can function individually, but dogs are happiest when they are in the pack and close to their soul family members. These are interesting facts for understanding the human soul because the human soul also likes being part of a pack.

There are many different groups within the Adam tree of life, which are reflected on Earth through the various religions and languages. Your soul group also exists on the higher plane, but many of your soul group members are also on this plane.

When I talk about soul groups, I have to talk about what I call closeness or affinity. Affinity means that there are other soul groups that are not exactly on the same branch as you, but they are close and they have an affinity toward your soul.

Often you can find that a soul group attracts other members or other people who are close to the branch but not exactly on the group's same branch. Examples of soul groups are seen all of the time on Earth. There are people coalescing or coming together in religious groups, and they frequently bond in other organizations such as political groups. There can be soul groups that come together for literature or movies.

Understand that some soul groups are higher and have a higher vibration than other soul groups. These soul groups that are higher often are accepting new members or are open to expanding their soul grouping. Sometimes people incarnate to be close to a soul group because that soul group is willing to work to expand and help raise the vibration of the other people.

Open to Your Soul Guides

We found that the existence of your soul group is more obvious when you go into higher states of consciousness. These higher states of consciousness include life-between-lives states, connection with the higher self, past-life regressions, and other such access to your soul information. When doing these exercises, you will immediately reach a point where you will be in touch with soul group members, including your guides and teachers.

It is possible that your guides and teachers are on higher levels (or dimensions), and when they are on higher dimensions, they are multidimensional. This means that they are able to participate in multiple energies and on multiple levels simultaneously. It is common for higher ascended masters to be a part of multiple soul groups and to be guides and teachers to multiple people. An example, of course, is Sananda, who is able to be a guide, a teacher, and a participant overall in soul groups throughout the planet. It would be very difficult (if not impossible in the physical reality) to count the number of soul groups that he is able to be a member of and to which he is able to provide guidance and be a soul guide. Certainly he is able to be a soul guide, but there are multiple other soul guides.

People on this Earth need great assistance. There are so many challenges and so many difficulties, and so much guidance is needed. I encourage people to open up to their soul guides.

Some of your soul guides may not be well known or may not be famous on this Earth. You may hear names that you have no recognition of. It is similar when you do past-life readings. Many people want to hear that they were part of Jesus's group in Galilee, yet that group was very small. Many psychics give readings saying, "You are the people who were there with Jesus and were with the Essenes." Of course there was a small group of people who were around him, but I want to point out that not everybody was able to be around him.

I also want to point out that it is not necessary that you work with just one family member or soul guide. Each person could have ten or twelve or even more guides. The guides know your soul history. They know why you came to Earth, and they are advising you. They are waiting to somehow contact you so that you can receive the information. It's always better to have more information about who you are and where you came from as well as to learn more about your soul family.

Healing and Separation

I want to speak about another aspect of the soul family, and this has to do with healing. Many of you are healers, and it so happens that your most effective healing often comes from those who are closest to you on the soul tree or on the same soul branch.

Don't expect to heal everyone. Be aware that there are certain people with whom you have special healing abilities and seemingly special healing powers, and these people are often part of your soul group.

I know that one of the big issues on Earth is being separate, the veil of separateness, which creates a great deal of anxiety and a great deal of discomfort.
It causes people to often feel lonely and disconnected. People need to learn
that everyone is part of a soul group.

Leaving a Soul Group

It is also true that some of you have actually left a soul group from a previous
lifetime and don't want to be associated with that soul group anymore. This
could be because the soul group was highly orthodox or highly rigid. Some
soul groups that incarnated on Earth may have been abusive to people and
controlling and even politically domineering. Sometimes people realize this in
their lifetimes and make decisions not to be part of that type of soul group in
this lifetime. Even though most of you have soul groups, there are these people
who have left soul groups and are open to aligning themselves with new soul
energy and new soul groups.

The idea of groups is part of the universe. The stars are in groups, the
planets are in groups, and the galaxies are in groups, and everything moves in
a system or group. It is only natural to find that souls are also in groups.

The other idea is that people want to think that their twin flames or their
closest soul members are on this planet at the same time. Generally, this does
not happen. It is rare for two people who are twin flames to incarnate together.
One will usually stay on the other side to help receive and monitor information.

I will stop for any comments or questions.

When you leave a soul group, how do you develop a new soul group?

When you leave a soul group, you usually make a decision to look at and
study other soul energies that are available. You then try to reach an incarnation in which you can be closer to that soul group and join. You feel the affinity.

It is harder to leave a rigid soul group because some of these soul groups
are very controlling. There are certain religious groups on the planet that want
to control your soul. For example, such groups might want to take you to
another planet when you die, and then you will be part of a hierarchy. Their
argument is that everything is preplanned. What is really happening is that
they are seeking to have you commit your soul to them after this life. Some
people realize that this is not good. This is a controlling thing because, basically, the nature of the soul is free.

The soul is a free spirit. The soul does not want to have that rigor or control. Control and rigor may be appropriate in some instances on this planet,
but it is usually not necessary on other planes. As I said, everyone of the Adam

species comes from the same tree, so you can still explore the tree and look for different branches.

Does the council that evaluates your life have any say, and if you are looking for a new group, will they help you find a new group?

The council can help you find a new group. The council does have a say, but remember that you also have free will and choice. The council will work with you, and the council will help you find the appropriate lifetime and appropriate place to incarnate. In this way, you will have the appropriate experiences through which you can meet new soul members or other soul members. Yes, the soul council is helpful and will do this for you.

The soul council is also involved in your dreams. Your guides and teachers are involved with helping to arrange things in your life. You'd be surprised to learn how much coordination is involved in one Earth lifetime.

I am Vywamus. Good day.

The Mission

Vywamus

ood day. I am Vywamus, a soul psychologist. We wish to discuss the personal mission that each of you has when you are incarnating on Earth. Humans have a great drive to find meaning and purpose in their lives. The worst and most unbearable idea is that your life has no meaning, no purpose. In reality, each person is contributing to the overall evolution of the planet, and everyone does have a contribution. The difficulty is when people try to measure their contributions compared to those of others; they compare themselves to others. For example, you can measure the work and the different accomplishments you achieve, and then in comparison, you might conclude that others might be seen to be doing more. Remember, more is not necessarily better.

Purpose and Mission

To understand the purpose and to work to bring yourself into greater clarity, it is important to explore and understand the ideas of purpose and mission. Without some understanding, without some grasp, you have feelings of being lost and of depression because you feel detached — like you don't belong. So the idea of having a purpose and a mission contributes to the idea of belonging.

One of the greatest punishments in ancient times was to be banished from one's tribe or group. In looking at missions and understanding them, you can find that there have been many lessons learned relating to being part of the group. For example, the past 2,000 to 3,000 — or even 5,000 — years have been a period of time that has often been dominated by male energies. The male energies have also sought to dominate spirituality. Women who have had spiritual insight or spiritual gifts were forced to keep those gifts silent or suppressed. In many cases when the women were unable to suppress the gifts and became more open, they risked being banished from the group, being punished, and sometimes actually being put to death. They could risk being put to death after false accusations such as being witches or being involved in lower-vibrational witchcraft.

To look at the soul mission, it is always helpful to look at past lives. If a woman had a past life in which she was forced to suppress her spiritual light and spiritual gifts, then often she will come back in another time and place where there is opportunity and freedom to express those soul gifts. This time on Earth offers many opportunities for freedom. This time on Earth offers many opportunities for women to freely express their spiritual wisdom and spiritual gifts. But I can also say that often women feel a self-imposed oppression. They may feel a discomfort in expressing their spiritual gifts, and part of this is remembering what happened in a previous lifetime.

For example, let's say that a woman was spiritually gifted and living during the Spanish Inquisition in Europe in the fifteenth century. Let us say that this woman had great spiritual understandings and great spiritual ideas. She saw a lot of the falsehoods that were being expressed at that time, and she began to express those observations. By doing this, she was endangering herself and her family. The family then exerted pressure on her to suppress her spirituality and psychic gifts. Now, she stopped this spiritual expression in that lifetime. Now, in her current lifetime, she notices something very interesting about spirituality: She never wants to express her spiritual ideas.

Once you open up to spirituality, psychic light, and spiritual gifts, it is almost impossible to go back and pretend you did not open up. So that means that the suppression of the spirituality in the case I'm describing becomes more painful and also life-threatening because the person is cut off from his or her energy source, gifts, and soul. They're also cut off from their mission because part of the mission of someone who has spiritual energy is to teach others. This was as true then as it is true today.

So that person may reincarnate in another place and time now in the twenty-first century, and the person will be working to uncover and to express his or her spiritual light and spiritual energy. So it is good for a person to know about the past life because that explains some of the hesitancy to become spiritual. It is an example of two things: an example of a mission and an example of how past lives can help you understand that mission.

Your Sphere of Influence

The mission can involve teaching, repair, and restoration. The overwhelming drive of the higher beings and the overwhelming healing for the entire planet depends on moving toward higher spiritual light and higher spiritual energy. This is a general mission statement and purpose for the whole planet, and it is a general mission statement for higher-minded individuals. So you have to understand that you are part of an energy force that seeks the raising of spiritual light and spiritual energy on the planet, and some of you now have the opportunity to teach that.

Others may find that they don't seem to be playing such a big role in the Earth drama. They feel confined to what they're doing, so maybe their sphere of influence is limited to just a few people. Therefore, they don't feel as deeply connected, and then they feel as if they don't have a big mission. This is not the correct interpretation.

It is important to look at many different aspects. You have to look at what was going on in the past lives. You must look at who you have an influence on now. Everyone has a unique sphere of influence, and each individual's unique sphere of influence is precious. So when you have a sphere of influence over a pet, over your parent, or over several friends, this sphere of influence becomes important. The idea is that the whole soul group of the planet is to move forward. There needs to be a core energy that moves the planet forward — that moves the species forward. And your sphere of influence, even if it is small, could be one of the major determining factors that adds enough energy to move the whole planet to a higher vibration.

So in speaking about mission, both personal and planetary, I ask that you look at your sphere of influence when you are trying to assess your missions. Don't measure or even try to calibrate your mission in terms of how many people you have to speak to or what large invention or political intervention you must perform. It is true that having a political intervention and influence on the lives of the people is good, but think of your mission and evaluate your success based on your sphere of influence, and then, when you become more comfortable, you will find that your sphere of influence can become larger.

Paradoxically, the first sphere of influence is yourself, so that means that one of the personal missions — and a very important one — is to influence yourself, to open yourself up to and bring yourself up to a higher light. In some cases, you may find that is the entire mission that you're going to be able to do on this planet. That is perfectly acceptable.

I'm thinking, in particular, of those people who have drug addictions and alcoholism and may appear to be (and in many cases are) wasting their energy and their spiritual light. Eventually, they will self-destruct. The self-destruction can affect other family members and people close to them. In most cases, people who have drug addictions and alcoholism had this problem in other lifetimes, and what you see in this lifetime is a continuation of that. It is true that they may have an extensive ability to influence others in this lifetime — that their sphere of influence in this lifetime is extensive, except on themselves. So they have come back in this lifetime in order to influence themselves and to heal themselves. This is a valid mission. It is a helpful lifetime when you are able to positively influence your higher self for growth.

When I look at the subject of spheres of influence, I can also say that some people have a greater sphere of influence than others. That is, some people's spheres of influence are enhanced. You, as a healer, can help people extend their spheres of influence. This is accomplished with humanitarian gestures through which people are helping others. For example, people can help introduce artists to greater audiences or introduce healers to a greater number of people. The higher your vibration, the higher your spiritual light energy becomes and the greater the sphere of influence you could have.

But then, of course, you could have the problem of dealing on an ego basis when your sphere of influence becomes large. You could develop an ego problem with it. This problem has been documented in the story of some of the yogis who moved from the East to the West and became famous, rich, and powerful. They struggled with how to deal with that level of sphere of influence.

In some cases, even though they have achieved a high level of spiritual energy, they become stuck at a level of ego, and that level of ego has to do with concepts of self-importance and abuse of personal power. You often see that some people who have created and attained a great spiritual light become withdrawn and more humble because they don't want to run into the problems of extended sphere of influence and ego problems. That usually indicates that they had some higher spiritual energy in other lifetimes and ran into those problems. So now they are learning their lessons.

Balance, Unity, and Nature of Self

One of the greatest ideas in understanding the personal and soul missions is the concept of balance. So if in one lifetime you were very rich and that prevented you from being spiritual, to counterbalance that you may decide to come back and be very poor — to learn whether that opposite energy will help you become spiritual. The soul psychologist wants to understand the sphere of influence and the balance. People then can think that part of understanding the personal mission in this lifetime is related to a balancing energy from other lifetimes, but it is also related to unifying the different components and the different energies of the higher self.

One of the personal missions becomes related to the holographic nature of the higher self. One personal mission is to unify all aspects of the higher self in harmony, and that could mean the aspect of the higher self that is a father or a healer, that is a spiritual teacher or a soul traveler. So a greater soul mission still can be defined in terms of the sphere of influence of the higher self and how one unifies the different parts of the higher self.

This concept related to ego development has even been described in modern psychology under the idea of the whole self, also called the gestalt. The idea is that there are other parts of the self that are disowned or not brought into consciousness. In this view, it is the conscious self in this lifetime that is being expressed in the world. However, there are different deeper levels of the self that go back into other lifetimes; therefore, the concept of the self in soul psychology has to be broadened to include the idea of the holographic nature of the self. This broadening will include using concepts to unify the self such as balancing, counterbalancing, and restoring parts of the self from this lifetime and from other lifetimes; extending the sphere of influence; and raising your energies in order to express your true nature.

I'm always fascinated by the concept of expressing your true nature. You can say that the overall goal from the perspective of the soul psychologist is to evaluate and see whether a person is expressing his or her true nature and what blocks or prevents that from happening.

One problem that emerges when talking about this concept of expressing your true nature is this question: What if your true nature is evil? What if your true nature is destructive? We have many examples of this on Earth — probably more than any of us wants to admit or acknowledge because, especially in the twentieth century, we have seen many destructive leaders. But in all centuries, there have been continual examples of people who have given full reign to their true natures, and their true natures happen to be very evil. At the same time, they have been able to extend their spheres of influence and spread their evilness. I cannot offer you a simpler explanation except to point out that in the third-dimensional world of free will, evilness can be expressed, and unfortunately people do exist who have evilness as part of their true natures.

Understanding Evil

We must look at the nature of reality and of the universe to understand evil. It is true that there have been other worlds before this one and that those worlds have ended because there was an imbalance. That is to say that the creation you see now is not the first Earth-like planet, nor is it the first third-dimensional planet.

On Earth, there is a balance of free will. One of the greatest beauties of Earth, from the soul perspective, is the existence of free will. That is why so many souls are attracted to coming here. So some people who have strong evil natures that seem out of control may have personal missions to learn how to control that evil tendency. It is unfortunate that they cannot control it and that they have the ability in a freewill planet to cause so much evil, hatred, and destruction.

It is also important for you to understand that everyone does have an evil impulse, so there is nobody who is totally pure. That is the nature of humanity's condition and the nature of the situation. So understanding evil means that you must understand that everything on the planet is a matter of degree, including the concepts of good and evil.

There are some people who have a lot of power, extended spheres of influence, and also aren't able to control their evilness. They are eventually going to have to control it on some level. But there are actually some souls who are so evil and so beyond repair that their souls could be extinguished. This is an interesting concept for soul psychology, the concept of extinguishing souls. In general, this means that when the souls are so far beyond any sense of repair because of their evilness, they just go back into the source energy.

The Overall Purpose

Even those people who have extended spheres of influence and have evil intention are serving some overall purpose and do affect people in some positive ways that promote soul growth. You know that there are people who have terrible things happen to them who become transformed. There are things that happen — such as car accidents or deaths of friends or any number of calamities or catastrophes that occur — and those events sometimes help people to positively restore their soul energy if they can survive. Some people want to have experiences of deprivation or poverty for their soul lessons. If there is too much wealth in one lifetime, the soul may decide to experience poverty in the next lifetime to help the balance.

I also want to speak of the planetary mission because when people are involved in planetary missions as many of you are, as many starseeds, it becomes an important discussion. I want to say that most of the starseeds are open and want to extend their spheres of influence to a planetary level. Earth now has tremendous opportunities available for people to positively extend their spheres of influence on a planetary level.

In earlier centuries, those who were going to have an influence on the planetary level, or on the larger level, really had to work hard. They really had to carry out some pretty amazing feats because there was not rapid communication or transportation. This time on the planet offers a great opportunity now for people who have the inclination to work on extending their spheres of influence. This ability is quite fascinating and remarkable. It was not possible 2,000 years ago to work globally as a planetary healer, but now, given mass communication and the Internet as well as the ability to travel, those starseeds who are so inclined do have the opportunity to extend their spheres of influence.

A Freewill Zone

The overall goal on this planet has to include the fact that this is a freewill zone. Soul psychologists need to incorporate this into their understanding of soul mission, soul purpose, restoration, and repair of this dimension. One reason why there is so much disrepair and chaos on this planet and in this dimension is because this is a freewill zone. Even those who are repressed by being in prison or by being in repressive societies still have the ability of free will. They still can choose many things about themselves and many of their actions.

The fact that this is a freewill zone explains why so many souls want to come to Earth now and why so many people incarnated on this planet and why so many souls want to continue to incarnate. It is well known that being on a planet that has a freewill zone offers the greatest opportunities for soul growth, because when you can choose certain actions, you can evolve much more.

If you have an evil impulse or a distorted desire to use drugs or alcohol and you come to this planet, then you will know that you have the choice whether to use those drugs and alcohol, and you will have the choice of whether or not to heal. Because this planet is set up as a freewill zone, there is more opportunity to repair the inclination toward acting out of uncontrolled lower vibrations.

I incorporate the knowledge of Earth being a freewill zone, and I use this fact to help people understand why they have come to the third-dimensional Earth and what the advantages are of being in a freewill zone. As I have explained, there are many advantages for soul advancement and soul growth here. Are there any questions?

What would a third-dimensional existence be like without free will?
A third-dimensional existence without free will is similar to that experienced by the aliens called the Grays. Everyone would be controlled, pretty much. It would be a place where everybody is just in line with the queen, so to speak, and there would be no individual trust. Everything would stay on the same level. Without free will in the third dimension, there would be no opportunity for soul evolution. However, there are opportunities for soul growth even in this experience. For example, I would say that some people who have been extremely evil end up incarnating on planets where they are under control and there is no free will. Such an experience can help them understand their evil inclinations, and they can learn to control their lower vibrations.

So having free will is like an opportunity for advancement. Some who come to this planet are experimenting with it, but others will bounce back into what is described as a third dimension without free will.

For what reason would a soul or being choose to have an incarnation on a planet without free will?

Let's just go back a second. Remember, there are soul guides and teachers, so it is not always the case that you are choosing your incarnations alone. Sometimes your guides and teachers are choosing for you. To be able to choose is a higher state of evolution, and that higher state of evolution is included in the Arcturian stargate, where you can choose where you will incarnate.

One primary idea in the stargate is that you go to this gateway where you can choose where you're going to go. Now, that is a privilege and a sign of higher soul evolution. But in the case of some of the lower beings to which we have just referred — especially where there's been a lot of evil — the soul would not be given the right to choose, and the guides and teachers in a life-between-lives situation would send the soul somewhere that they thought would be in its highest good.

So they would learn from that experience ultimately?

Yes, they would learn from that experience, but sometimes it takes a long time, and they will incarnate into lifetimes where they become like soldiers. Sometimes people reincarnate from those lifetimes and become cogs in the wheel of armies. They repeat the experience of being without consciousness and participate in some type of mass warfare.

So remember, look at the concepts of spheres of influence and the concepts of soul evolution in the context of Earth being a freewill zone.

This is Vywamus. Good day.

Finding and Learning Soul Lessons

Vywamus

*S*halom, *Shalom, Shalom*. Greetings. I am Vywamus, a soul psychologist. We would like to talk about soul psychology. As much as we talk about the higher energy levels and as much as we talk about the light, you still come back to many of the psychological problems that you have on the lower and middle soul levels. These are the problems you are wrestling with from day to day. Problems that elude you or that you don't want to recognize in yourself usually have spiritual significance.

In previous lifetimes, many of you have gone to higher energy states only to tumble down because you didn't work out these "minor" problems. At that time, you called them little blocks, and you didn't really think they were important. However, you found yourself in a rather embarrassing position — a position from which there was no way out. Then you lost the spiritual powers and the ability to vibrate on higher energy frequencies. That is why it is so important to work out these problems from the lower self now. Don't think that because it is a problem of the lower soul or the lower personality that it is not crucial. Don't think that the middle personality isn't important. These problems you are having — some of which are psychological problems — are important.

Now some questions come up: Why do these problems occur for people? Why are you having these life problems? What is their significance? Some say you wanted the problem in order to teach yourself a lesson. Wasn't that nice to offer yourself such a difficult lesson? Well, that is an interesting way to look at it. When you are in the middle of the lesson, it seems more difficult. You wish that you could terminate the lesson immediately. Actually, you can drop the lesson if you move and expand your consciousness. Then you can take the next growth step. When you expand your consciousness and recognize the necessary personal lesson, the problem and its significance will no longer dominate your life. When you recognize the personal lesson, the problem you are struggling with will take its proper perspective.

Your reaction to the problem is as important as the problem itself. Think about the number one problem in your life today. Right now, think of your reaction to it. Can you report what your reaction is to the problem? You now have had a chance to learn a great spiritual truth. You could be wiser and spiritually alive if you learned to solve this problem. What is your reaction? Are you open to solving this?

Many might be reluctant. It's true that you want to gain spiritual knowledge. You want access to higher knowledge. You want access to higher energies. Yet when it comes down to working on the personal problem, there is resistance. Why? The reason is that you are reluctant to go through a difficult experience. It is that reaction that is creating the resistance. On this plane, you know a lot about resistance. The resistance is self-generating. Resistance is like a snowball coming down a mountain, getting larger and larger.

Many psychologists have developed a great idea that has spiritual significance: To help people grow psychologically, you have to help them deal with resistance. What a beautiful thought!

Most of you did not want to come into this incarnation. You wanted to stay. It is like being in your mother's womb and then getting kicked out! Who wants to leave that comfortable place? You know that if you are too comfortable, then you don't grow, yet no one wants to leave that comfort. There is no guarantee that the comfort will continue forever. I have great respect and admiration for your courage to come back and deal with this incarnation to continue struggling with your soul problem.

I will say that there is an inverse law: The greater the reaction, the more important this problem is on your spiritual path. What a great indicator you have! I would guess that the problems you have are problems you don't want. Even though you know they have the potential to give you great spiritual gifts and great path openings, you still might not feel that it is worth the struggle you are going through.

You are back to the basic principle of belief systems and your mental body. This is the source of much of your conflict. You need to put yourself at peace with these problems. You can change them by working with your belief system. You can also open yourself up to what it is you need to learn.

I am going to share some common lessons you need to learn from your personal problems:

• Do not be attached to the outcome.

- You are not in control.
- Accept the truth of your body.
- Let go and trust.
- You will be guided to where you need to go with it.
- Have faith in yourself.

What beautiful lessons! If I told you that I had a group of people who were working on these lessons, wouldn't you be impressed? Wouldn't you think that they were highly evolved? So why aren't you impressed with yourselves? These are core soul issues on which you are working. You are right in there with the "meat and potatoes" of your spiritual growth.

Sometimes the resistance is easier to overcome when you can share it in a group and you are able to gain a different perspective on yourself and the problem. Then you will be pleased. You can accelerate the problem to a quicker conclusion. Being stuck simply means that there is no movement.

You Have Control

There are only two ways to get out of a problem: You change, or the people who are creating the problem change. You have control over yourself, over how you change and how you are interpreting the events. You have minor control over the other part. When you change, the energies interacting between the problem and you become different. How many of you believe that you can affect the outcome by your whole attitude, your perspective, and how you are thinking about the problem? Your thoughts can create possible outcomes. How many of you are focusing on negative outcomes? Don't be afraid to admit it. We won't hold it against you.

If I told you that focusing on negative outcomes increases the possibility that they will come true, would you still hold that focus? There is a way to work around the problem of negative thinking. You have to get a soul perspective on why you are in the situation and what the lesson is.

It would be a good idea to write down the lesson and post it on a wall so that you can look at it every day. Remind yourself of the lesson. You are in control of your reaction to the problem. Beliefs are that powerful. Beliefs are so powerful that they can even affect outcomes.

It is true that you are not in control of everything, but you are still a player in this, and you can have an effect on the outcome through your attitude. You know that people dying of cancer have miraculous remissions. That often occurs when they have changed their perspective.

You have come into this incarnation to work on these problems, and when you are able to state the lesson, then you are at least 50 percent of the way through the process. The next question is, what do you need to do to learn the lesson finally? The last word is so important: "finally." You probably had this problem in another lifetime, but you didn't learn it. Now you have another chance to do it. Let's finally do it.

If you cannot answer the question of what you finally need to do, then meditate on it. Your soul involvement is such that you want to solve this problem as soon as possible. It is possible to be done with it once you are able to learn the lesson. The whole problem might not go away, but you could find some remarkable relief. Your energy field around the problem will lessen, and you will be surprised by the amount of negative energy that will stop coming your way. Then you will have more energy to focus on spiritual work.

I am Vywamus. Good day.

Uncovering the Mystery of the Mental Body

Vywamus

reetings. I am Vywamus. As a soul psychologist, I am here to work with you on your mental body. I know that there are exercises for the physical body in which you build up your muscles. Many of you are worried about the condition of your physical bodies and how they look. You want to make sure that they have the right shape and so on. But how many of you are really paying attention to your mental bodies? Remember that you are not going to be able to take your physical bodies with you when you leave this planet. I always try to understand why people are so concerned about their physical bodies when they realize that they cannot take them with them. Your mental body, on the other hand, has a part that will go with you. So would it not make more sense to work intensely with the mental body? I have been asked today to talk to you about your mental body and help you to condition it so that you will be able to use it most effectively throughout the time that you are here on Earth.

How many people even think about exercising their mental bodies? The answer is not many people. So let us go into the roots of the mental body and how it works. This is not going to only be a "sit back and listen to Vywamus" time. This is going to also be a time when you will have to participate. You are going to have to do some work with me so that we can uncover together the mystery of the mental body.

The Power of Belief

The mental body is based on beliefs and thoughts, and beliefs and thoughts are powerful. Beliefs that one holds on to can totally change a person. For example, this channel knows of a man who was told that he had incurable brain cancer and had a given amount of time to live. This man believed the doctor — that the cancer was incurable — and he believed he had a limited time to live, so he went out and killed himself. Now, that early death was in part based on a belief. The question is, was it really true that he had incurable cancer? And how do we know that it would proceed the way the doctor predicted it would proceed? Everybody might say that this man had a cancer. There is no way to even know whether he could have overcome this cancer. But we do know that the beliefs and thoughts that he was given by the doctor were so powerful that he could not deal with them anymore, and he tragically ended his life.

There are other people who believe that they have incurable cancer, and they too have been told that there is no hope for recovery. However, by some rare opportunity, these people with incurable cancer may meet a doctor with higher consciousness. This doctor could say, "Well, sir, we have this new amazing drug that has just been discovered based on a plant in the remote part of Tasmania. This plant was recently discovered by an aboriginal research team in a cave, and it has been used only five times, but each time, it has miraculously cured the cancer, and we only have ten tablets left. We are going to give you the tablets, and you take one of them every month for the next ten months. They are very powerful, so please be careful. Do not drive after you take the pill." So the doctor gives the patient the pill.

The patient comes back a month later, and the tumor has shrunk down, and the doctor is totally flabbergasted. He says, "Okay, we will keep you on the pills for an additional period, which would total ten months. The pills will run out, but it does not matter because the tumor is gone. Sorry that all the pills that were brought from the Tasmanian trip have run out, but you are cured." The doctor never told the patient that the pills were actually placebos — pills that had no actual medicine but were simply sugar pills. However, the patient believed that the pills contained a powerful, new cancer-curing medicine.

The patient has to stop taking the pills after this ten-month period. Amazingly, the cancer comes back. The patient believed the pill was curing him, and now that he has run out of the pills, he believes that he has no way to fight the cancer. So this is another example of the power of the mind.

There are many ways to influence a patient's belief system. When the doctor talked to the patient and said, "This is a very rare pill based on a plant in Tasmania" and so forth, this set up an expectation for a miracle type of medicine. Then the doctor continued and said, "Oh, this is very rare — from the deep forest" and "Oh, this is from the ancient plants." It probably was not even anything, but the doctor presented it in a way that was so powerful and so mysterious that the patient's belief system was open to accepting a wonder medicine. The doctor further affected the patient's belief system by saying, "You are lucky that you were chosen to receive this." So again, we have the power of the mind, but what is even more mind-boggling is that when the pill was stopped, the man's cancer returned. The cancer returning makes you really think about the power of the mind.

Controlling Your Thoughts

The mental body is really powerful and sacred. How do you treat your mental body? We know we can learn how you treat your mental body by looking at what you are telling yourself. We can learn what your self-talk is or what your personal mental conversation is with yourself. We also know that the current state of the media, the TV — including the commercials — is trying to train you to talk a certain way to yourself. They are trying to corrupt your mind to think that you need to smoke this cigarette so that you will be cool, or you need to drink this pop so that you will feel refreshed. Commercial ads work with how your body looks. Ads tell you what you should think. The one thing that is totally yours is what you are thinking, and it is what you are thinking that is the basis for your belief system. Your belief system creates so much of your reality.

I have heard people complain. They say, "Why do people come to Earth?" And we say, "Well, Earth is a freewill system." What are we talking about with free will? Everything is preprogrammed. People believe in predestination. The idea of karma seems to support predestination. You also have severe limitations on what you can and cannot do in this reality. But the truth is that you are free to think whatever you want. I want you to think about that: *You are free to think about whatever you want.* When people say this is a freewill zone, I want you to remember that you have the freedom to think what you want. Even in the darkest darks of concentration camps, the darkest darks of imprisonment, you are free to think what you want.

In our opinion, one of the greatest tortures is to try to shape and control your thoughts. That is exactly what is happening. That is exactly what has been occurring often in many parts of this world during the past fifty or one hundred years. Actually, thought control has been going on for centuries in some civilizations. That is not new. What is new is that the power of the thought control, the methods of thinking and controlling your mental body, are getting more sophisticated and more technical.

Reclaiming Your Mental Body

So how do you reclaim your mental body? Are the thoughts and the beliefs that you have about yourself based on reality, or are they based on information that was wrongly given to you by someone you really believed and whom was in authority? Obviously, the earliest authority figures you had were your parents. Were they enlightened? Were they giving you the correct information about yourself?

Equally important, were you giving yourself the correct information about yourself? Do you believe that you are worthy? Do you believe that you are worthy of ascension? Do you believe that you have all the things necessary to complete this life process and the lessons in this lifetime? What do you believe about yourself? Can we really be honest about that? And if we can get in touch with what we call the core belief about yourself, are you willing to look at it? And how can we change your core belief? It is powerful to work with your core belief system. To find your core belief about yourself, you must access the deepest part of your belief system.

I love computers for many reasons. They are a metaphor for the self. There is a core operating system within a computer, but access to the core system is often denied unless you have a special privilege to go into the system. You certainly do not want to manipulate certain files in the core of the computer unless you have permission and you have special knowledge. So the computer is an interesting metaphor for you. Number one: Are your core beliefs about yourself accessible? And if they are accessible and you look at them, do you want to change them, or do you want to allow them to continue to dominate you? Do you want to update your belief systems about yourself?

So, to demonstrate and work with this idea, I would like somebody who would like to volunteer to talk to me, Vywamus, about his or her belief systems. Is there somebody who would like to do that? [Pause.] Okay, we have a brave soul who is willing to volunteer. Can you come up a little closer so that we can hear you? When you think about your belief system, do you have a sense of your core belief system?

Volunteer: I do not because I do not think very well of myself.

I see. So we got an indication. You say that you do not think very well of yourself. Correct?

Yes.

So that is a core belief about yourself when you say you do not think very well of yourself. But is that thought your thought or someone else's that was given to you? Do you know why you have that thought about yourself?

I think it is somebody else's thought that was given to me.

Well, that is possible. But you said, "*I* do not think very well of myself," so you are describing your core belief that you now seem to have about yourself. So that means that we have to go beneath that layer of "I do not think very well of myself." And I agree that it is probably true, but what is the belief? Can you go beneath that? Is it "I am a bad person," "I am a confused person," or "I am 'whatever'"?

Oh! I do not think I can.

So this means that access is denied. This belief is so powerful that even here, with this very bright and determined woman, who is also brave —

And foolish.

Pardon? No, that is not one of the terms that I would use to describe you, but maybe you would use that term. So she is trying to get into her belief system, but the access is denied. The closest we can come is "I do not think very well of myself." Is that correct?

Yes.

How does that belief system affect you? Do you remember the case of the man who received the medicine from Tasmania? I could go back into the jungle or the forest or the bush and say, "I have this pill that I want you to take, and if you take this pill, then this feeling you have, the feeling that is 'I do not think very well of myself,' will change." Would you take the pill?

I think it would depend on some of the circumstances surrounding me. I would be skeptical.

Of the pill?

Yes, of the statement about the pill.

Then the pill would not change you. I could assure you that I had given it to many people and that they all changed their opinions and beliefs of themselves.

Can I have some client numbers?

We have client confidentiality. I cannot reveal the names of the other patients. So access is denied, and there is a resistance to change. Would that be correct?

Change can be difficult for me, yes.

So the question that we have to ask you is this: How does that belief affect your current life? And how are you doing?

It makes it tough. Like I said earlier, I am questioning any decision I make, which I think goes back to my childhood.

I see.

That is one aspect of it.

So we have a little bit more information. We know that the original belief system came somewhere in the childhood. She is willing to admit that, and that is a big step. And we know that one of the effects of the belief system is that it affects her ability to make decisions, so she does not believe that these decisions are right. Is everything I said correct?

Yes.

And you are sure you do not want to try this pill?

I prefer not to take pills unless I really, really have to. I would ask my doctor.

Well, I thought that people are trained in this culture to take pills.

Not this one — not me.

Ah, you do not go along with those thoughts.

No, not necessarily, no.

Ah! How interesting. You go along with the thought "I do not think very well of myself." You can accept that, but you will not accept the thought "I have to take a pill."

There is quite a strong streak of independence within me.

So what is this other belief about this independence? We have the primary belief, and now we are getting the secondary belief. So you said that you have a very strong source or streak of independence.

People call it stubbornness.

Stubbornness? But stubbornness is based on the protection of the integrity of the self. So somewhere in this deep belief system, there is another belief, another thought about the protection of the integrity of the self. I hope you do not think that I am going to cure you today. Is that why you came up here? We are just using this as information, as an example of the belief system.

Now I've become interested in trying to get at the strength that is behind the integrity of the self and the protection of the integrity of the self, because I have perceived that belief — that core belief she has about herself — and it could be something as simple as "I have the right to protect myself at all costs, and I will not give up my integrity." I believe that that belief, wherever it came from — maybe it came from her father — this belief is so strong that it is able to override the other beliefs. And certainly it is strong enough to provide a strong core of thinking and a strong belief foundation. So here we are demonstrating that you can have one belief that is maybe a problematic belief, but you can have a secondary belief that is able to override the primary belief and protect you. Are there any questions you want to ask me?

I cannot think of anything at the moment.

Okay. I appreciate you coming up here and sharing this, and I would encourage you to maintain that stubbornness because it is based on a strong belief about the fact that you are right. And that is good.

As a youngster, being stubborn was the only way to save myself.

Well, I would just recommend that we modify that belief slightly. Instead of calling it stubbornness, you could say, "I have the right, and I am capable of protecting the integrity of myself."

That sounds nice.

That modified belief is more effective and more powerful for your development than "I am stubborn," which has a kind of negative connotation. If you tell yourself that you have the right to protect yourself, that will override the other primary belief: "I do not think very well of myself."

So I did not need the pill, did I?

Well, I guess not. I will have to give the pill to somebody else. Maybe somebody else needs the pill and you are saving it for them.

I am very generous.

Good. Feeling generous is a good belief.

Thank you, Vywamus.

Looking at Core Belief Systems

Earth is a place where one of the lessons is to work with the mental body. Fortunately, everything that you think does not happen immediately. Some of you have very catastrophic thinking, but it does not materialize because things are slowed down on the third dimension. On the higher plane — remember that Juliano was doing an exercise with you about being at a special energy place where what you are thinking can manifest quickly when you are in a sacred place? But generally you are not able to be in that kind of sacred place often. Normally, your thinking is slower, and that is for your protection. Things are slowed down because, a lot of times, people have thoughts that are not in their best interests. There are also false beliefs such as "Well, you have to think right, and then you will get a million dollars," but the truth is that it is more complicated than that. There would have to be a series of special thoughts and karmic circumstances to make things manifest. This is for your protection.

Is there someone else who would like to look at their core belief systems with me and who has the courage to come up and sit here? You may be the lucky one to have that pill from the Tasmanian bush.

[Pause. A volunteer is selected.]

Your name, please.

New Volunteer: Lisa.

Okay, Lisa. What is your core belief about yourself?

I like myself, but I have a few issues with fading memory.

A few issues of what?

A fading memory and not remembering names.

What do you believe about your memory? You said your memory is fading?

A lot of things I used to remember, particularly names, now I have trouble remembering.

So what is the self-talk about that?

I think, being a crystal person, I am usually very busy looking at people rather than taking in what their names are.

You are critical of yourself for that?

No, I enjoy people's company, but I would like to remember their names.

So that is an observation of an ability rather than a belief. In other words, there might be some lack of a neurological chemical in your brain, such as acetylcholine, which could be causing minor memory loss. Maybe the pill of the Tasmanian bush has an activation of acetylcholine in it.

I would love to use it!

But your idea is that your memory is fading, and this is due to some circumstance — possibly biochemical changes in your brain?

I think it is just aging.
 What do you believe about aging?

Aging is a very pleasant state of being. Unfortunately, people do not expect as much of you. But aging has its advantages.
 But your basic core belief you say is "I like myself."

Exactly.
 So does that mean you think you are a good person?

Yes.
 So what part of your belief system about yourself needs to be changed, or is there any part? Is your mental body in really good shape?

It is just the forgetting thing. That is really the only issue I have, and I do not know whether this is physiological or psychological.
 What do you believe?

I hope it is something I can change.
 What do you *believe*?

I do not know. I think we have been conditioned to believe that it is just our age.
 So it is physiological.

Yes.
 Do you think you have a disease?

No.
 That is good. You did not hesitate one minute. So I do not see a relation-ship between the fading memory and your belief system. Do you?

No, but then what is the cause?
 You have just told me the cause was aging.

Okay. I have said that.
 You said aging is a very pleasant experience.

Except for the fact that you lose those bits that you treasure.
 You what?

You lose the bits that you treasure. I like remembering people's names. That is one example.

Why do we not develop a new belief about your memory?

That would be very nice.

Would you be willing to develop a new belief about your memory?

I hope so. Yes, I would.

Well, I would be willing to help you with it. It seems — like with the last person we worked with — maybe you do not need the pill from the Tasmanian bush either. How about this affirmation: "I am able to compensate for the loss of any memory I have due to aging."

I like that. That is good.

Do you like those words? Can you say them?

I would like to believe …

No, no. Not with "would like to." That does not go with beliefs. We have to either believe it or not believe it.

Like a statement?

Yes.

I accept that I will have perfect memory without the use of the pill.

Is that what I said? I do not think so.

I cannot remember what you said.
Another Participant: "I am able to compensate for any loss of memory that I may have from aging."
Lisa (the volunteer): I had forgotten what you had said. "I am able to compensate for any loss of memory I may have."

Due to aging.

Lisa: "I am able to compensate for any loss of memory that I may have due to aging."

Okay, say it again. Let us make sure you have it.

I cannot remember! "I am able to compensate for any loss of memory that I may have due to aging."

Could somebody please write it right now?

This is why I type things.

That is okay. You are under a lot of pressure now. We are putting you on the spot.

No, this is normal.

So, "I am able to compensate for any loss of memory that I have due to aging." What does "compensate" mean? That is a big word. Do you know what that means?

It usually means you give something up to allow something else to happen.

You give something up to have something else; that is interesting. I look at "compensate" as "I am able to find alternatives to improve." I like that better. Let us remove the word "compensate": "I am able to find alternatives," alternative methods — whoever is writing this down, because she will not remember it — "I am able to apply alternative methods to improve my memory due to aging issues." Do we have that down? Can we say that again?

Another Participant: "I am able to find alternative methods to improve my memory due to aging issues."

Well, let us just leave out "due to my aging." Read it without the last part.

Lisa: "I am able to find alternative methods to improve my memory."

Period. I want to change the words "to find" because what good is it to find it if you do not use it? "I am able to use" or "I am able to implement." Is that too big of a word for you?

I can remember that.

Okay, can we change and remove "to find"?

Other Participant: "I am able to implement alternative methods to improve my memory."

Period. Now that is a new belief that I am offering you today. Are you willing to use that belief?

Lisa: Yes.

It is actually considered an affirmation in your language. One of the things about beliefs is that you can change your belief system by repeating an affirmation, and then eventually it goes into your subconscious. Once it is in the subconscious, then it can be implemented. Let us look at that one more time to make sure that it is said in the best way and that you are comfortable with it. Can you read it?

"I am able to implement alternative methods to improve my memory."

Notice that you are not saying what these alternative methods are, but what you are telling your subconscious is that you are able to do that. And now you will be attracting, learning, and finding those alternative methods, and then you will be able to implement them. How does that sound?

It sounds very good.

So we are demonstrating several principles. The primary principle is that the affirmation to change the beliefs must be short and concise. And then you can begin to download that belief system. So in your case, you will have to repeat that 5,080 times.

If that helps, I will do it.

What I am most worried about is whether you will remember to do it and whether you will remember the affirmation. I am glad your friend wrote it down.

I will write it down and repeat it so that I can say it.

I assure you that it will have a dramatic effect on this.

I might just add that I have a sister who is only eighteen months older than myself and she has Alzheimer's, and my mother has no memory at all. So it is probably fear based.

So we get into another issue — because I asked you earlier if you thought you had a disease, and you said no.

I do not think I have one, but I can see that there is a pattern that might be repeated.

So do we need to create another belief to deal with the fear?

No, I can now see that it is fear based.

Fear is based also on a perception. So if you just say, "It is fear based," that does not really heal the energy. You have some reasons why you have that fear, correct? Because you said your sister has some issues?

Yes, she has Alzheimer's. It is actually worse than that, but it is something like Alzheimer's.

And you said your mother does?

Yes.

But you believe that you do not have it.

Yes.

Okay, I appreciate very much that you have been honest and shared this information with us.

You are welcome.

And please use this affirmation.

I will certainly do. Thank you so much for it.

So that is the second one who does not want to take the pill.

Participant: You did not offer it to her.

Well, she is amenable to working with the affirmation. Can you say the affirmation again, my friend?

Lisa: "I am able to use or implement alternative methods to improve my memory."

That is a beautiful affirmation, if I may say so myself. I think the core message I want to say to you is this: These belief systems are usually quite simple statements. Notice that the first person said, "I do not think very well of myself." It was pretty simple. Then the second belief system was "I am very stubborn." The belief systems are quite simple, but it is in their simplicity that their power comes. And when you wish to change and work with the core system, it is much better to work with and create a simple belief. We also demonstrated that some beliefs can override earlier beliefs; even though one belief might be a core belief, a secondary belief sometimes can overcome the first one. But even in the first case, we talked about how we still would like to get to the main issue and change the core belief.

I am Vywamus. Good day.

Thoughts and Sensitivity

Vywamus

reetings. I am Vywamus. Let us talk about thoughts. I would like to use the metaphor of radios and compare thought waves to radio receivers and radio transmitters. There is a concept in radio called sensitivity. This is the function of the radio receiver describing how it picks up many different signals. The signals are always there in the air, so there could be many radio stations transmitting signals, but if you don't have a receiver, you cannot pick them up.

In some cases, the receivers are not sensitive. They do not have the ability to pick up weaker signals. To do that, we need a more sensitive receiver. To pick up weaker signals, you also have to have a radio antenna that is very high. It has to be high in the air because the signals come from far away. So you can see some metaphoric images there in terms of thought, vibration, and thought reading.

You can increase your receiver sensitivity, but there is another concept in radio theory called selectivity. Selectivity means you will be able to pick up only the signals that you want — not all signals. If you turned on the radio and ten stations were broadcasting on one frequency, you might pick all of them up at the same time, but you wouldn't be able to make any sense of any of them. Selectivity helps you choose which signal you want to hear. Without selectivity, the received bandpass would be overwhelming.

Many of you are experiencing a broadening of your telepathic powers. This is the ability to have more sensitivity in your receiver. You may not have developed the ability of selectivity, which is the ability to push out unwanted signals, but soon, through practice, you will be able to do this. There are many empaths now who are awakening to their psychic gifts and will open themselves up. They also need to develop selectivity.

Let's talk about thought invasion. This occurs when you lack the ability to stop people's thoughts from coming into your energy system. Everybody is a transmitter and a receiver for thoughts. Ultimately, all of your thoughts are recorded in the akashic records. The akashic records are records of every thought of every person who exists.

All of your thoughts are received by entities and energies, and they are recorded in the akashic records. You can put a protective energy field around your aura so that people cannot get into your thoughts. If you want, you can also put a white light around your head, which is representative of your mental body. Other techniques that protect you from thought invasion include using a sacred shield from the Native Americans that serves as protection. You can also wear the Star of David as a protective shield or a crystal.

Many different procedures can protect your thoughts. At certain times of the day or certain times in your life, you are more vulnerable to others' thoughts. The problem is that as you are developing your sensitivity, in the beginning, you may lack the selectivity; therefore, you are more susceptible to a thought intrusion or a thought invasion.

Let's go back to the radio. Good radios have filter protection, so for signals that are too overwhelming, the radio can actually shut the sounds off or filter them out so that you do not hear them.

Thought filtering is something empaths need to develop. This is a very intriguing subject. Sophisticated radios, if overloaded with other-frequency thoughts, vibrations, or frequencies, could be shut down as a protective measure if the signals are too much for the receiver to handle. This shut-off feature protects the radio from damage. Empaths need to have their human mind receivers turned off when they are being overloaded. You are learning to do this. There is an educational aspect about your sensitivity. Remember, each of you is transmitting, and each of you is receiving.

In radio theory, the higher your antenna is, the better your reception. If your antenna reaches fifty feet, you're going to hear signals from farther away than you could hear if you just used the short whip antenna on your table radio. It's the same way in the psychic world. Many of you are sending your etheric antennas way up into the fifth dimension, into the etheric realms, up to the Arcturians, and to many other higher places. So you are receiving a lot more signals than you did earlier in your lifetimes.

Sometimes receiving so many signals can be overwhelming. Because your etheric antenna is high, this means that you can receive signals from far away. At the same time, you may receive many more signals that are close. Those close signals would also be stronger. Some close signals you probably don't want; you don't want to receive the lower-vibrational signals from people who may be in your work environment, for example. But again, you haven't yet learned how to be discriminatory. Being discriminatory is called, in radio technology, "wide dynamic range." It's the ability to select those signals you want to hear and notch out, or remove, the unwanted signals. This principle of dynamic range applies to the psychic world as well.

I am Vywamus. Good day.

Dealing with Traumatic Memories from the Soul Perspective

Vywamus

reetings. I am Vywamus. I am a soul psychologist. I know you have high expectations for me to be able to explain soul psychology. At the same time, maybe you should have high expectations for yourselves as well. But actually, I know that you have high expectations for yourselves, and sometimes you may feel as if you don't meet those expectations. I know that you had high expectations when you came to the third dimension, and you probably did not realize how difficult it was going to be.

The third dimension is quite confusing, and there are many surprises here. Everybody would like to know the future, and everybody would like to know what is going to happen. For example, people always ask, "When is the ascension going to happen? What will happen tomorrow? Should I invest my money in the American stock market?" People think that a soul psychologist understands the American stock market. I try to explain to them that we are not supposed to use our psychic powers for gambling or investing.

"Is it true that if I think correctly, I can become rich? All I have to do is think correctly and say the right affirmations, and then I will become rich?" People ask me to read their akashic records, and then I read the record. The record could say you were rich in your past lifetime, and you decided to come to this lifetime to be poor and then see whether you still could be spiritual despite being poor. Everybody thinks it is easier to be spiritual when you are rich. When you are rich, you must really prove that you love Spirit and that the material world is not important.

People have expectations of how their lives should be and over what they should have control. Some people do not give up the idea of control and expectations easily. One person said to me, "Vywamus, here you said that one key to spiritual development is the ability to manifest, so that means that one key for my spiritual success is to manifest more wealth." That's a good point! And he said, "I am ready to release the karma connected with poverty, and I am ready to manifest."

Something occurred to me, so I answered him, "Well, it depends on how you define wealth. Wealth could be happiness. You could be living in a beautiful place next to the ocean or next to a lake without much money. Do you define wealth by how much money you have in the bank? That is a big mistake people make — defining wealth by how much money they have in the bank."

The person who asked this question went into meditation and said, "Oh! Maybe you have a good point here, Vywamus!"

This person started to realize that there was truth in how one defines wealth. Many rich people — that is, people who have lots of money in the bank — are unhappy because they don't know what to do with themselves. So wealth is also really doing what you want to do in this lifetime. Wealth is being where you want to be — living where you want to live.

Of course, it also helps to have money and to have some type of support from the universe. People approach the issue of money in various ways. Some people want the universe to take care of them lavishly and without effort on their part. They think that the money will come to them without doing anything, and sometimes it comes and sometimes it doesn't, and then they say, "Oh, well, it must be God's will." Or they say, "Spirit will take care of me."

Detachment

That is a curious and interesting approach. This approach of letting Spirit take care of you illustrates an important principle in soul psychology: to not be too attached to the outcome. In other words, you do whatever it is that you need to do, then turn over the outcome of your efforts to Spirit. This approach certainly takes a lot of courage and faith.

One problem of the third dimension is understanding how much control you really do have. Is control an illusion, or is it real? Do you really have control over the outcome of events, or is everything really preplanned? And if everything is preplanned, then why should you try to change anything?

The answer has to do with not being attached to the outcome, because the real answer is a combination of both. It is preplanned that you are going to do some action, but you can actually decide not to follow through. You can decide whether you should give your full effort. Now, I will tell you it feels better when you give your full effort and when you put all of your energy into something. This means that you are in the present. This is the biggest problem of the third dimension — that is, being in the present. All of the great spiritual teachers, including Vywamus, say the solution to your problems is to live in the present. In fact, the society in the third dimension is really confusing because there is such a focus on the past and on the future. So release the past, accept the future, and live in the present, and you will be okay.

But if this is the truth, then why is this planet so screwed up? If everything is preplanned, then doesn't that mean you can do whatever you want? From the planetary perspective, that should mean you can use all the coal you want — that you can use all the oil and the coal you want and put pollution into the atmosphere: "Let's burn all the nuclear power and have all the electricity we want. Let's live in the present! Who cares about the future? The future will be taking care of itself."

Can you see that solely living in the present like that can represent a problem too? So the great teachers are saying: "Live in the present," but if humankind continues to pollute the planet, then everyone could die. So living only in the present is not the total truth, either. If you just continue to take all the fish out of the ocean and not think of the future, then pretty soon there will be no fish. So this leads to one of the challenges and greatest lessons of the third dimension: balance. You have to balance the future with the present.

Past Trauma

Now, what about the past? Many past events on Earth have created a lot of trauma. I know a lot of bad things happened in the past. I know that the memories of the bad things create lots of trauma. Trauma is a complicated, emotional reaction. When a bad thing happens in the past, you can experience trauma from it. One thing that often happens is your mind tries to forget it. You don't want to remember it. Imagine that you were beaten by your father or maybe that somebody sexually molested you or maybe that you saw some terrible violence as a child. Your mind can block all memories of that past. This is a pretty good psychological defense.

People who suffered trauma as children often say that they do not remember anything that happened to them before they were ten years old. When this happens, I say, "Well, you may have some kind of trauma. It could have been that a bad thing happened to you when you were younger."

They reply that they don't know, or they say, "I don't remember."

What can I say to them? "You don't remember because you were traumatized. Wake up! Remember, remember!"

They say, "I can't remember."

In the psychology world, this reaction of memory loss is called a defense. There is no easy way to break through the defense, so forgetting is the mind's reaction to protection — protect by forgetting. Many people use this defense.

However, if I look at the person's akashic records, I can see that the trauma still is in the memory. It still is carried inside and still can have an effect on a person's life.

So the memory of the past can be blocked, but nevertheless, the event can still be hurting you. So what do you do about it? Well, first, you must respect your defense because your mind, your personality, wants to protect you. This is a good thing. Your personality made the decision that if the memory continued to appear when you were younger, then it could have been too much for you to deal with. With a trauma, you might not have been able to develop. So your personality, your middle self, made a decision to block the traumatic memory so that you would be able to survive and continue. Note that I used the word "survive." That's because the trauma is perceived as a threat. The trauma is a danger, and if the memory of the trauma in your early childhood were to remain in your awareness, then you might not survive. That is the way a child thinks, and you have to say that the child is trying to protect him- or herself because the child wants to grow up and be an adult. As an adult, the child then believes that possibly there will be strength to deal with this.

So you now want to heal. To heal means to make whole again, but to do that, you may want to recover traumatic memories so that you can repair yourself. You must talk to your inner child and say things like this: "I have the resources now to deal with these bad memories. I have the strength to deal with these traumas. I give my memory permission to remember. No matter what the memory is, I know I will be able to deal with it." So you see, you are preparing your mind to heal and to release these traumas.

I want to talk about the different levels of consciousness, because when you go into altered states of consciousness, you can go around the normal psychological defenses to recover the trauma and recover the memories. But remember, you must always tell the inner child that you have the resources to deal with it. In altered states of consciousness, such as in deep meditation or a light trance, you want to soften the defenses and then go to what can be called the middle or higher self. From that perspective, you can then access information that you cannot access in normal consciousness. You can even access information from other lifetimes. This is how strong your altered state of consciousness can be.

Can you give us advice on how to put light on and access the cellular memories where the traumas are residing?

The memories of the past before this lifetime or the memory in this lifetime?

Both.

The first role is to tell yourself that you have the resources to deal with it. Also, I would like to ask you, why do you want to access those memories? Because there has to be a purpose for you to want to access those memories. It must be some healing or some problem you want to fix. You don't want to go back and recover traumatic memories just for fun, because going back is also like surgery. When you do a surgery, it has to be something really important that you want to fix. I also suggest that when you go back into these memories that you approach doing so with the seriousness of physical surgery. So you want someone — a therapist or a soul psychologist — to help you.

A soul psychologist is somebody who understands that there are past lives that can affect this lifetime. So let's say there is an agreement that you are talking to yourself correctly and that you are preparing yourself for psychic surgery and going back into your past. Then you will have to find the right person who is oriented toward soul psychology to guide you.

The next step is going to an altered or higher state of consciousness where you can try to go back into the past memory in different ways. You could do an age regression, which is where the therapist says, "Okay, you are now thirty-five years old. Let's go back to thirty, twenty-five, twenty, then go back to the point where you feel the trauma happened. Then describe what you see — what you are doing. Then many memories should start coming back."

If you want to go back to a past life, you can go back to the age of one or zero (in your mother's womb). Then we go back to lives between lives. For example, in accessing past-life trauma, here is a possible scenario: "I am in Yugoslavia in 1853. I am sitting in the palace, and I am a prince in the court. Suddenly, my enemy comes up behind me and stabs me in the back. I've been betrayed again! Oh! This is why people are betraying me now in this lifetime. I should never trust people."

This is a past-life scenario that could explain why you have a problem trusting in this lifetime. This could help you understand the problem. But you really must do this type of regression with somebody you trust. You must be able to keep your ego out of it because the ego has a strong desire to censor information. You need to connect to your higher self. The higher self recalls experiences from other lifetimes. The higher self remembers everything, and the higher self is not ego-involved in what is happening. The problems that you are having in this lifetime often can be the result of imprints and experiences from other lifetimes. So you carry in your cellular memory the imprints from the other lifetimes.

Is every trauma or everything that happened in other lifetimes lodged in the soul? If the soul is timeless, why would psychological wounds persist in this lifetime?

The soul has access to all the information from all lifetimes. The soul itself is still pure. Please remember on the highest level that the soul is perfect and the soul is pure. Imprints and wounds are imprinted on the lower levels of the soul. To answer your question, we must first talk about the different levels of the soul.

At the highest level of the soul, there are no imprints. They are not there. But in the lower levels, the memory and the imprints from previous lifetimes are there. These imprints are in the form of memories and traumas, and they are part of what I call soul lessons. Let's take the example of a past life in which the person was a prince in Yugoslavia who was betrayed by somebody and then stabbed in the back. There are several soul lessons to learn.

Now, we have to ask, did that person learn the lesson in that lifetime? The best possibility is that he did learn the lesson in that lifetime. Let us say, then, that the prince did not die; he recovered and went to psychotherapy. He understood that he had mistakenly let his guard down. He learned the lesson and continued to grow, and he was fine.

So that original trauma was bad, but he did resolve it, and he healed himself in the lifetime in which the trauma occurred. If he did not heal himself, if he carried a lot of resentment and was not able to resolve the issue, then he would carry that imprint with him on a lower soul level to his next lifetime. Then the soul would look for the right time to incarnate to find the right circumstances to resolve and heal that problem. This means that the imprint is carried from lifetime to lifetime. The soul finds the right time to incarnate and to see when the right circumstances exist for those problems to come into consciousness again for healing and resolution.

I want to use another example. There were many people in Atlantis who participated in the military experiments, which resulted in the destruction of their civilization. These people were bright and scientifically minded. Many of these people reincarnated in America in the 1960s and 1970s. Some were even born earlier. They became scientists in the early 1980s and 1990s, and then they found themselves doing the same thing as they did in Atlantis — using their scientific knowledge for military purposes. They had to wait for thousands of years to find the right circumstances to reincarnate and resolve earlier soul lessons. It is hoped that they will learn the lesson not to use the scientific technology for military purposes.

At the same time, there are people who died in the Nazi Holocaust. They chose not to come back and be Jewish again. However, they found that when they were thirty or forty years old, they accidentally went to synagogues and they listened to the prayers and felt moved. Soon they had memories of being in temples and in synagogues in Germany. Here is another possible example:

Five years after the Holocaust and after dying in a concentration camp, several people reincarnated into another country where they were safe to experience their Jewish heritage.

The point is that you don't know from the third dimension when the right reincarnational circumstances will manifest for your soul lessons. Your higher soul makes a decision on when to reincarnate based on what you need to learn. Now, you all have been reincarnated at this time in the twenty-first century when the ascension is going to occur. There are soul lessons for you to learn during this ascension.

A Clean Slate

Are there any teachings we can learn or improvements we can make when we go to the spiritual world?

Yes, there are teachings in the spiritual realm also. In the spirit world, you talk to your masters, guides, and teachers. You begin to learn from them about the mysteries of the third dimension. When you get ready to return to the third dimension, your guide touches your forehead in a ceremony and activates an energy whereby you will forget everything that was told to you in the spiritual world about your journey. You will come in with a *tabula rasa*, or black slate. So when you enter the third dimension, everything is clear and clean.

One of the rules when you come into the third dimension is that your soul memory will be suspended. It is not in your highest interest to remember everything. For example, if you remembered everything, then you might become very confused.

Let's go back to the prince in Yugoslavia. He sees the guy who stabbed him in the back in his last lifetime. Now the prince is walking down the street, and he sees the guy again, and he will say, "Here you are! You killed me in my last lifetime! I am going to kill you now!"

Then the man says, "But you are crazy!"

You can imagine the chaos that could occur. So that is one reason why the soul memories are forgotten or repressed. It is more accurate to say that the memories are protected rather than erased because, with the right approach and the right perspective, the memories can be retrieved. Without the right preparation, this information will be useless and could cause damage. So there needs to be a certain spiritual light/energy quotient developed to retrieve such memories.

Parallel Lives and Universes

Can there be, besides past lives, simultaneous or parallel lives during which you are having experiences that come to this life so that you can fix them?

We know the concept of parallel lives, and we are talking also in modern physics about parallel universes. In parallel universes, you are driving down a road and you turn left in this world, and then, in the other world, you turn to the right. Then something happens to you on the right, and something different happens to you on the left.

It's not like that, really, but you see, it's an interesting thought. In fact, there are other universes. We talk about multidimensions where we say that you can be in different dimensions simultaneously. Your soul is so beautiful and so complex that you have the ability to be in multiple dimensions, and yes, what you are doing in the other dimensions can affect what is going on in this dimension.

The perfect example is the dream world. That world is like a multidimensional reality. What happens in the dream world can affect what is going on in this world. Some societies encourage the memories of the dream world. In these societies, people talk about their experiences in the dream world and then use the information. Western society does not do that unless you go to a psychologist and pay a lot of money to talk about your dreams.

The idea of the dream world is based on time and cycles of consciousness. You have eight hours when you are awake, eight hours when you work (you may not necessarily be awake when you work [laughs]), and then you have eight hours when you sleep. So this is the timeline of being on the straight line. But in the multidimensions, time is like a circle, which means that the dream time is interacting with the waking time. It means that the multidimensional life can also interact with this life. It can mean that your future self can interact with your present self so that you have different aspects of yourself that are on different dimensions.

Vengeance from Past Lives

Is that not interfering with the free will?

No, it is not interfering with the free will because you have the choice to integrate it. You have the choice whether to study it and whether to use the dream information. You have to be in a level of high spiritual advancement to integrate and use this type of dream experience. If you are not at a high level, you can easily become mentally unbalanced.

I want to talk on a related subject. Sometimes you see people who murder other people for no obvious reason. It reminds me of a case in Yugoslavia in which one person was betrayed by another person from a past life. You have an example of a person thinking, "Oh! You are the person who betrayed me in my last life! Now I will get my revenge." In soul psychology, we call that a "bleed over," because the murderer's thinking became confused from a past life to a present life. The murderer remembered her past-life situation but unfortunately acted irrationally in a present life and killed someone for reasons related to what was going on in another lifetime.

Negative Cohabitation

I want to expand these ideas more to help you understand why certain irrational and evil events occur. Lower spirits are living in the fourth dimension, and many people on the planet have weak auras. Because some people have weak auras, the lower spirits can cohabit with them. We call such cohabitation "negative cohabitation." Through the negative cohabitation, the people can commit bad things such as mass murders. You are seeing many examples of this now on Earth.

Are they lost souls — that is, the lower souls from the fourth dimension?

Yes, I would say they are lost souls, but I would also say many are misinformed souls. There are a lot of lost souls there in the lower fourth dimension who are trying to get into the auras of people on Earth. These lost souls are trying to make people on Earth do strange things, such as assassinations at schools. These terrible events have no logic from the third-dimensional perspective.

Can it help us in this life to become conscious of what we are doing in our other multidimensional lives?

Yes, it can help you. Let me give you an example: Say that you are in the dream world, and you are in a beautiful temple praying, and you are receiving enlightenment energy. When you wake up from the dream, you say, "Oh, Boy! I am doing very well now." Then you decide to find a teacher who can help you with meditation.

So yes, connecting to the other-dimensional worlds through dreams, for example, does help you. Juliano and the Arcturians' teachings also help. They teach how to direct your multidimensional life and bring the energy from those other lifetimes into this lifetime.

Soul States and Levels of Self

Could you explain the different states of the soul?

I would like to start by talking about the different levels of the self: the lower, the middle, and the higher selves. The higher self is directly connected to your soul, and most people never have the experience of the higher self in this lifetime. Many starseeds, of course, are changing that now.

The lower self is your animal self. You act from instincts, and you act, really, without thinking. The middle self is the self that is trying to do well, to be ethical, and to be of service.

There are higher levels beyond these three levels. Your soul has a direct connection to the Creator because, ultimately, you will stop incarnating and will merge with the Creator. The soul is involved in that evolution having to do with incarnations. Some souls have reached the top levels, and they are ready to merge.

When I am teaching soul psychology, I am trying to help people understand that they incarnated in order to learn certain soul lessons. When they find out what that lesson is and they learn that lesson, they become happier and more at peace with themselves. So your soul does not really care if you are rich or poor. The soul is more interested in doing and learning your soul mission.

People may think that the third dimension is too dense and that you cannot attain higher energy here, but there is always the possibility of full integration with all parts of yourself on the third dimension. You can manifest and experience enlightened states of consciousness on the third dimension. You can access all the parts of yourself and the spirit of unity and manifest that on the third dimension. We can bring this higher awareness and this higher state of consciousness and this higher method of fifth-dimensional energy into the third dimension.

I am Vywamus. Good day.

Restoring the Self

Vywamus

reetings. I am Vywamus. I am the soul psychologist. This is the moment you've been waiting for: the ascension! It is right now. We are now on the fifth dimension. All of your troubles are over. Let it be.

You don't have to worry about unpaid bills, and you should have no worries about unemployment. You don't have to worry about retirement. You don't have to worry about Earth's changes or asteroids hitting your planet, and best of all, you've avoided all of the big Earth changes. You didn't have to experience them. You didn't have to experience the upheavals and the darkness that is coming from the photon belt. What else did they scare you with? Fire and earthquakes! There are earthquakes even in Oklahoma! You know things are bad if there are earthquakes in Oklahoma.

But ask yourself, "Where is it safe to be anymore?" What makes you think it will be safer anywhere else? If I told you that the safest place on the planet right now is the North Pole, would you go up there?

Why would the soul want to come to this planet and go through all of this — this duality and separation from the Source? I think this is most challenging. As for the anxiety, the fear, and the suffering that is now occurring on this planet, it is totally unimaginable.

I understand you've reached more than 7 billion inhabitants. That's really "inhabitation," isn't it? When your planet reaches 7 billion, there are a lot of people inhabiting. That's really something. There must be cheap rent here on planet Earth! When you think about your galaxy, our galaxy, and all of the different galaxies and universes, there are a lot of choices of where people can go. So why are they coming here? That is a good question. You want to find the answers to that question. Seven billion people have all of that soul energy.

People used to say that these billions of people are all reincarnating from other lifetimes on Earth. If you add up all of the populations from ancient Greece, ancient Egypt, and Atlantis, throw in a few of the Neanderthals and Cro-Magnons and all of those societies, China, Australia — does all of that equal 7 billion souls? If you add it up sequentially from 30,000 BCE until now, you have to reason, "I don't think that adds up to 7 billion. Where are all of these souls coming from?"

Cosmic Karma

I've given lectures before on karma. I've mentioned certain karma. It's remembered as karma from the past or cosmic karma. Let's talk about cosmic karma. That's among my favorite subjects. People may say, "We couldn't have done that many bad things in the past to equal the negative events that have occurred in the twentieth century. Look at all of the terrible things that happened in the twentieth century. Now those must have been some bad dudes in the past who are dealing with karma!"

There have been some bad things that have happened on Earth in the past, but how can it equal all of the terrible things that are happening now? Then we come up with cosmic karma. It's bad enough to have karma on Earth to work out, but now we have cosmic karma. This means that many things that are happening have a cosmic relationship — a cosmic connection.

Some souls on Earth are actually incarnating from other planets. You feel good as a starseed because you come from another planet. Being a starseed has a positive connotation, but we need to come up with a new term now, because what about the bad guys who are incarnating here? Do you want to call *them* starseeds too? We need to come up with another name for these guys. Maybe we could call them the "bad seeds"? How about the "groundseeds" (as opposed to starseeds)?

This is actually quite serious, as there have been planets that have imploded or exploded because of these "bad" beings. There have been planets that have had quite a variety of negative things. Now some of these same lower beings have decided to incarnate on Earth, and they are bringing their problems with them. If you think you have immigration problems in Arizona, this Earth has big immigration problems here with some of these souls. Maybe we should put a halt to it, don't you think?

The reason why they wanted to come to Earth is the same reason Juliano mentioned about this planet being in a freewill zone. There is the possibility of soul evolution here because you can do more soul evolution on Earth. You can learn more soul lessons and resolve more soul lessons when there is free will.

What is amazing is that we have found, in our travels throughout the galaxies, that there are not a lot of other planets that have 7 billion people on them. We have lost count of how many religions there are on this planet. If there is one God, there are certainly a lot of different interpretations. You would think that unity thinking would create unity, but no. That has not happened on Earth.

There is quite a complex language system that you have too. How many languages do you have here? This is truly an amazing and a complex planet. This planet is called the Blue Jewel because there is so much beauty, so much biodiversity and human diversity, and so many opportunities for learning. If you have a specific lesson to learn, I guarantee you that among the many countries, religions, and languages, we will find the right situation for you. Don't worry. You'll be downloaded into the right family to learn just these things.

Repeating the Past

With cosmic karma, you have more choices and more alternatives. People think that the karma goes exactly from one lifetime to the next. So if you did a bad thing in this lifetime, then you will be born immediately into the next lifetime and the same thing is going to happen to you again.

However, the concept of cosmic karma means that your guides and spirit teachers have to find the right circumstances for you, and sometimes those right circumstances may not be for thousands of years. I know that some of you were around in the Atlantis time. I know that there was a lot of guilt. Some scientists, philosophers, and politicians in Atlantis really tried to stop the destruction.

There were great prophecies about the upcoming destruction in Atlantis just like now at this time. There is no shortage of prophecies of doomsayers on this planet. Everyone from the Maya to Edgar Cayce — and we can think of other ones, such as Nostradamus — have predicted coming destructions. Do you notice how much money doomsday prophets have been making lately on television? It seems that even Cayce and Nostradamus should receive royalties from those television programs. There is no shortage of doomsday predictions.

Some of you tried to change the course of events in Atlantis, and you were not successful. Some scientists who were developing this military technology in Atlantis that was directly related to their destruction have come back to this lifetime. They are now developing the same bomber and drone technology, and God knows what else they are doing — but almost exactly in the same way as before.

You say, "Hello, don't you remember what you guys did before? Yet you are doing the same thing now?" Where did all of this scientific knowledge and information about this military technology and how we use it to dominate the world come from? You would think that scientists would learn their cosmic lessons. You would think that one lifetime of being destructive or responsible for destruction would make them change their ways. But people tend to repeat the past. One of my favorite lines is: "If you think it's bad on Earth now, do you want to come back in fifty years?" Do you want to learn the lesson now and resolve it? Or will you say, "Well, I'll take care of it in the next lifetime"?

Mormons and Reincarnation

From what we are seeing, fifty years from now on this Earth, things may be quite a bit worse — unless there are some major turnarounds. Remember, souls often reincarnate in groups. Many of you know each other from past lifetimes, and it's not as accidental as you might think to come into this lifetime and meet these certain people from your soul group. Some of you have made contracts to work together before as a group.

One of our favorite groups is the Mormons. They really have this group consciousness down great. They are programming their members to reincarnate together on another planet after this is over. It's pretty sophisticated to program your members for how they are all going to live on another planet. Their planet is there; that group is there already. This channel has worked with Archangel Moroni, who brought down the teachings and the tablets, the plates, to Joseph Smith. There was a lot of high energy and very high connections.

Moroni (many do not know of Archangel Moroni) has a very high vibration. The concepts of reincarnating for this particular soul group really came from Moroni. This is a very advanced soul technology to work with as a group and to have them link together as a group, to form that link throughout other lifetimes. This is irrespective of whether you agree with what the Mormon teachings are or how they want to formulate this life. I'm not commenting about their roles and practices but rather on their ability to create a group cohesiveness that will allow them to reincarnate as a group after this lifetime.

Make the Choice

The Arcturians are teaching that you have a choice of wherever you go or with which group you are going to be. The teaching is that the Arcturian stargate will give you the opportunity to choose where you will go. Will you go into the Pleiades? Will you go to Sirius, X-terra, Sagittarius, or many other different places?

I think it is appropriate that you look at the experience in this lifetime as part of your soul journey. Your soul has manifested and appeared at this point in this lifetime, and there are certain things that you need to experience and learn on this journey. Once you learn the lessons on this journey here, you can free yourself of the incarnational cycle and from the necessity of having to return here. You can travel onward to other realms and higher vibrations.

The question is, what lesson is it that you need to learn? Why did you come here? What was it that was important for you to experience? Some of you came here to experience the ascension. Some of you came here to experience this open conflict and these people in this time, and you wanted to learn and participate in that process. Some of you came here for personal lessons. It could be relationship issues. It could be how you relate to the planet and this current upheaval. It could be related to whether you had karma to release.

Sometimes we find that many of you were warriors, which is quite common when you look at lifetimes before. Now you've come back as doctors and healers. You might have been responsible for the death and destruction of many soldiers or peasants or villagers in one lifetime. Now you are coming back and devoting a lot of time to healing to "undo" that karma. There are those of you who lived in a strict society in which you were being repressed. You look back on the history of this planet, and there weren't great living conditions. It is true that in ancient Rome, for example, they had some Roman baths, but how many people were able to take baths? There were a lot of slaves, many warriors, and so many different problems in that ancient society.

Sometimes a lifetime is restrictive, and you come back to experience a lifetime with more freedom. What I have found is that some people are having a really hard time with the freedom. For example, they could have many choices and lots of freedom now: "Let's see ... I could study Buddhism. I could study Arcturian technology. I could become a Mormon. I could do Taoism. I could become an atheist." There are hundreds of choices. And some starseeds who are now healers have to work with the groundseeds. Some starseeds have been perplexed about what to do with their freedom as well as the need for some type of structure.

Dealing with Spiritual Trauma

We found another interesting phenomenon that is especially prevalent among female starseeds. Many female starseeds had other lifetimes on this planet in which they were teachers, shamans, astrologers, or prophetesses. They might have been working in fortunetelling or esoteric energy work. Some were actually punished by society for doing that work. One of the really hard things to grasp in this society is the continued prejudice against women and how women have been treated over the centuries on this planet. This is especially true of women who earlier had great shamanistic powers. If the woman was a stronger shaman than the man, then the men may not have liked it. Some women were stronger and had great psychic powers. Sometimes the men put the women to death or punished them so that they wouldn't be able to practice their shamanistic powers anymore. Now, when these women come back into this lifetime, they have a hard time relating to their powers and coming into their powers because of the memories from past lifetimes.

These memories are soul imprints. Traumatic events that have happened in past lifetimes leave impressions on the soul. These are like genetic transfers of energy from down the family line. Memories create soul imprints that you carry with you. The memory of Atlantis is still strong among many of you, as are memories of traumas from that civilization. Traumas from past lifetimes leave soul imprints. One of the healings is to come into contact with some of these traumas and clear them.

There has been a lot of trauma associated with spiritual beliefs on this planet. Some traumas on the planet originate when people think that a certain way is the truth and that others better believe it; otherwise, they have a way of dealing with you, and it isn't nice. What kind of spirituality is that? That's pretty primitive. That kind of approach is still prevalent on this planet in many parts of the world. Such an experience will leave a traumatic imprint on you.

When you are coming to the point of realizing your spiritual powers, you will want to reach out, expand, teach, and do soul work. Then there is a little voice that says, "Wait a minute. Don't you remember? The last time you did this in a past lifetime, you suffered."

We are happy that the Native Americans are speaking of the return of White Buffalo Calf Woman because it is a sign of the return of the feminine light and the power of the feminine. I'm not trying to be prejudiced, but I think the male energies have had enough of a rule on this planet. I'm not saying that the men are bad, but the male energy — this energy of domination of nature, this energy of control — is not going to solve the current Earth problems. It's going to lead you down the same path.

The Rise of Feminine Energy

In the 1960s, they were singing the song "The Age of Aquarius." The Age of Aquarius is the acknowledgment of the feminine light — the feminine Mother. The energies of White Buffalo Calf Woman are announcing that at this time. Let's not confuse feminine energy only with women because men have feminine energy too.

There are women who became rulers, who became male-like, started wars, and tried to dominate the world. But generally, the men have followed the path of domination on this planet. Unfortunately, being feminine usually means that you've lost power. Even though you may be right and spiritually sensitive, you wind up being dominated. The return of White Buffalo Calf Woman and the coming into this age of feminine energy are actually part of this new alignment.

One thing you are going see is a period in which the feminine energy is going to become more prevalent. In addition, those who feel the feminine energy are going to become more powerful. One thing that is clear in this world is that you don't get things done unless you have power. People will not listen to you and make the changes just because you have knowledge.

Learn to Use Your Gifts

Certainly, as my friend P'taah likes to remind me, when Jesus came to the Pleiades, he received a much better reception than he did here on Earth. They didn't crucify him in the Pleiades. This, I can guarantee you. It is interesting why the spirituality and the differences in spirituality led to so much conflict on Earth. It really has to do with power, domination, and control of this planet.

One of the lessons for a lot of you is how to find your power in this type of reality. I like the teachings of Chief White Eagle. He likes to teach you about gathering personal power. As starseeds, to fight the groundseeds, you need to have personal power, energy, and focus.

I think it is interesting that not only do the imprints in other lifetimes come but you should also understand that one of the lessons in this lifetime is to integrate who you are now. In a lot of past-life work, people often want to focus on what they did in their past lives as well as the trauma that they experienced in those past lives. An example would be Pompeii, where the volcanic eruption happened and people became engulfed in the lava, becoming statues.

I want to point out that when you go back into a past life, you should work also on recovering good past-life memories, as some of you had great powers in past lifetimes. You will want to bring those powerful energies, those powerful strengths, and show them and integrate them in this lifetime too.

Some lessons in this lifetime are to learn how to use your strengths, your powers, and your gifts. Some of you in other lifetimes did not take advantage of developing your gifts or using them correctly. You might have even been crucified for trying to do good. Remember that in the higher self, the self will try again. But from the higher self's perspective, this is just one lifetime. Think about that: This is just a lifetime. The higher self thinks that you can have another lifetime, if you want to. You can manifest somewhere else.

That sounds like unusual thinking when you get into that kind of viewpoint, doesn't it? It's a strange detachment when you experience that your higher self has, and you have, your stuff together to go to that perspective. It would be easy to misinterpret this perspective as justification for evil, to say, "This is just a lifetime." It can be a trap.

You need to have a greater level of spiritual development to go to that place of the higher self. If you go to that place, just realize that your higher self has a detachment and objectivity about this lifetime and about all of its lifetimes. The challenge — and one of the greatest lessons — is how to bring the knowledge and teachings and energy of the higher self into this lifetime to maximize all of your gifts and do what you came here to accomplish.

Many people also get confused because they ask, "Well, what is my lesson here? What am I supposed to be? What did somebody call them — super rock-star spiritualists? Or spiritual rock stars? Spiritual rock stars, yes, we can now be spiritual rock stars, like Vywamus." What if you came down just to learn to be a peasant? What if you came just to appreciate Earth? Some of you actually came down not to have responsibilities but just to be able to experience what it is like to be in duality in a third-dimensional world — no responsibilities, just learning. It's not hard. It sounds like a nice lifetime, as long as you can arrange it, you are living on a nice beach, your food is taken care of, and everything is pretty.

Some of those we are working with actually have that situation. They have all of the bases covered — such as money, food, shelter, and freedom — yet some people don't know how to deal with this situation. Others don't have the financial means to have all their needs taken care of, but they want to have a better situation. I want to mention that some people use their spiritual affirmations toward making money. They have thought power, but they just don't have any effective power of thinking; otherwise, if their thinking were really effective, then why would they have to repeat the affirmation 1,000 times? Why are Earth people repeating affirmations over and over again?

Money and Spirituality

Some of you are coming into this lifetime to learn how to experience spirituality and, at the same time, to have money and wealth. Some are like Siddhartha, who came here and found out that he didn't need wealth because it was a hindrance to his spiritual development and his spiritual mission.

There are two ways to look at this: One lesson is to have wealth and be spiritual, which everyone wants; the other is to be spiritual and to not have wealth, as wealth seems to be a deterrent or hindrance to spirituality. If you came into this lifetime and, say, you were some great duke (or duchess), wealth could really blow your chances for spirituality. Many of you came into this lifetime stating that you wouldn't be hindered by having all of this money in order to be spiritual. The soul lesson is that gaining a lot of money may not be in your best interest. We always say to stick to the affirmation of having lots of money, but only if it is in your best interest. Or you can phrase it so that you don't let the wealth interfere with your spirituality.

There has to be some understanding of what is in your highest interest. For example, it may or may not be in your highest interest to experience poverty. Some of you have imprints or soul impressions from previous lifetimes when you were poor, and now it's hard for you to break out of that. This is getting to be a big problem now in the world and in this culture because of the perceived poverty that is occurring as well as the great sufferings that are coming from poverty. There are certainly a lot of lessons regarding money and poverty.

Cycling Lessons

The Earth changes are part of these lessons. The way the soul works is in cycles. For example, say you are twenty to twenty-two years old and life gives you some hard lessons, but they are not too bad. You deal with it and don't really pay close attention to it. Then, at around thirty-five years of age or so, the spirit tries again to have you learn the same lesson. This time it gets a little bit harder on you. However, you are able to solve it, and you don't have the problem anymore. Pretty soon, you are fifty-five or sixty years old, and your soul says, "Hey, buddy, you don't have too much time left. If you are not going to totally learn this lesson, then I'm going to throw something at you that is really going to make you think about it. How would you like to have a disease? Are you ready?"

In doing soul psychology, we like to work to prevent the big catastrophe or the big uproar. If you really look at personal history, then you will find that people have earlier signs of certain issues before the big uproar. I'm not saying this critically. It's pretty hard to solve major life issues unless you take a soul perspective. It's pretty hard because all you want to do is solve the immediate pain without addressing a broader perspective.

Restoring the Self

This leads me to the subject of restoration of the self. Many of you have had traumas in your lifetimes. Many of you had traumas in your childhoods. Those traumas, whether they are of sexual abuse, physical abuse, or a whole range of abuses, left an imprint on this life and this ego. Traumas can distort the development of the self, in which case you can feel like a victim of the abuse. More importantly, you can become identified with this abuse.

Now you are waiting to release. You meet someone like Vywamus, a soul psychologist, who can help you release the trauma. But then the problem becomes that after the trauma is released, there's a big hole, a big emptiness in you. You might not know how to fill that emptiness because you've spent all of your earlier lifetime developing yourself around that concept that was based on being traumatized. This goes along with issues of low self-esteem and other personal problems.

However, now you receive this new spiritual technology. There is a tremendous advantage for personal healing when you use spiritual technology and integrate that with soul psychology. You can achieve dynamic releases. The entire trauma can be released; it's not as hard as you may think. But there is an emptiness that could follow after the release. So this is where the idea of restoration of self plays an important role. What would the self have been if you had not been blocked or traumatized? Sometimes restoring the self is more difficult than releasing the old blockages.

We want people to understand that restoration of self also implies allowing the real self to come through. It does take some work, and it could be difficult. It is good work. That could be one of the lessons that comes through — that is, to learn how to restore the self. Some of you may wonder why you had to have that trauma in your life. You might think, "I thought I was done with abuse in the last lifetime," but you come back to this lifetime and see that you have the same problem again.

Maybe the lesson that you have to complete is not only to learn how to release yourself from abuse but also how to restore yourself. Releasing yourself from the abuse is one part of the process. You also must be able to restore yourself. Releasing yourself from trauma is good; you don't have to suffer as much. But there still can be some personal suffering if you don't have to complete the job, which is the restoration of the self.

Release Trauma to Restore the Self

I will now take your questions related to soul psychology.

The question I have concerns what you were just speaking about: victims of trauma, especially childhood trauma, needing to fill in the gap that is left after the release of that trauma, which is something I relate to very personally. But I was wondering: Is there another concept called "generational grief"? It hasn't been used in this concept, but what it relates to is that we have had soul imprints in all of our lifetimes. When you talk about releasing and restoring the self, are you talking only about this lifetime or about all lifetimes?

It is possible to unite all of the lifetimes. You can solve problems in this lifetime and achieve a unity that links you to all of the other energies in other lifetimes. That is pretty overwhelming for someone dealing with a childhood trauma in this lifetime. You might think, "Okay, not only are we going to resolve this, but now we must resolve all the other ten traumas from past lifetimes." What I am suggesting is that all the energy is releasing. They want to go back and release the energy from all the past lifetimes. Is that what you are hinting at?

I'm just asking if you are talking about just this because I'm hearing you imply that there is a thread or style that connects all of the traumas.

There is a thread, but the beauty and the reason why so many people want to incarnate on this Earth is because you need to resolve it in this lifetime.

Then it travels back?

It does. That's part of the release. That is why so many people want to come to Earth. This is a freewill zone. In a freewill zone, the problems that you are experiencing really do have a history, and you do have a choice. But you can resolve them here and now, and then you are done. That's what a lifetime can accomplish. It's truly fantastic, and one of the beauties of coming to Earth focuses on having the freedom and choice to resolve traumas. That is what happens.

There is benefit for some people — not for everyone — to go back into the past lifetime. There is a benefit in working with the energy of life between lifetimes, which is the ability to talk to guides and teachers between lifetimes. Sometimes, when going back into the past lifetimes, you re-experience the same trauma that you experienced in past lifetimes. You can feel stuck here. So life-between-lives therapy (which is part of the soul psychology work) focuses on talking to your guides and teachers about what you are going to try to fix this time. Perhaps this time you came into this experience and now you can free yourself from the trauma. However, to directly answer your question: Solve it here and now, and then it will take care of the past energies as well.

How do you start the restoration of the self?

Well, first you have to release the trauma. You may ask the question: "Do I release it all at once?" It sounds like a nice package, but sometimes the release takes a process. The way you restore the self is to ask yourself, "If I don't have to deal with this problem anymore, then who am I?" The real question is, who are you without the trauma? You know who you are based on your likes and dislikes and based on your inclinations. You start to focus on where you are getting your greatest energy, your greatest power, and where you feel you are guided to go. That is bringing you to the restoration of your self.

Everybody thinks this release happens all at once. Sometimes this release happens as a process because those blocks, those traumas, also blocked you from growing, much like a flower blocked from fully blooming. Now you get to say, "Who am I?" For instance, the restoration of the self starts as you are re-creating who you are, who you want to be, and who you came to this planet to be. You can put aside that information that was given to you by those people who traumatized you. Those people who traumatized you were not giving you the right information about yourself.

I am feeling this feeling, and I didn't have a name for it until now: self-restoration. It is as though I have accessed my first lifetime and I have released it — almost everything. Now I have to go back to where I was before the traumas. The question is, how do I access who I was before?

It is not always necessary to go back to earlier traumatic lifetimes. But it could be helpful because it could provide some good clues. But you just have to resolve the blocks from this lifetime. The circumstances that you have in this life provide the information and the threads of the representation of the whole problem. Isn't it true that you had some abuse and pain in your childhood in this lifetime? And isn't it true that you had some pain and abuse in past lifetimes also?

The pain and abuse of the past lifetimes did contribute to you coming into this lifetime with this pain and abuse of your childhood. The experiences from the past lifetime provided you with the foundation for the trauma and damage to yourself in this lifetime. If you can release and work on this pain and trauma in this lifetime, then that will help you to release all you need to. Now, I realize that there won't be as much work for me as your soul psychologist because, if you go the other route, then you will work on many lifetimes and need more help. It's complicated because a lot of people want to go back to all of those other lifetimes.

But the thing is, sometimes I think I am so identified with the abuse or pain myself that I lose the clue of who I am.

Exactly. And to make it simple is why I'm suggesting that first we just focus on this lifetime. Believe it or not, if you can resolve everything in this lifetime, wouldn't that be easier? That would take care of the past lifetimes, and you wouldn't have to come back and incarnate with the same problem again because you'll have resolved it in this lifetime. That's really positive information.

Okay.
You don't sound convinced.

No. Not at all. But I will think it over. I will consider it.
You can go back and do all of the other lifetimes. Think about all of the money you've spent on therapists who helped you out in the past lifetime.
No, no, I don't want to. I think I just have to rescue me from myself before the trauma.
What I am suggesting is that you restore yourself because you have inklings already of who you are now. Despite the trauma, you still have been able to

survive, to become who you are, to do spiritual work. You have a lot of clues — a lot of inklings — about who you are. You need to restore that part and bring that part to fill in the emptiness.

Okay. Now work on me. I will invite you to work on me, okay?
You still don't sound very convinced.

No, I'm not. But I'm working on it.
Another Participant: Hello Vywamus. My question is the extension of everything that's been discussed in a way. So we can drop all of our karmic imprints and everything if we are able to separate our bodies and our minds. We have to be able to release and to come to the ultimate truth of who we are as beings. We have to understand the true nature of our being and the ultimate reality of truth and understanding of our true nature. The mind, the ultimate self, and the body are separate. Each provides experiences. So are we able to realize our true nature? Can we realize our ultimate nature and truth of our being?
In essence, yes.

What do we need to do to drop this body?
The confusion is that the body should be viewed as integrated with everything. There are emotional, mental, physical, and spirit bodies. The best way to describe this is that you have a chance to bring all of the aspects of yourself into unity in any lifetime. Any lifetime concerned is an opportunity for enlightenment, if you want to call it that.

In this lifetime, you have the opportunity to do that through the ascension. The thing about the ascension is that you're going to skip a few grades. Most of you are probably not going to get it all together because it is quite a task to graduate with total integration. To get a glimpse of who you really are, yes, you can drop the ego, but talk about the self in balance with everything else. By restoring the self, you are allowing the energies of your true self to come into the earth. This includes your higher self.

This is Vywamus. Good day.

Negative Self-Talk

Vywamus

reetings. I am Vywamus. I am a soul psychologist. What is a soul psychologist? A soul psychologist is someone who is in the fifth dimension and specializes in understanding the psychological nature of the human condition. So right away you tell yourself, "It must be difficult to be in the human condition if you need a specialist to figure it out." I think you will agree, for you have been here for quite a few years, that Earth is a pretty weird place to be.

There are a lot of paradoxes and contradictions on Earth. It is supposed to be a logical world, but illogical things happen. There is a lot of density here, and there are many people with low vibrations. I cannot believe how many people always ask the same question: "Why am I here?" Even after being here for forty or fifty years, people are still asking that question.

You would think that after being here that long they would know why they are here, but it is kind of confusing because you do not get a letter when you are born telling you, "You are here to learn this lesson." Maybe the guides should start that.

When babies are born, they should get letters from the spirit world saying, "You are here to learn this Earth lesson. Do not open up this letter until you are eighteen years old." I do not know whether they would wait that long or whether they would believe what the lesson is. What if the lesson was: "You are here to learn how to be spiritual while you are in poverty"? Who would want to have that lesson?

There are people who had a lot of money in previous lifetimes and, because they had so much money and wealth, the wealth interfered with their ability to be spiritual. So now, in the next lifetime, maybe they decided — or their guides decided for them — that they would come back in this lifetime without any wealth to see whether they could be spiritual. Personally, I would say, "Give me another chance. I can come back rich, and I can show you I can still be spiritual." Would you not rather be rich and spiritual together?

Many of you are using your powerful spiritual affirmations to get wealth. We know that there are many teachers around the world saying, "Use my meditation techniques, and you will have wealth in six months. And please give me 2,000 euros so that I can teach you this technique, and I can become wealthy with you." Is it that important to be wealthy in order to be spiritual?

The Power of Self-Talk

Earth has the opportunity for free expression and free will. I know that you are here to study the ascension, and you may wonder, "Who is this guy Vywamus? What is he talking about? What does wealth have to do with the ascension?"

You know that you have a mental body besides your spiritual body too. I know you like to work with only the spiritual energy, and maybe you think that the mental energy is a little bit lower and beneath you. But one of the healings has to be on the mental body as well. The mental body is one of the four bodies. It has a powerful effect on all of the other bodies. What you believe about the mental reality has an effect, and what you believe about yourself has an effect.

One of my favorite topics is self-talk. This is one of the most important psychological discoveries of the twentieth century. Everybody thought that the most important psychological discovery was the Oedipus complex, but that is minor compared to what I am going to tell you now. And remember that you heard it from Vywamus, the soul psychologist.

The biggest change you can make in yourself is your self-talk. Self-talk is the words that you are silently telling yourself in your mind all the time. Did you know that you are having an ongoing conversation with yourselves almost twenty-four hours a day? Some of the things that you are telling yourselves are pretty bad. For example, here is some typical negative self-talk: "I am stupid. Why did I do that? I should have known better than that. The way I am going, I will never ascend. The ascension is only for more-worthwhile people. I am not worthy enough. That person over there is much more spiritual. They will ascend, but I will not. I meditate and meditate, and I still do not see the auras. What is wrong with me? I have been trying to hear the guides for twenty years, but I still do not hear anything."

Does any of that self-talk sound familiar? What effect do you think that negative self-talk has on your development? Part of your ascension work involves clearing up the mental body. If you cannot solve this problem, you can always come in another lifetime and try again. But one of the things that the guides have been fond of saying lately is that if you think Earth is a difficult place to live in 2014, wait until you come back in 2050 and see what it is like here. If you think that the weather is weird now, wait until you see it in 2050. The idea is that you will want to learn and clear as much as possible now so that you do not have to work out any more psychological issues later. It sounds simple enough, but it is difficult to get a handle on what to do with your personal problems.

It is like a computer. When the computer was born, it was given a program to operate. When you were born, you were given a program. Some of the program came from a past lifetime, but a lot of the current information came from the program your parents gave you. Now you are trying to solve all of these complicated problems, but you are using old software. You could try to put in a new program to see whether it will work. You know what it is like when you put a new program into an old computer: All of a sudden, it freezes, and you have to press Control+Alt+Delete to get out of it. The computer freezes. So how do you change your self-talk, and how do you change or download a new program into your mental body?

By the way, the new program should be something like this: "I am a starseed, and I am ascending." That is certainly better than the old program that you probably grew up with. But there are other issues even with that program that make you more sensitive. Sometimes there are other problems.

Vywamus Answers Questions

I know that we do not have a lot of time, and I know that you want to experience my wisdom as much as possible. And I cannot blame you for that. If you have any particular problems related to self-talk or changing your programs and life lessons, let me know now, and I will see whether I can help you.

I am a very mental person. When I try to do a meditation, my mind always goes somewhere else. I cannot stop my mind.

This is a case in which you have to work with your body to stop your mind. If you try to focus on the mind, you are fighting fire with fire. Some people think that you just have to sit there and that maybe after twenty years the mind will slow down. I find that, especially in this age, there are so many things to keep your mind occupied, so you sometimes have to work with the body.

Let me give you an example. You might find that it will be more helpful for you to do yoga or some type of physical exercise that will help you shut your mind off for a while. This was a standard practice in some of the ancient temples in China, and it was one of the main intentions of yoga many years ago. They would do certain body exercises and movements in order to move the energy away from the mind. After doing those exercises, they found that people were able to meditate better because they had discharged the energy.

You would have to find out what physical exercise suits you. Maybe weightlifting would be good for you. Have you thought about that? That was a joke. There are different types of exercises, and you have to see what is suitable for your body. For example, you might do well at swimming, and you might find out that you can more easily turn your mind off after swimming. Would you be willing to try one of those exercises? I am not sure which one would be suitable for you, but I think you get the idea. You might be surprised. Half an hour of exercise enables you to do two minutes of quality meditation, a depth in meditation that you could not achieve before.

My self-talk is usually "I am not perfect. I have not done things well."

I am glad that you are aware of your self-talk. A simple solution is to use another affirmation, such as "I am doing things the best I can with the ability I have for my highest good." You could change that sentence to suit you better. One idea for changing the self-talk is to create another talk for yourself. Who knows where that message you are saying comes from? It might not even come from you. It might come from your mother. It is not the most important thing to find out where it came from. The important thing is to shift the negative thinking so that you can create a better message for yourself. After what I told you, can you come up with a better message? I would like to hear it.

I will try. "I do the best I can with my present ability."

That would work, and that would give you more compassion toward yourself. Remember, Juliano was talking about the Planetary Tree of Life. He talked about judgment on one side and compassion on the other. Too much judgment is not good. You need more compassion toward yourself for your progress.

What about controlling fear?

This is a big issue. From my experience as a soul psychologist, I find that the fear is based on feeling cut off from the unity that is present. One thing about coming into the third dimension is that you lose the eternal contact with the oneness. If you do not feel connected, you obviously feel alone, and that is uncomfortable. One of the severest punishments in primitive societies was to be excommunicated from the group. In many situations, that person would prefer death to being kicked out of the group. This is the first place to start looking at fear.

The truth is that being cut off from unity is an illusion, but it feels real. There are other reasons for fear besides feeling disconnected. I would have to work with you in more depth to find out which type of fear you have that might be different. All the fears really come from being cut off, even from your own power and unity. When you do have something that bothers you, if you are in connection to your personal power and connected to your guides, teachers, and unity, then it is easier to deal with whatever the problem is.

You can also use this affirmation: "My personal power is getting stronger, and I am able to deal with (say whatever the fear is)." We have a special technique we use to increase the power of affirmations. You may have been saying other affirmations that were perhaps counterproductive for many years. Even if you are given correct or newer affirmations, how do you overcome the years of using the old affirmation? The answer is you use a fifth-dimensional light with your new affirmation to counterbalance the older affirmations of your subconscious.

Another Participant: When there are different paths to take, how can we make the right decision?

The fact that there are different paths to take is a good sign. There is a saying in spirituality: "There are many different paths, and they all lead to the same place." You have to connect with your own inner power and guidance. Then it becomes apparent what you should do. In your case, I do not think that any of the paths that you choose will be bad for you. Maybe one will be a little bit better than the other, but even if you choose the one that is not the best, it is still okay. I always say — and this is something very similar to what I told the other woman at the beginning — "Choose to the best of your ability what you think is your best path." Even if two paths are really close, use the best of your ability to choose. You can tell yourself this affirmation: "I will work to the best of my ability to choose that path that I think is best for me." But it is good that you have choices. Some people do not even see any choices.

What about things we have in the subconscious that we are not aware of and that are blocking us?

If there are things in the subconscious that are blocking you, you will see a symptom of the block somewhere in your life. There is always a thread in the conscious life that will lead you to the deeper block in the subconscious. Look for the threads and the link in the consciousness; there is always one. If you look hard enough, that will lead you to the subconscious block, and then you can easily remove it. But we do not recommend going to the subconscious first; we recommend using the conscious thread and using that connection to go to the subconscious.

Blessings to you all, my friends. This is Vywamus.

The Multidimensional Self

Vywamus

halom. Greetings. This is Vywamus. Let us look at the multidimensional self and its relationship to soul psychology. Soul psychology attempts to deal with the inner self, and the inner self is more than what is in your awareness. The inner self is more than what is in this incarnation, more than what is in this dimension, so there are different levels that need to be considered. In this lecture, we want to look at the multidimensional self — that is, the self and the parts of the self that are living in and experiencing other dimensions.

First, it is important to know that you have to have a certain stability of mind and stability in the third dimension to explore the multidimensional self. The multidimensional self is not considered part of your survival necessities, even in this age of 2014. You can say that the multidimensional self is not essential at all for survival. We could say that the multidimensional self is not necessary for the primitive human, and it's not necessary for the earlier development of humanity. However, even when we look at those aspects, I will point out that there are some benefits to the multidimensional self.

So the multidimensional self includes those aspects of you that exist on other dimensions. In particular, we are looking at the fourth and fifth dimensions. In soul psychology, I talk to many people whom we call starseeds. Starseeds are those great souls who are expanding their awareness to other realms and even have participated in experiences on other planets and on other star systems.

I am going to speak today more directly about the fifth dimension because each of you has a presence in the fifth dimension. Even though you are predominately in the third dimension, your soul has links to all the dimensions that exist.

Now you're focusing on the fifth dimension. Some starseeds are reporting that they are commanders of certain areas, and other starseeds are reporting that their multidimensional selves are doing healings, organizing groups, meeting with their soul families, or meeting with their guides and teachers. These are examples of the experiences of the multidimensional self.

Multidimensional Interaction

When we are involved in higher consciousness, it is useful and necessary to more directly connect with the multidimensional self. The ascension, the process of graduating from Earth and going to the fifth dimension, also involves the multidimensional self. As preparation for that process, it is necessary and helpful to experience, relate, and receive information from that fifth-dimensional self.

To more directly understand how it is possible that you're living in other dimensions, we need to look at time. Time on the third dimension is linear; therefore, the multidimensional self, the fifth-dimensional self, is that part of you that will be in your future. The fifth-dimensional self is that part of you that will ascend. The future self can't be described using linear technology.

In reality, time is not linear but rather circular. From this circular perspective, the past, present, and future are all interactive. When you take that perspective, you are interacting with your future self and with your higher self. In this view, you are interacting with your past self and your fifth-dimensional self.

The question is, what percentage of your incarnation or of your presence is in this dimension? You have a limited ability to participate in this dimension. Your conception of yourself and your ideas of who you are and how you can function limit you.

You have the ability to go into these other dimensions through meditation. Other methods include going into altered states of consciousness, astral projection, and thought projection. Other fifth-dimensional beings are coming to Earth using their technology and their spacecraft. They are working with you to help you experience the higher aspects of yourself.

There are great benefits to being able to experience these other higher-dimensional aspects of yourself. For example, there are great scientists, musicians, sculptors, doctors, and healers who have been able to bring down to Earth higher skills and artistic talents by connecting with their fifth-dimensional selves. One of the contributions necessary in this time is to find ways and links to connect with your fifth-dimensional self. It is important to bring the information and the experiences from the fifth dimension back into the third dimension. One of the overall goals of healing the third dimension is found in the energies and links of the fifth dimension, and one of the major roles of the starseeds is to continue to provide links to their fifth-dimensional selves. You can bring down that perspective to the third dimension so that it can be healed and become more unified.

Examples of people connecting with their fifth-dimensional selves include Albert Einstein, Mozart, and Beethoven. Some of the great discoveries in medicine and science, such as the discovery of x-rays by Wilhelm Röntgen or the discovery of the polio vaccine by Jonas Salk, were achieved through these scientists using their higher-dimensional contacts.

There are many examples of people who allow their multipresence to be experienced in the other dimensions and then bring that information and those experiences back into the third dimension. Going to the fifth dimension in thought projections, for example, helps you to prepare for your eventual graduation to that dimension. You have to have a perspective and knowledge of other dimensions before you can actually go into those other dimensions.

From the fifth dimension, you still can have a powerful perspective of the third dimension, and interestingly, with the proper mind expansion, your third-dimensional experience can offer you a perspective of the fifth dimension. This means that your fifth-dimensional self can offer you a greater perspective on your third-dimensional self. Perspective is everything in mind expansion; perspective is everything in soul growth and in the evolution of yourself. In essence, I can say that the perspective of your fifth-dimensional self can give you the complete picture of who you are, how you are developing on Earth, and what all the outcomes of your actions are going to be.

The fifth-dimensional self can also help to arrange guides and protection for you as you are going through the third-dimensional trials and tribulations. The fifth-dimensional self has access to other higher beings who are also seeking connections to you. There are other humans who are in the third dimension who are projecting themselves and wishing to contact their fifth-dimensional selves. People who are projecting their energies into their fifth-dimensional selves can more easily meet other people on the planet who are doing the same thing.

In modern psychology, having multiple aspects of the self emerge at once is often considered a serious mental illness. This has been called multiple personality syndrome and is even a disorder according to modern psychology and psychiatry. We must make a distinction: Experiencing your multidimensional self is not the same as having multiple personality disorder. Multiple personality disorder is often characterized by confusion, irresponsibility, and lower consciousness, and accessing your multidimensional self is characterized by feelings of harmony, heightened awareness, and contact with your higher self.

You need to have mental stability to engage in the experience of the multidimensional self. You will begin to receive messages from your higher self, from your guides and teachers, and from the ascended masters. There are other body experiences that you will begin to have, including time changes and time and space shifting. You will see that your current space-time continuum is linear, and you will begin to experience the space-time continuum as circular and have a higher perspective of reality known as unity consciousness. Such higher perspectives can cause problems in your daily living if you are mentally unstable because these higher experiences are often confused with "hearing voices" and "seeing visions." But if you are stable and are formally rooted in the third dimension, then all these experiences will be exciting and will make you feel very creative and stimulated.

Learning about One Dimension from Another

Let us again look at the story of Adam and Eve. In the beginning of the story, Adam and Eve were in the fifth dimension. However, their actions resulted in them being thrown out of the fifth dimension. They had to enter the third dimension. When they were in the fifth dimension, they did not understand the benefits of being there. When they came down to the third dimension, they realized the benefits of living in the higher dimension. From the third dimension, they uniquely had the perspective of what it was like being in the fifth dimension, or the Garden of Eden. Because they were in the fifth dimension, they continued to have special powers in the third dimension. In fact, they had special powers throughout their lives.

The story of Adam and Eve gives you information and instructions about the multidimensional self. They lived in two dimensions. The perspective and the experiences of the third dimension help you appreciate the fifth dimension. The third-dimensional self is related to the fifth-dimensional self, and likewise, the fifth-dimensional self is related to the third-dimensional self.

As you go deeper into yourself and deeper into your meditations, you will become more comfortable in opening up the veils of perception. You will have more experiences with your fifth-dimensional self. You will have more understanding that you're a multidimensional being. You will be able to draw the information and power from that energy of the higher dimension and bring it to the third dimension. You will be able to solidify your links to the fifth dimension by using your third-dimensional perspective. This will make you a better person in this third dimension, and it will offer you better preparation for your graduation from Earth and your eventual entry and merging with your fifth-dimensional self. But even in your fifth-dimensional self, you will be multidimensional with the higher dimensions, which includes your seventh-dimensional self.

I am Vywamus.

The Past Self

Vywamus

reetings. I am Vywamus, a soul psychologist. So you want to learn more about yourself and why you are here on Earth. You want to learn who you are, what your mission is, how much time is left in this Earth, and what the easiest way is to get out of this planet without any pain. Well, remember a little bit of pain is okay.

I know that you do not like pain on the third dimension. There is so much pain going on. I imagine it's very uncomfortable for you on Earth. You see pain from other people. I know that you are particularly traumatized by seeing pain in animals and plants and all the living beings. It is a mystery why the population in general mistreats animals, plants, and Earth. This is one of the big mysteries of the whole Earth experience. I'm sure you will agree.

Why does everyone want to kill each other? You certainly have seen enough of this in your cowboy movies and detective movies. It looks like so much fun to kill everybody. I've never quite understood that either, but the movies certainly like to glorify pulling out a gun and shooting people. Maybe it is understandable why people kill each other. Maybe they think it's fun or they think they have the right to do it. It makes them feel strong. But it never seems to make sense to me why they want to hurt the animals and the plants.

Incidentally, I do want to say something about the plants. People on Earth don't seem to make the connection between plants and breathing. I always find that a big mystery. I don't think you need to study quantum physics and entanglement theory to see the relationship between plants and air. It always seemed pretty clear to me, the importance of plant life for the air. Yet I still notice that people are arguing about whether it is okay to cut the trees down. They think that just replanting trees in a line, in a row, is going to solve the problem. They don't seem to understand that Earth needs a forest, not a garden.

But I'm hoping that there will be an "aha" moment. You know that "aha" moment when suddenly everything becomes clear? Everything seems to fall into place. Maybe we could start a movement in which instead of saying "amen," we could say "aha." *Aha!* We'll try that a little bit later as a mantra. *Aha!* You want to have that "aha" moment when everything is crystal clear.

Why the Past Is Important Now

You want to know why you are here, who you are, and what more you have to do on Earth before you can graduate. In order to help you understand the answers to these questions, I'm going to discuss a very controversial subject in this lecture: the past. I know modern metaphysics, such as Zen Buddhism, teaches you to focus on the present. In fact, in modern Kabbalah, there is a beautiful Hebrew term for focusing the mind on the present: *He'nei'nee*, which is pronounced "he-nay-nee" and in English means "I am here" or "I am ready to interact with the Creator now, in the present." So the current mantra is "be here now." The idea is not to "be there then," which is a cute way of stating that your mind is focusing too much in the past. A follow-up question to "be here now" and "be there then" is "Will you be there in the future?"

I am going to suggest to you in a very radical way that the past does matter — that who you were in the past does have an important relationship to your present being. There is a great benefit to knowing about your past lives and even knowing what star system you may have come from and what you have done in previous lifetimes. Working with your past lives is more than just trying to help those people make a living who are doing past-life therapy! [Chuckles.] The true conception of the self includes an integration of the past, present, and future.

This is expressed even in Kabbalah concepts in which they talk about the name of God and the Creator's relationship to time. One sacred name of God in Kabbalah is actually expressed in the future: "I Will Be." People commonly express this name as "I Am That I Am." What would you think of the expression, "I Was That I Was?" [Laughs.] That sounds like Popeye, doesn't it? "I was that I was, I am that I am, and that's all that I am." (For those who don't know, Popeye is a cartoon character in the United States.)

But why would you want to know your past, and why is the past important? There are some people I hear who say, "That's all in the past. I'm leaving my past behind me, and I am moving on." That sounds like a powerful position. You can't do anything about the past anyway, right?

Well, let me give you some arguments for working with the past, and you can certainly disagree with me. I won't be offended. Maybe your arguments will be more convincing than mine, but let me start with a simple concept from Alcoholics Anonymous in which they emphasize that they want to make amends for the past. They recommend, as part of the healing process, that you ask people for forgiveness for wrong deeds that you have done in the past. Why would forgiveness be important if somebody has done bad things and then they totally renounce the bad behavior? They already stopped the drinking. Why would it be important to make amends? Making amends means that you now admit your bad behavior in the past, and you are going to ask for forgiveness. This helps both people go through a healing process.

Why, for example, does Germany want to make amends with Israel and pay reparations if the past is not important? Why would the past be important, and why would admitting that you were wrong be important? Why would you have to make amends?

I believe that your past lives are your history. It's the growth of your soul. I believe that's important, although I've heard a lot of people saying, "Well, that's ego going back to who you were." But I think that the growth of your soul is related to where you've been. It reflects your history of what you've been inclined to do in each lifetime.

So do you think it's important to make amends for things that you've done in the past if now you realize they were wrong?

I think stating the fact that you are sorry is important, yes.

Have you ever apologized for something done in the past?

Yes.

So there is something that strikes you now that, when you look at your past, you want to make amends for. Have you been able to do it yet?

I've pretty well worked through that with the help of someone.

Okay, good. So you see the value in working with the past?

Yes.

Good. So that's one on Vywamus's side.

Stored Trauma, Denial, and Repression

I think it is important to work through our past because I believe that it is still part of us energetically. If you work through it, maybe you can work through your energetic knots.

Very good point. Many of you are body therapists. Most body therapists know that emotions from the past are stored in the muscle tissues. Is that a fair statement?

Even though you may think you have resolved the past, the body still has a memory, and it still may carry a lot of the trauma and a lot of the pain that was in the past. But the human body also is very adaptable. That means that the body and the mind are integrated. The body remembers all traumas, but you, in your conscious memory, can forget them. You can think that everything is resolved in your mind, but the memory of the trauma may still be your body.

So my question to you is this: Do you think a trauma that is resolved in your mind is also resolved in your body? Is the trauma still stored in your muscle memory even if you have worked out the trauma mentally? Would you consider a mental resolution a complete healing?

A mental healing is a step on the way to a total healing.

In other words, the trauma can still be in the body. I want to point out in my deep study of the human condition that I am intrigued by the defense structure of humans. There is one universal defense, and if I could have only one defense, can you guess which one I would choose?

Audience: Denial.

Yes, of course. I love denial. Denial is worth its weight in gold. You can get so far with denial. You can deny so much. In fact, you could deny that the biosphere is dying. You could deny that global warming exists. You know the arguments. I think you call them "rationalizations," and they are wonderful [laughs]. I listened to some of the arguments about Earth being okay, and you're right. You're absolutely right. Everything is fine on Earth.

Fracking is not causing any problems. Radiation leakages are not a problem. Yeah, you've resolved all your problems. You told me you have. That's all I need to know.

I'm always intrigued that people want to go to psychics, because a part of them knows that they are in denial, and they are hoping that somehow the psychic will see through the denial and tell them what's really going on. That's so obvious. But there's always a part that really knows that you are experiencing denial. It might be a part of you that's hard to reach.

There's another favorite defense mechanism I like: repression. That's a great one. The basis of repression is that you just stuff it. That goes a long way too. You just swallow it; you put it away somewhere; you sweep it under the rug. With denial and repression — boy, you'd have to be pretty sharp and motivated to break through these two defenses! You need a lot of strength to push through them and get to the truth. At the same time, you might be surprised to hear me say that these defenses can be useful.

Using Your Defenses

Some of the circumstances that you have experienced during this lifetime had no immediate solutions. I mean, if you want to talk about painful experiences, let's talk about childhood. There you were as a child — pretty powerless and with two crazy parents who had no understanding of your spiritual sensitive nature yet were totally in control of you. They might have been doing weird things. They might have been drinking, they might have been physically abusive, or they might even have been sexually abusive. There were a lot of painful situations during your childhood, especially if you are a starseed — because being a starseed means that you have a sensitive nature.

Most of the starseeds I have met are psychic even though they don't want to admit it — denial again. Why do they deny the positive? Have you noticed that too? People think that defenses are only to be used for negative things, but you can use the denial for positive attributes as well. For example, you can say, "Oh, I'm not very psychic. I'm not very sensitive. I'm not very spiritual." So the denial also works there, even though you have a psychic gift.

You have come into this planet and culture with great sensitivity. Sensitivity is required to be a starseed. A starseed is a person who has been incarnated on other planets. In most cases, the starseed is an older soul and knows a great deal about the galaxy. Remember, being more sensitive also means that you experience much more pain.

You can deny your sensitivity and make yourself less sensitive. The problem is, when you make yourself less sensitive, you don't feel as much, and you are not psychic. You lose your ability to connect to the other realms. Blocking that connection is a very high price to pay. One thing that would be terribly painful on the third dimension focuses on being cut off from the Source and from higher light. It is hard enough to experience duality and the pain and suffering that go along with it. If you are connected to the Source, then you know that duality is just a temporary experience. You know that duality is an illusion, that there is greater purpose to this appearance of duality.

Soul Retrieval

I've talked about the past and the resolution or integration of the past self. I now want to talk about soul retrieval, because soul retrieval is a tool for understanding the past self. By the way, as a soul psychologist, I know about the importance of soul retrieval. It is based on retrieving lost or dissociated parts of yourself from other lifetimes. These parts need to be reunited with your current self in this lifetime. For example, imagine that in a previous lifetime you were sensitive and were involved in interesting but culturally unacceptable spiritual pursuits. In that past lifetime, there was a period when you were punished for your spirituality and psychic gifts. You were traumatized, and you were forced to go underground and hide yourself. You had to deny yourself and your spirituality for survival.

An example of this situation is being a witch in medieval Europe in the fifteenth or sixteenth century. People had mistaken ideas that women who were psychics were witches. There were 2–3 million women who were killed for being accused of being witches. That is a tremendous number of women who were killed over several centuries. Imagine that you were a psychic, spiritually minded woman in that time in central Europe. You would have to protect yourself from the dangers of being accused of being a witch. If you engaged in psychic-spiritual energy work, then you could be falsely charged for being a witch and be burned at the stake. So during this lifetime, you denied and repressed your spirituality as a means of survival. That's a pretty high price to pay; you decided to suppress your spiritual side and deny all of your psychic abilities so as not to be mistaken for a witch. You left that part of your soul there in that lifetime. You continued to live your life without any spiritual practices. When you died, you had so repressed and so denied that part of yourself that you became disassociated from that part of yourself and left that part there in that lifetime.

I will try to explain "disassociated" because that term has several different meanings in modern psychology. Generally, disassociation can be considered a coping mechanism for dealing with an overwhelming trauma. When you are faced with a trauma such as physical or sexual abuse, you disassociate yourself from that part of you. By using this defense mechanism, you do not have to directly experience the pain and suffering of the trauma. In essence, you leave behind the part of yourself that experiences the pain. Therefore, when you die, you do not bring that part of yourself with you.

Now there is another important concept related to disassociation that is called soul imprinting. This is another important term in social psychology. Soul imprinting refers to the process whereby experiences, both positive as well as negative, are imprinted on the soul so that they carry through from lifetime to lifetime, or through each incarnation. Soul imprinting also includes the "imprinting" of skills and gifts, such as psychic abilities, healing skills, and even musical abilities. The existence of soul imprinting is seen most prominently, for example, in musicians, mathematicians, or scientists who have extraordinary skills at a very young age and are considered child prodigies. They actually bring these skills and abilities in from previous lifetimes, and this represents an example of gifts imprinted by the soul from a previous life-time and then brought into this incarnation.

So here you are in the present in this lifetime. You disassociated yourself from the part of you that was the spiritual side and psychic side because of fear of being punished for your "witch"-like powers. The imprint of fear of punishment is now with you in this lifetime. Now in this lifetime, you are beginning to feel safe and comfortable, so you begin to explore your spiritual side. For some reason, you find yourself feeling uncomfortable as you explore spirituality. Then when you can go back through soul retrieval work, you find that part of yourself that had the fear of being punished for spirituality and psychic abilities. That part of you was blocked. During the soul retrieval, you bring back that part of yourself and reintegrate it into your current self. In this current lifetime, you now feel safe to explore your spirituality and spiritual gifts. So this is an example of bringing disassociated parts of yourself back from a past lifetime and integrating them into the here and now.

Making Amends and Disassociating

Participant 2: If you don't mind, just go back for a moment about making amends whenever possible when you injure someone or others. I think that's important to add on there. The training that I've been exposed to recommends that we amend the list. The first person that you put on the list for making amends is yourself!

So it is important to look at your past, and it is important to make amends in the past to yourself. I like the word "amends" because it implies that there's some correction that you can do to yourself. Many of you were warriors in your past lives. You may have had experiences in which you were out of control.

If you harmed somebody in this lifetime, then you can make amends now. You also can stop the karma by making amends. If you have harmed some people in this lifetime, then you might find that behavior could tie you to Earth's incarnational cycle. Making amends can help you become free from karma. You, as an aspiring ascended master, want to free yourself from the Earth incarnational cycle.

Are there any other comments or questions, especially about the witches? Is there anybody who remembers a past life as a witch?

Participant 3: I had a memory of a death experience. I saw myself being burned, and I had three children telling me, "You promised you would stay this time." And in the middle of this death situation, I knew I wanted to stay this time. I made that promise. It also reminds me that I have that memory now, so when I become discouraged, I remember I made a promise to get through this life, so …

You made a promise to stay, so were you burned at the stake?

I was burned at the stake. The memory is of those three children who lost me and what I heard them saying: "You promised this time you would stay."

I think that the soul is more intriguing, more complicated, and more beautiful than you might even know — and more complex. To me, it's fascinating that parts of the soul would stay back in other lifetimes, and it's fascinating that you could retrieve that part of yourself from that lifetime. I like that concept, because what you will find is that people have left parts of themselves behind in previous lifetimes. The same concept of soul retrieval in past lifetimes works in this lifetime. So if you were physically or sexually abused when you were a young person in this lifetime, then it is safe to assume that you disassociated. "Disassociation" is a keyword, and the idea of soul retrieval is linked to this concept of disassociation.

Disassociation, to explain it simply, is taking the self and sending it up five or ten feet above you, watching what is happening to you but not feeling it. That is a coping mechanism, but it also implies that part of your self is left there at that experience. You have distanced yourself from the trauma so that you do not have to feel the pain from the experience.

Participant 4: I have had several lives as a witch and a pagan. I recently took a walkabout in London visiting known places where witches and ghosts may have been. I was taken to the very place where they were drowning witches or people they suspected of being witches. If you sank to the bottom of the water, you were innocent but dead, and if your body floated, you were a witch and deserved to die. The tour guide demonstrated this punishment by asking me if I was a witch, and all of a sudden, all the blood went down to my feet and I thought, "Oh no, not again." To this day, I don't swim well because I'm afraid to be out of breath. So did I leave a part of myself back there?

Yes, you did leave a part of yourself back in that lifetime, and yes, you can deal with it in this lifetime because it is a part of you. One of the goals in this lifetime is to integrate as many parts of yourself as you can. What I like to emphasize as a soul psychologist is that you are multipresent, you are multitalented, and you are multidimensional.

This may sound like the condition known as multiple personalities, which is a diagnosis for a mental disturbance. I would like to talk about multiple personalities. Multiple personality disorder is a true case of disassociation that was carried through. In this condition, integration was never done in the lifetime. Having multiple personalities is a true verification of reincarnation because, in this condition, a person has brought back as many as seven or eight disassociated and unfinished parts of the self into this lifetime.

But in your case, I would say that the skills that you had as a witch were repressed in this lifetime. I know you're deeply spiritual. You have deep spiritual gifts, but because of your previous traumas, there still is a reluctance — and understandably so — to allow those skills to emerge because of the memory from the previous lifetime of what could happen.

So in the soul retrieval, that part of yourself that blocked or was blocked can be brought back to you and integrated so that you can be more of who you really are, which includes the psychic side of you and your spiritual side.

Resolving Past Trauma on Your Own

Participant 5: I don't remember my past lives, of course, but sometimes we have some insights. What I would like to know is — okay, now we have difficulties because we left some parts of ourselves in the past. But I don't feel I would like to do a past-life regression, and I would like to know whether there is some other type of integration.

First of all, if you don't feel like going back to your previous lives, then you do not have to. But you have to ask yourself this question: Is my not wanting to go back to past lives a denial or a repression of previous traumas? Am I really integrated? Have I really repaired myself? It doesn't mean that you have to go back if you answer, "I am not repaired." It doesn't mean you have to go back to do past-lives work. If you are not oriented to do that, then do not pursue past-life work. This is like how everybody doesn't have to have the medical treatment of penicillin. Past-life therapy is a valid method. Soul therapy can focus on looking at what is happening in this lifetime. Remember, because what happens in this lifetime is in resonance with the past lifetimes, treatment can occur by accessing events in your current life. You — we — can still work on soul problems from the perspective of the present lifetime.

I would like to be sure that there are a variety of different kinds of treatment or therapy for my problems.

First of all, we need to find out what the problem is. You say "cure." Well, what am I curing? Do you feel okay? Do you feel that you're intact, or do feel that you are repressing something? Do you have a problem? Maybe you're totally enlightened and have had the "aha" experience and don't need the intervention of a soul psychologist.

I try to help myself the way I know would be better for me. These are people trained in clearing your conscious records. Each time I go to a therapist, I'm aware of what I need to be working with.

The other idea you must understand in doing soul psychology and soul retrieval and healing is this: Do you feel blocked? That's a simple question. Is everything flowing in your life, or do you feel blocked? Is everything going the way you want? Is your health fine? How are your relationships?

But everything is not fine. I have problems in many of these areas.

Do you feel blocked? Maybe you are not expressing your spiritual gifts in this lifetime.

Yes.

So what do you want to do about it? Do you want to be unblocked or stay blocked?

No, I don't want to stay blocked, but I guess I can try to see. I'm looking for a way to cure myself.

So you're looking for a way to cure yourself as opposed to trying to find help from someone else?

I am open for a healing both from someone else and from inside myself.

Let me say that, based on your past-life experiences — which you don't want to remember — you were dominated and controlled by other people, and you want to solve all this by yourself by learning how to trust yourself. This means that you have done a fantastic job in arranging this lifetime so that you now have the freedom to do this. And I think that's wonderful. Can I tell you what the problem is?

Sure.

The problem is you may be running out of time. You may say, "Well, I want to try to fix this, and I want to do it myself," and that is noble. I encourage everybody who wants to fix it by themselves to do so, but do you have enough time left in this lifetime to fix it by yourself?

Well, when I realize I don't have enough time, then I just let go. I try to forgive myself and just let it go.

Well, does that work?

In many ways, it works, yes. But in other ways, it does not work, and I am left with the feeling that this is just something that I have to solve by myself.

Don't be shy about getting help from other people. You have been hurt before in past lives. You've trusted people before in past lives because you thought they were going to help you, and they didn't. They betrayed and harmed you. So you have a reluctance to seek help from other people in this lifetime, and that's understandable. But I just want to tell you that it is okay to seek help now from people in this lifetime. The people you are seeking to help you will not harm you anymore. It will not happen.

You may need some outside help. If you see somebody you feel attracted to whom you think might be able to help you, then go for it. Time is accelerating now. Looking at the condition of Earth and the planetary crisis, I can say that time is running out. Try to solve this problem as soon as possible.

Participant 6: In this lifetime, I have dealt with a lot of imprints from other lifetimes. For me, I decided to go back and do the healing from these imprints by myself, but of course, having somebody guide you always makes it that much easier.

The fact is that you are not overly guarding from pain. If there is a lot of pain in these imprints, then there's always reluctance — because people always want to avoid pain — to go back and experience pain. Incidentally, there is also a side effect because, to go back and experience the pain, there's an accompanying fear that you will be stuck in that pain. But what I'm saying about you [to the participant] is that you don't have that fear. You're not going to get stuck, and you're more open, and that's good.

So I don't tell people that they should ignore their pain. They are fearful of the pain, and they don't want to go back and reexperience the pain. They are fearful because they might get stuck, and that is a good reason to avoid going back. Pain is a good teacher, but it also makes you avoid things, and it makes you very careful.

In summary, soul retrieval exists both in the past and the present lifetimes. Indeed, there are parts of your soul that can be retrieved even from this lifetime that became stuck due to a trauma in your childhood.

I am Vywamus. Good day.

The Future Self

Vywamus

reetings. I am Vywamus, a soul psychologist. I will talk about the future self. I think it's important to have a conception of time because, on the third dimension, time is linear. You know this. You have the past and the present and the future, and it's like a line progression. But in reality, time is a circle or sphere, and the energies of the past, present, and future are actually interactive. In fact, your past self does interact with your present self, and your present self also can interact with your future self. In a more complicated way, the future self can interact with the past self.

These are not normal perceptions that are used in your philosophy or in your religion. Some of the basic core beliefs that have become the foundation of the major religions in the West and the East are based on the concept that your past actions will affect what happens to you in the future. Actually, many people readily accept that the future self exists. What is controversial is, what actions and what effect does the past self have on the future self?

It is a great step forward to understand that your future self exists. In the animal world, for example, the animals do not know that. They do not know they have future selves, but at the same time, the animals are living in their present selves totally. In your future, you are ascended masters. You are on the fifth dimension in your future selves. You are working in higher light. The question is, how does that energy in the future affect you now?

A simple way to look at this situation is to imagine that you are going to inherit money in the future. If you know you are going to be a millionaire in two years, then you might buy things now knowing that you'll have the money later. You might not go into debt, but you know you are saving money, and you might say, "Well, if I have $1 million in the future, then I could spend this money now because I will have a million dollars in two years." That's a simple example of how the future self affects the present self and its behavior.

Now, if you know that in two years you are going to ascend and you are going to be an ascended teacher or master, you might decide that you are going to totally devote yourself as much as possible to studying religion, spirituality, and energy work. You might want to have as much background or experience as possible in preparation for your future work. In fact, your work coming from that knowledge would actually encourage and help that future self arrive earlier. That is to say, you might ascend quicker. You might achieve what I call the "aha" experience at an earlier time because you have gained a confidence in yourself that you did not have. You gained a certainty in yourself that allows you to bring this knowledge of your future into your present.

Imagine that you knew you were going to write a spiritual book two years from now on the Tree of Life. You are not going to write the book now because you don't have the knowledge yet to write the book. But you know you're going to write it in two years, so you think, "Well, I better prepare myself for my future work and the fact that my future self is going to do this." This sets into motion certain things that are necessary so that you can do the best job possible in writing this book. Your future self can influence how you are in the present.

A Relationship with the Future Is Important

I want to teach the concept of future self to the planet, and I want to have the planet understand that the projected future of Earth does not have the most positive outcome. Therefore, the present behavior of the planet must change so that the future changes. This is a difficult concept to instill on a planet, but it is part of the planetary stages of development.

I will go back to the idea of writing the book. So you study now in preparation for the book after you decide that you are going to write it, but you're not going to get any reward for it. There is no reward until the book is written, and that's not going to happen for two years. So what is the motivation to do anything now?

Well, the answer is that it requires a higher order of thinking, a higher order of experience, to understand the relationship between your future self and your present self. It requires a higher order of consciousness. The reward for your efforts will come later, which is sometimes referred to as delayed gratification. This is where humankind is stuck right now. Humankind does not understand as a planet the effect of the future Earth on the present Earth. The solution to Earth's problems is rather painful because Earth's problems become accelerated as humankind neglects the relationship with the future self in the present. As events become accelerated, the length of time between the events in the future and the present diminishes to a point at which you will see simultaneously that a present action has an immediate effect.

This phenomenon has been referred to as the "butterfly effect" in environmental science. One butterfly moving in a different direction suddenly changes everything — all the weather patterns and other Earth events shift dramatically because of the seeming shift of how the butterfly has changed its behavior. Of course, the butterfly did not have all of that power, but its behavior was an accumulative shift of all events, and the butterfly's shift represented the "straw that broke the camel's back." But there are also positive events in the future self. The fact that you acknowledge the future self exists means that you believe in your eternal nature. Belief in the future self means that you do have a future.

Knowing that you are going to be successful in writing this book in the future will make you feel better in the present. It will raise your self-esteem knowing that you will earn $1 million in two years; that's definitely going to be a helpful prediction for you. You have to learn to be more mature by incorporating the concept of delayed gratification into your behavior.

In conclusion, I want you to understand that the future self is important for your present self. There are healing methods for accessing the energy in the future so that you can bring the future knowledge and information into the present.

Isn't it encouraging to know that you're going to be an ascended master in the future? And that your time here is short and you want to learn as many things as possible? You can even travel to your future self. The self is multidimensional, which includes multitime dimensional.

I am Vywamus. Good day.

Soul Inclination and Reincarnation

Vywamus

reetings. I am Vywamus, a soul psychologist. In this session, we will talk about the training necessary to be a soul psychologist and about the proper perspective that a soul psychologist must take.

When you look at the term "psychologist," you will naturally think of modern psychology. If you look at modern psychology and how it has developed, then you might conclude that modern psychology has severe limitations. Basically, modern, mainstream psychology does not want to deal with reincarnation. It does not want to deal with soul energy.

When you look at the soul energy and the previous soul imprint, you have to look at some of the mystical approaches to psychology. For example, we know that in the Kabbalah, some of the ancient rabbis were able to look at people's foreheads and tell what their previous soul lives or previous incarnations were. They also were able to tell what their inclinations are in this lifetime. Every soul actually has an inclination, and this inclination is manifested in every lifetime — even in your different lifetimes. So, for example, we may say that your soul is oriented toward compassion, or it might be oriented toward humor. Or it might be inclined immediately toward spiritual matters. This liking is what I would call the "soul inclination." The early rabbis were able to look at a person and tell what the soul's inclination was.

Understanding soul inclination is important for a soul psychologist because some people are not following their soul inclinations. For example, let's say that a person's soul inclination was toward music and creativity. Then let us say that the person did not follow that. She decided or was forced into studying something like engineering or mechanics. She may be good at those subjects, but it's not following her soul inclination. So the soul psychologist is interested in learning what the soul inclination of the person is that they are working with.

How do these people, these mystics, these rabbis, teach themselves to read the soul inclination from the forehead? Well, actually, there are several methods. You could read the soul inclination from hand reading. The handwriting also can reveal the soul inclination. So we have reading of the hands and the lines of the hands. The handwriting, the forehead, and the configuration of the lines on the forehead are evidence of soul inclination, but more importantly, it's the third eye. You can connect with the person's third eye as a soul psychologist, and when you do, you can receive information about his or her soul inclination. In fact, as a soul psychologist, it is always good when you are with the person to visualize that your third eye is connecting with his or hers. Using this method, you should be able to receive a great deal of information about the other person.

The soul psychologist is also interested in past lives and the lessons from past lifetimes. The soul psychologist is interested in higher levels of consciousness and how to access those levels of consciousness. The soul psychologist is interested in what the soul lessons of the person are. Helping the person identify what the soul lessons are can be one of the key ingredients in the work of the soul psychologist. In other words, the soul psychologist wants to identify to the client what his or her soul lessons are.

The Soul Lesson and the Freewill Zone

When a client is facing difficulties in a situation, the soul psychologist knows that the information and the circumstances from those difficulties give the soul psychologist immediate information about the soul lesson of that client. From this perspective, we say that everyone has some soul lessons on Earth now. If there are no soul lessons, and if the person has learned everything he or she needs to, then really there is no need to incarnate. In fact, from our perspective, the fact that you have incarnated here means that you have a soul lesson and that you have some circumstances and situations to work through, to learn. I think that it is a good analogy to say that Earth is a school, a freewill school, because people do have free will, and because of that, there are great opportunities to learn.

If you have learned everything there is to learn on Earth, then you might conclude that there's no reason to come back. However, in returning you could focus on having a commitment to provide service to this planet. So I want to emphasize that some starseeds — especially ones who are coming to Earth now — are here particularly to be of service. The mission can be how to go about service, how to present that service, and how to be an effective server on a planet. Service can be focused on working as a planetary healer.

This suggests that many starseeds have come here to learn how to be planetary healers. Some starseeds have come here to learn how to be healers of humanity. From the soul perspective, there are many different planets, and there are many different circumstances on other planets that are good for soul learning. Sometimes people are even coming to Earth for training in how to work with a planet and how to work with a whole species and its people.

Incarnation and Karma

Now I would like to look at soul psychology from the perspective of incarnation and karma. When people look at karma, they also look at punishments and cause and effect, which is accurate, but karma is more than that. Karma is also lessons. Karma is also learning how to experience both sides. For example, karma can include how to experience the masculine, the feminine, homosexuality, and heterosexuality, or how to experience being disabled versus being able-bodied. There are many cases in which people were making fun or being hypercritical of people who are homosexual. But then they could be setting themselves up in the next lifetime to be homosexual so that they could experience what it is like on the other side of that.

Karma is complicated from the soul psychologist's perspective. We are interested in learning what the past lives of a client are because, a lot of times, we can understand why certain circumstances exist in this lifetime. What is relevant and important to understand is that people are usually reincarnating in soul groups. I like to use the term "karmic groups."

Soul groups are people who are from the same soul family or from the same soul tree. They reincarnate together because they help each other. It's also important to note that healers are usually the most effective in healing people from their soul groups. So all healers have a particular range of people with whom they can work, but as they get more experience in lifetimes, their range expands, and they are able to heal even people who are not in their soul groups. The range of healing ability then becomes broader.

There is also the phenomenon of reincarnating in groups that have karmic history together. For example, you could reincarnate with the same type of family over again even though they are not in your soul group. This happens because there are certain lessons and certain information that you have to learn, and sometimes the lesson is finished when you learn how to free yourself from a certain level of vibrational group energy from these families. So I find that many people always question, "Well, why did I choose this father? Why did I choose this brother?" And many people say, "Well, I'm not particularly connected to my family. I don't feel connected to my parents on a soul level at all." In fact, people often say, "I really want to get away from my parents as quickly as possible."

Try to understand that sometimes the families you choose are able to provide you with certain lessons. These could be lessons in self-esteem or codependency. They could be lessons in serving people. Maybe you also have some certain service to teach the family. Maybe in another lifetime, you had some kind of karmic debt to them, and now you're paying them back.

Don't automatically think that your parents come from your soul family because in many cases, they do not. In some cases, the parents just wind up being convenient because they are able to offer the right circumstances. Your parents might be able to offer you the right geographical location, or they might be able to offer you the perfect balance that will give you the Earth experiences you need. So I just want to clarify that often the parents are not soul members.

On the other hand, there are many circumstances in which parents are soul members, and it's not unusual to see a mother and child or mother and daughter very close. It's not unusual to see a father and son be really close. When you see such a closeness, you can see that they come from the same soul group. Sometimes they even switch roles in the family hierarchy from one lifetime to the next. For example, in one situation, one is the father, but in the next lifetime, the son may become the father. The soul psychologist is aware of this type of role reversal in incarnations.

Psychic Impressions

Now the question is, how does the soul psychologist get this information? Well, it comes from a two-step process. The first step is that you get what I call "psychic impressions." These impressions come from conversations with the person. The soul psychologist gets the impressions from seeing the person. Basically, it means that you put yourself in contact with the person's energy in some way. It can even be done remotely. So soul psychologists open themselves up to their own psychic abilities and intuition. They seek to become as psychically sensitive as possible toward their clients so that they begin to receive the information about the other person's soul journey.

Now, I know this is a leap for many people. They say, "Well, I'm not psychic." Many people will say, "This is being made up," or "I'm supposed to be a channel for that person, but I'm not a channel." The answer is that channeling and psychic abilities are learned skills. That means most people can learn how to increase their psychic awareness and their psychic skills. There are certain procedures you can follow to increase your psychic skills, and I will go over some of those procedures in these lectures. The most important point to understand at the moment is that soul psychologists use and access their psychic skills with the client and, in particular, they seek to connect with the client's third eye. The third eye is the area that can provide direct information about the soul.

Accessing Spirit Guides

Frequently we suggest that you ask the client the following question and give these instructions: "Would you please give me permission for my spirit guides to access your spirit guides so that I can bring down the highest information for your highest good?" This is an intriguing statement because, first, if the client can give this permission, then it is an excellent start for the healing process. It means that the client is acknowledging that he or she has spirit guides and that you, the soul psychologist, are accessing these spirit guides, who are willing to give information. We are talking about a beautiful connection. This brings the next important issue for the soul psychologist: You can use your spirit guides in order to directly access the spirit guides of the client. Using spirit guides is a great advantage in doing soul psychology work.

When you use a spirit guide, that spirit guide cohabits with you in a positive way. Remember the basic concept of positive cohabitation is that the positive guide has higher energy than you. Therefore, when the guide comes into your energy field, that guide is able to help you raise your vibration so that you can maximize your psychic ability, your spiritual abilities, and your abilities as a soul psychologist. That's why we recommend using very positive guides such as Archangel Michael, Chief White Eagle, and P'taah. There are many other spirit guides who can be used in soul psychology work, including Archangel Metatron.

Many different guides can be used, but remember each person has a specific guide who can be most helpful with specific tasks. This means you each have a specific guide who could help you with your soul work. For example, you have a guide who could help you as a medical spiritual adviser. You have a guide who could help you as a teacher. You have a guide who could help you as a healer. Many spirits are involved in guiding people who are doing Reiki healing work, for example. A spirit guide could help you as a spiritual philosopher. When doing healing work, the soul psychologist wants to connect with the spirit guide that he or she has who is oriented toward being a spirit guide for soul work.

So people might say, "Well, Vywamus, I don't have a soul psychologist that's around me," but I would say there are soul psychologists who are spirit guides among each of you. Ask your spirit guide to raise your ability, your sensitivity, your intuition, and your psychic ability. After a while, through repeated requests, encounters, and repeated work, you may find that your abilities have been so raised that you begin to feel a strong connection to your spirit guide. You may also find that you can use your spirit guide at the beginning of the session and then, after you are connected, information and healing energy will comfortably flow through you to your client for healing.

Removing Your Ego

The importance of spirit guides is that they help you to move into the right fifth-dimensional framework. Once you are on a higher-dimensional right track, then you can remove your ego from the encounter. I want to emphasize this important point about soul psychologists removing their egos. It's important that you step aside and allow the energy and the intuition to come through you without censorship.

Some people might say, "Well, as a soul psychologist, you can access your psychic impressions. Does that mean that you should have 100 percent accuracy?" But remember that 100 percent accuracy is a very high standard, and it is difficult for anyone — no matter how well trained and sensitive — to have 100 percent accuracy. In most cases, you can work and increase your accuracy. Seventy percent is a very good level of accuracy for a psychic reading.

So that is why I always suggest that you, as the soul psychologist, understand that you are accessing and receiving psychic impressions from the person. Use these psychic impressions together with basic third-dimensional information that you receive from normal perceptions. We are not of the persuasion that soul psychologists should do their work cold. (In this context, "cold" means doing the soul work without doing a basic interview during the work.) Doing a cold reading means clients just present themselves to you without giving you basic information about themselves.

There are some psychics who could do such cold readings. For example, Edgar Cayce was able to do cold readings with extraordinary ability. You must remember that he did so in full trance — that is, he lost consciousness and went to sleep during his sessions. He actually had no conscious memory of what he was channeling.

A soul psychologist offers more than a psychic reading. A soul psychologist helps people identify the lessons and different issues they are here to learn. Then the soul psychologist can help people integrate and learn the lesson and, in many ways, heal themselves so that they are more in balance with the lessons.

The Soul Journey, Directing the Self, and the Warrior Self

Many people have been warriors in previous lifetimes, so when they come into this lifetime, they still have the warrior energy and they want to exert their warrior powers. They might find that some kind of disability happens and they can't be as physically strong as they were in the other lifetime. Suddenly, they have to change their whole orientation.

So maybe they were going to be football players or soccer players, and then something happened and they weren't able to do that anymore, so they became devastated. They felt their whole world come to an end. From the soul psychology perspective, the soul is saying, "Look, we don't need to do this warrior self anymore. You do have the gift of the body with certain energies, but that's not what you need to do in this lifetime. Since you're not that spiritually oriented so far, and you've been so oriented toward football and physical things, we're going to have to help you out, to direct you, and the best way to direct you is for you to lose that warrior ability for a while."

Many times, when people are injured, they are suddenly able to get in touch with their soul purpose and soul energy. I know this is a difficult lesson for some people, but it's a good example of how the soul may work and how the soul psychologist can work with learning, understanding, and helping the person identify this. The soul psychologist may say, "Look, if you hadn't lost that ability to be a football player, then you never would have gotten into spiritual work" or "Maybe the spirit is directing you to another path, and this is how it's being shown."

Discussing the Soul Inclination

The soul works in interesting ways, and I think part of the problem is that your culture, your society — the Western society — does not emphasize, nurture, or encourage people to follow their soul inclinations. In fact, the whole subject of soul inclinations is not deeply discussed.

Just imagine that on some other planets, especially in the Pleiades, they spend a lot of time when a new person is born to understand what the soul inclination is. They work with that person to make sure he or she has the right circumstances and education to fulfill the soul inclination.

Many people on Earth do not even begin to deal with their soul inclinations till their forties or fifties. Two-thirds of their lives already have passed by then. Many people do things, including work, that have no relationship to their soul work or their soul inclination. So not dealing with your soul inclination is definitely a disadvantage — possibly even in terms of getting involved in relationships.

Levels of Consciousness

I want to also mention the relationship of psychic abilities to the level of consciousness because the soul psychologist also must study levels of consciousness. The soul psychologist must study the different levels of the soul: the higher, middle, and lower soul. Soul psychologists must study how people can enter alternate states of consciousness and use that to help themselves. Actually, soul psychologists want to go into alternative levels of consciousness so that they can access higher information more effectively. At the same time, soul psychologists want to help the clients reach other levels of consciousness.

Soul psychologists are also interested in shamanism and ceremonies. They're interested in chanting and in any methods used to change levels of consciousness or to go to higher levels of consciousness. This is because soul psychologists know that, when a person gets out of the normal state of consciousness, that person is much more open to higher input. In fact, this is really a key factor. You want your client to be open to higher input.

The Relationship between Soul Psychology and Illness

Vywamus

reetings. I am Vywamus, a soul psychologist. Now we will look at the relationship between soul psychology and illness — in particular, physical and mental illness.

There are many theories about physical illness. Some people believe that the soul made a decision before it entered the body that the body would experience a certain illness. There are other views that say, in a similar vein, that the person wanted the illness as a certain form of punishment. Then, of course, there is also the theory that the illnesses that occur are random and beyond the person's control. I want to look at all of those ideas because some truths are found in each of them. Our review indicates that there is no clear-cut answer, but rather it is often a combination of factors that lead the soul and the physical body into illness.

The first level I want to look at is using illness as a learning tool. It is true that the soul comes into a physical body to learn certain lessons. There are many opportunities in a lifetime to learn lessons. You have opportunities in your youth, you have opportunities in the middle of your life, and you even have opportunities at the end of your life. So I can say that there is a great deal of generosity in an incarnation, because you get more than one chance to learn a lesson.

It is not just, "This is it, and if you don't learn it, then you don't have a chance to learn it again." Many people do not learn their lessons the first time, and later on in life a similar lesson returns. They may take and learn the lesson early in life. But when it gets later in life, the soul realizes that there is not a lot of time left. Under these circumstances, there is often an agreement that an illness can force the person who is incarnated to shift and to make a reassessment of his or her life. When I'm talking about illness, I want to talk about injury as well. So an illness that occurs in a lifetime can be related to a soul lesson that would not be learned if the injury or illness had not occurred. As a soul psychologist, one has to assess whether this is the situation.

Illness Is Karmic in Nature

The second case is that an illness is karmic in nature, and here are several examples: There could be an illness or an injury that was directly related to a battle or to the warrior status that the person had in a previous lifetime. So it is possible that, in a previous lifetime, you might have been a warrior, and you might have injured or maimed many people. Now, in this lifetime, you could come back to experience what it is like to be maimed.

Another example would be that you might have been overly critical of people who were suffering from illness. If somebody had multiple sclerosis or Parkinson's disease and you were very critical or mocking toward them, then karmically, the soul could bring that illness to you in this lifetime. So that illness becomes karmically related to your earlier criticism of people who had the same illness.

The idea is that the soul psychologist has to make a diagnosis or assessment of the origin of the illness. There is not one diagnostic tool for everything. In other words, every illness doesn't fit neatly into a karmic lesson from a previous lifetime. For example, your soul could decide that illness would benefit you because it would limit your physical activities and allow you to use more mental abilities.

The karmic punishment is a third example, and in some ways, it is related to the first two. "Punishment" means that there were certain things that you did that caused injury or damage to another experience, and now, as punishment, you are experiencing an illness or injury. For example, say you were the owner of a chemical factory that released chemicals into the water and the air. And the only reason you did that was to make money more quickly. Well, if the chemicals created disfigurement in many people, in your next lifetime or in an appropriate lifetime, you could come back and experience the disfigurement.

The issue becomes more complicated if you ask, "Does this mean that all people who are being disfigured are now karmically suffering?" The answer is: not necessarily. Some people are in a primary state of experiencing karma (young souls who are just starting out on their journeys), whereas others are in a secondary or third state. Does the soul know what illness or energy it is going to experience before it incarnates? The answer is yes. However, there also is always an unknown factor in an incarnation. There can be unexpected events and newness. Not knowing all that will happen to you is an important factor in countering a fatalistic view of reality.

As soul psychologists, we do not take a fatalistic view of all events. That means not everyone is destined to live out all this suffering. There are intervening factors. Some of the intervening factors are spiritual energies or grace or a learning experience. So if you were in the type of lifetime in which there was an opportunity to learn and you took that opportunity early in life, then it is very possible that you could avoid the illness in the later part of your life.

Assessing Illness and Karma

I hope you are getting the idea that this assessment of illness and karma, in soul psychology, is complicated. I know there are many people who would say, "Well, this person got cancer because the person wanted to. That was part of his or her soul decision." Actually, you would have to make an assessment of the person's past karma to see whether he or she fit into that category. You also would have to make an assessment of whether this was a learning experience. Then again, you would have to make an assessment of whether this is, what I call, a primary karmic issue. This means it is something that happened by chance and was not due to past mistakes. It is not due punishment or a lesson that the person needed to learn; it's something that may have spontaneously or coincidentally occurred.

Now, some people may have difficulty with that because they think that everything is predestined, but just remember one thing: This planet is now filled with chemical toxins. This planet is filled with high doses of radiation. There are many intervening variables because the biosphere is greatly compromised, so many people will be experiencing illnesses that are not necessarily related to karma.

Therefore, I can say that your soul knew before it came in that it would be exposed to a great many of these issues. The soul was also learning or considering that it would become aware of the dangers of this environment and that it would take the necessary steps to activate and strengthen your immune system. For example, if you had a serious accident in a previous incarnation, then your soul might resolve to be more careful while traveling or driving. Or a necessary lesson might be not to use certain drugs so that you'll be more alert.

The soul knows there are dangers in coming into any lifetime — dangers defined as illnesses, injuries, and other issues that cannot always be predicted. Not everything is known. We were talking about soul psychology and coming into a family. It was discussed that the soul chooses the family to come into, but families are not a perfect match. So you could say that the soul wants to learn a lesson and that a certain family offers the best opportunity for that at this time.

Sometimes the exact match — the exact circumstance — is not present, so you take the best opportunity. There are intervening variables and unknowns. You might ask, "Well, how could that be? Why are there unknowns?" The answer is at once profound and complicated. There are many unknowns about the Creator. You have heard Juliano, Archangel Michael, and others speak about how the Creator cannot be totally known and that here on Earth and in the third dimension, you are seeing one side of the Creator only. This means that there are karmic aspects and aspects of this lifetime, including diseases and illnesses, that fit into the category of the unknown.

I have given you some guidelines with which to look at illness. I do not think it is helpful for a person who is suffering from an illness to say, "Oh, I am being punished for something that I did in a past lifetime," or even, "I am being punished for something that I did in this lifetime."

A better approach might be: "Well, what am I to learn from this experience of illness?" I know there is also a lot of suffering and pain, and sometimes people cannot transcend the suffering and pain. In many ways, it is very difficult, at times, on the third dimension to perceive the higher perspective. But it is always possible. If you need assistance with your pain, then it might help you to use medications such as drugs and painkillers. If you need some assistance from medication to help you rebalance, then that is acceptable, because in many cases there will be relief.

Another category of karma occurs where people experience immediate karma in a current lifetime. For example, say you did something that was very bad and hurtful to others in this lifetime. Then in the later part of that current life, you suffer an illness that may be related to something you did in the earlier part of your life. I think that you need to have a broad perspective on this because it does take a higher perspective to be accepting of your fate. Knowing that an illness is karmic may help you endure the situation better.

Challenges and the Higher Perspective

What helps in negotiating the illness is asking yourself this question: "What is it that I'm supposed to learn? What new perspectives can be assimilated from this experience?" I acknowledge that's quite a challenge. It is also quite a challenge knowing that there are many compromises in this lifetime because of the environmental factors that everyone is familiar with, namely pollution and energy radiation.

It is clear that humanity's immune systems are compromised on a major scale on this planet. Frankly, the immune systems of the species are susceptible to mass extinction from an unusual flu, such as bird flu or AIDS, or immune system attacks — organisms and bacteria that your immune system is not capable of combating. You knew that you were coming into an environment like that, but also, in some cases, I could say that one of the challenges, one of the lessons, is that you need to learn how to strengthen and prepare your immune system for such intrusions.

Everything is in the balance. You may think that humankind can dominate Earth, and you may think the biosphere can be destroyed. But remember that the biosphere does have a way of counterbalancing energies that are creating a huge imbalance on the planet. For example, the outbreak of a mass illness or a virus, on a global scale, can be interpreted as Earth rebalancing itself and rebalancing the species so that the species does not continue to destroy the biosphere. That is one interpretation of why some of these other immune-attacking illnesses can overtake the population.

Mental Illness

I also want to speak briefly about mental illness. In most cases, mental illness comes from not feeling connected — from being disconnected from the higher self. I know this is a great generalization, but being unconnected means you don't feel connected to the group. You don't feel connected to the universe, and you don't feel safe because you are not connected. Of course, there are many variations of this, but many of the people who are mentally ill are also extremely sensitive.

One great reason why people come to this planet is for the emotional energy and to learn how to control it. This can also be defined as the ability to experience love, which is a fifth-dimensional emotion. It is clear that in order to evolve into the fifth dimension, you have to open up your heart and you have to be in a very loving heart energy. So when we talk about life lessons, we could talk about the ability to experience emotions, to experience the heart energy, as being one of the major lessons — if not *the* major lesson — involved here.

Emotional Illness

Emotions can also create illnesses. Unexpressed emotions, especially emotions of anger and hatred, are actual energies that are carried in the body. Then each body has a certain amount of energy that it can carry. If that energy cannot be released or transformed, there are occasions when the emotions also create — or I would rather use the word "contribute" to — illnesses. It is not fair to say that emotions alone create illnesses.

There is already an energetic predisposition from pathogens in many people's immune systems. It could be an energetic predisposition from past-life karma. It could be an energetic predisposition from some injury or other weakness. Then the emotions can weaken the immune system, allowing it to be invaded.

The greatest pain is being cut off — being cut off from family, being cut off from the soul group, being cut off from the Creator. When a person who is mentally ill experiences being cut off, then that person suffers. So, in most cases, helping the person connect to a higher energy and his or her soul group will create a very powerful healing effect.

Questions and Answers

You have mentioned all the complexities of any certain condition in a lifetime. What would you recommend, or what methods do you suggest, to discover what the etiology is, the source is, of any condition?

What I would recommend is that the soul psychologist do the interview and look at all the factors. Discuss all of them with the patient. And there are other circumstances. These are not the only ones, but I'm just giving some broad interpretations. So ask, "Is this a spontaneous event that occurred without your knowledge and your coming into this planet?" Know that also is a possibility. "Is this something that is karmic? Is this something related to a lesson?" What I suggest is that you, in discussing an illness with everyone, look at all of the factors, and then the person and you together will reach the proper conclusion.

So one of the gifts of the soul psychologist, one of the great perspectives of the soul psychologist, is that they are open to all of these possibilities. But don't be totally rigid. There could be, as I said, general things because people knew before they came that there were going to be problems. People knew when they came to Atlantis that there was going to be destruction at the very end, but they came anyway because there were still things to learn.

Are there also conditions that are just purely genetic?

"Purely genetic" usually implies that there are some kind of karmic conditions and a choice to come into that. That would be a higher indication of a karmic factor there. Now, the karmic factor also could be learning. Sometimes the soul is curious, and it is not a punishment, but the soul wants to know, "Well now, how will you deal with this?" or "What perspective is this going to get you?" For example, there are cases of higher evolved spirits who come in mentally retarded or quite mentally disabled. Those souls want to have that experience because of the unique perspective that it would provide. So, again, these are other examples that show it is not always punishment.

But it's always some sort of lesson.

It's usually some kind of lesson or a desire to have an experience in which the soul is interested. In summary, the soul psychologist is always looking at past lives for karma. The soul psychologist also is looking for lessons in this lifetime that can be assessed and based on where the person is in this lifetime. Even if the person is ill and dying, this does not mean that it is a failure, because, from the soul psychologist perspective, we know the soul is evolving. So this is just one lifetime, and we have to take the perspective of the higher self.

The higher self just sees this as a lifetime. It doesn't see this as an end. Sometimes there is even a great lesson at the very end of life. There is a great lesson at the moment of death, or right before then, so the lessons can continue right up to the very last breath.

Schema and Personality

Vywamus

chema is the complex environmental stimulation and programming that people receive when they are growing up. This programming really determines the formation of the lower Earth personality. It isn't part or a reflection of the higher self or the soul self. People incarnate in order to find imprints or patterns that they need to experience, so they will choose a certain family for these reasons. Sometimes the reason is that the family will give them a conflict that they need to resolve for their soul evolution. They are exposed to the programming and the parenting and the situation that will make them experience and have the programming they need so that they can resolve the situation.

I suggest that when you first talk about programming with a client, you do it on a general basis. Then talk about the programming from the standpoint of the schema. Talk about how that programming sets up a personality pattern that is in part related to what some of the soul issues are. Talk about the fact that the higher self, and especially the multidimensional self, is coming from a totally different perspective.

These issues of the programmed self do need to be resolved, so please emphasize that you cannot just ignore the issues of the programmed self. And remember that people who ignore the programmed self often get into problems when they get more into their higher selves. The programmed self is still part of the foundation, and if the foundation is not built right, then there will be problems.

Thought Fields and Programs

I also want to talk about thought fields because one of the things — especially about the programmed self — that is important is that the programmed self does attract people who have the same program. It is a very complex and not-well-understood phenomenon. So a victim, for example, can attract an abuser.

Now, I don't want people to think that the victim is guilty or responsible for this, because that really confuses the issue. You have to deal with that issue delicately. There is this important process where people have certain thought programs, and these thoughts attract other people playing the same programs.

I know of an American psychiatrist named Eric Berne who called programs "the games people play." For example, there is the alcoholic game. There are many different games and programs, so the thought fields are actually a conglomerate of programs. Somebody wants to be a child, and that person needs to find someone who's going to parent him or her. There are many examples of this, so part of the idea is to overcome the program, to transcend the program. But you first have to gain an awareness of what the program is and understand that these programs and games are part of what we call the Earth self. People say, "Well, I want to work on my fifth-dimensional self," but you have to work on the foundational energy of the Earth self that I'm talking about.

This in itself is important because many starseeds find themselves in conflicts in marriages and relationships that are not satisfying and that were started or programmed or engaged in when they were younger, when these people were making their decisions based on their programmed selves. This means that the people, the starseeds, don't become aware of their fifth-dimensional selves until they are older. And then they might find that they become very spiritual and are working in a multidimensional self. Then they wonder, "Well, why am I in this high energy and this high spiritual process, yet I'm still working and still struggling with these older issues from the Earth self?" The answer is the programmed self still wasn't processed enough, and it wasn't worked out enough.

So this means that you need to do things with your body. There are certain different exercises you have to do when you are older, or there is different care you have to take of your body. So remember that you still have to take care of this programmed self also. We want people to have an understanding of the programmed self that will help them overcome it.

Overcoming the Programmed Self

We also want to talk about the higher-dimensional psychology of working with the programmed self. In other words, there are shortcuts and innovations that come from the fifth-dimensional self that can be used to help overcome the programmed self from the earlier times. One of those methods that Juliano talked about was using power affirmations, fifth-dimensional light, and the omega light.

I think that you need to learn about affirmations, but you also need to talk about another concept that is very prominent in simple psychology, which is the concept of self-talk. In fifth-dimensional interventions, you can use specific interventions in your self-talk, such as "I am connecting with my higher self. I am connecting with my fifth-dimensional self."

One of the big interventions is the concept of the multidimensional self. This concept has to be extended into talking about the programmed self and about the Earth self. Let us look at it from a broader perspective.

What is the human personality? What is the higher self? I think the higher self is a key concept. For example, you have the self from the Freudian standpoint — the conscious, the unconscious, and the superego. You also have the concept of the self in the Kabbalah of the lower self, the middle self, and the higher self. In the ascension work we are now talking about, there is the multidimensional self.

We need to talk about the multidimensional self, to include it in our discussion. Let us look at alternate states of consciousness, because nothing is a stronger support for the multidimensional self than alternate states of consciousness. You can use the example of dreaming to understand alternate states of consciousness. When you are dreaming, you are in another state of consciousness, and you are in another reality.

In multidimensional consciousness, you are also experiencing another reality, but the truth is that you now have the ability to be on different levels of consciousness, and these different levels of consciousness are part of yourself. I'd like to use the example of a person having different aspects of the self. You could have your mothering side, your friend side, and your wife side. You have different aspects of yourself, and nobody really has any problem in understanding that concept.

So how do you integrate the fact that you also exist on different dimensions? You look up to the higher dimensions, and you interact — especially with the fifth dimension — because you have a part of yourself on that dimension. But this is an important concept for people to integrate in their sense of self. I think it has a great benefit, especially when you're talking about integrating the self, about bringing down these higher aspects of the self, and about finding ways to connect with the self.

Multiple Selves and Multiple Personalities

Now, part of the confusion is that we have this concept in modern psychology called multiple personalities. So you understand that you have to be at least cautious that some people do not confuse hearing voices and talking to other parts of themselves as suffering from multiple personalities. The difference between what we are talking about and the illness of multiple personality disorder is that when you are connecting with these multidimensional parts of yourself, these are the higher parts of you. They are the parts of you that are very wise and transcendent as opposed to just being lower parts of you.

I want to mention something about multiple personalities. One issue with multiple personalities is the psychiatric illness and why it occurs. You know that you have had perhaps, let's say, 150 lifetimes on Earth at least, but just for the purpose of this discussion, we'll say 100 lifetimes. With multiple personalities, first of all, each lifetime has developed a different personality because, as you would say, the schema, or the programming, in each lifetime led to different circumstances, a different environment, and different parents. In multiple personality disorder, the gateway between those other personalities a person has had in previous multiple lifetimes gets carried back into this lifetime, and there is a mix-up in the neurological patterns. This results in the person being unable to understand and differentiate between some of these other personalities that he or she has had in other lifetimes. I think that is an important distinction to make for people who have had these multiple personality experiences.

A psychologist or therapist would perhaps want to understand why somebody would have this disorder. We encourage people to explore their fifth-dimensional selves through trance, through going to sacred places, through being with their groups, and through trying to find ways to access their higher selves. One problem is that the ancient ways of accessing these parts of the self have been repressed. You have ancient ways of using sweat lodges, chanting, or going into sacred temples, and these are traditional ways of going into altered states of consciousness. People did not have what we call the spiritual technology that is now available. There are new spiritual technologies available for the development of the self.

But the current psychology is primarily focused on the development of the programmed self, the Earth self, and how to resolve the issues. We are on the forefront with you in seeking ways to develop the multidimensional self and how to bring that multidimensional self into this Earth and into this dimension using new spiritual technologies. The important thing to remember is that your fifth-dimensional self has energy and power that can really help you overcome the problems of the programmed self. So gaining this perspective of your higher self is important.

The Fifth-Dimensional Self

I want to explore the following subjects: the thought field, the emotional field, the spiritual field, and the physical field. The emotional field is part of the program, and it is focused on many of the same principles because it is not just the thoughts. It is the emotional energy that is interacting with other people and other fields. So this is a brief overview, and I will stop for any comments or questions.

When David channels, is he connecting with his fifth-dimensional self or even higher?

Both. In channeling, you are connecting to your fifth-dimensional self, but you are maintaining your third-dimensional self because you are connecting and bringing it down into the third dimension, so another way to put it is you are connecting with your antenna to bring in fifth-dimensional energy.

But does it go even higher at times?

He can go higher, but generally he stays at the fifth dimension. But it is possible to go higher.

Is the fifth-dimensional energy for the starseeds available right now? Can we connect with our higher selves?

Yes, and I know there are people who are talking about connecting with the eighth dimension and the tenth dimension, and the point is that people need to solve these issues on Earth and the fifth dimension. That is the goal. So why would you go to these higher dimensions unless you could first make sure that you have the process down for the fifth dimension?

Everybody has a different approach to this, but our approach to working with the guides and teachers is to just stay focused on the fifth dimension. If you wanted to, you could look at certain third-dimensional patterns in the psychiatric sense. For example, depression from this approach is usually seen as the denial of self. A person is given a program that is against his or her nature. This view is opposed to looking at depression as a genetic illness. So then there are negative patterns that develop, and in almost all cases, the depressions are caused by negative programming. Even schizophrenia is caused by people neurologically losing the program and the ability to discriminate between realities.

There is caution that needs to be taken when working with this fifth-dimensional energy: We are working with higher energy, but remember, you are splitting realities. You are working with other higher realities, and that is what the multidimensional self is: working with higher realities.

But you know that some people get confused about the lower realities, and it takes over, or they misinterpret the reality. We also want to look at other exercises such as bilocation and thought projection and how those are incorporated into the sense of self. Generally, we're saying that the sense of self has to be expanded to the multidimensional, fifth-dimensional self.

I am Vywamus. Good day.

PART II

RELATED CHANNELINGS FROM OTHER BEINGS

Intermediaries and Soul Psychology

Juliano and the Arcturians

reetings. I am Juliano. We are the Arcturians. We will look at the concept I call intermediaries. Intermediaries are spirit guides, prophets, and other people who are able to bridge the energy gap between dimensions.

There have been many different intermediaries throughout the history of Earth and this galaxy. There is a good reason why intermediaries are necessary. We are now in a time when the messages, information, and energy from intermediaries are vitally important to your development and even to your survival on the planet. Certainly, the use of and interaction with intermediaries is essential for your ascension as well as for your understanding of soul psychology and your evolution.

The intermediaries are able to go to higher levels of dimensional experiences. There are several assumptions and ideas that must be explained so that you can get a better grasp of intermediaries. The first level of understanding has to do with the nature of the reality. When I say "reality," I mean all dimensions, all living creatures, all universes, all galaxies, and of course, all the different realms that are subsets of these different dimensional spaces.

All of the nature of these realities is hierarchical — that is, the universal reality is based on a hierarchy. There is a hierarchy of dimensions. For example, the fifth dimension clearly is above the third dimension. The sixth and seventh dimensions are above the fifth dimension. I know that this concept of the hierarchy seems to contradict the assumption of the fifth dimension and how the fifth dimension interacts with the third dimension. The assumption is that the third dimension is based on linear thinking and the assumption of the fifth dimension is that dimensional time and space are in a circle and are interacting. Therefore, if I talk to you about a hierarchy, that is a linear description — not a circular model.

Of course, linear can be horizontal or vertical, but nonetheless, vertical still is a linear progression. How is it that we can reconcile this difference when describing the concept of the hierarchy? Frankly, the answer is a paradox.

There are many paradoxes in describing these realities and the nature of this reality. Having a vertical linear hierarchy that is also fifth dimensional and incorporates the characteristics of fifth-dimensional ideals seems illogical. Yet the vertical model seems to express the basis of reality because, as you go to a higher realm, you are experiencing a different and higher hierarchy. In fact, the whole basis of personal ascension rests on the fact that you are going to a higher level.

You can dispute this paradox. You can say that everything is interacting on the same level and all is one. I would actually agree with you because, by the very nature of this reality, of this universe, everything is one. However, you have to grasp that from the perspective that you are now experiencing on the third dimension — that there appears to be a vertical hierarchical system.

One aspect of this system, of course, is the different and higher dimensions. Another aspect of this system has to do with different levels of dimensional beings. These dimensional beings include the angels and the angelic hosts.

There is a hierarchy of angels. There is a head angel, and this head angel is called an archangel. There are levels of the angelic world in which you can go up or down different levels.

I want to also tell you that these levels of dimensions present a paradox. The paradox has some points of unity and resolution because, by the nature of your being — that is, by the nature of being part of the Adam species — you are able to experience both parts of the dimensional hierarchy simultaneously. You are able to experience the top of the hierarchy and the bottom of the hierarchy. But you only can have this experience in expanded consciousness. With expanded consciousness, you have the ability to access and experience the different levels of this hierarchy.

The hierarchy goes beyond the angelic world. The angelic world is only one part of the hierarchy, and as you know, the angelic world is part of the Sacred Triangle energy because the angelic world includes fifth-dimensional beings.

Intermediaries on Earth

Throughout the history of this Earth, there have been other intermediaries. In fact, the angelic world is considered an intermediary world because it is between the third dimension and the fifth dimension. The angels can exist between the dimensions, but they also exist in the fifth dimension.

Understand that there are different levels of intermediaries. There are intermediaries who are living in the fifth dimension, but they are able to bridge the gap and come down to the third dimension and appear to you. These beings include the sightings or apparitions of, for example, Mother Mary. These include the sightings of the archangels. These include the sightings of the extraterrestrial beings who are sometimes observed through UFOs.

These intermediaries also include certain prophets and masters who have been asked and have accepted the role of being intermediaries on Earth. You call these higher beings prophets. Sometimes they are called even higher names than prophets. There are several examples of these types of higher intermediaries: Moses, Buddha, Confucius, Lao Tzu, Jesus, and Mohammed are examples of such beings. There have been numerous other beings who can be considered higher intermediaries. They come down from the order of a hierarchical system to bring information and healing energy to Earth.

We now are in a time when there are many intermediaries coming to Earth. There have been periods in the history of Earth when there was spiritual darkness. There have been periods when there were no intermediaries, or very few, and the intermediaries have only been available to certain people. Now we are in a period of unparalleled access to intermediaries. Even though this is a period of great change and disruption and upheaval, it also is a period when the intermediaries are able to manifest through various techniques. This includes, for example, the ability to appear in this reality. That is, fifth-dimensional beings can appear on Earth. Another way intermediaries interact with the third dimension is through walk-ins. Still another method intermediaries use is cohabitation or the ability to share spiritual presence with higher Earth beings. There are now those spiritual beings on Earth who are able to have prophetic visions and prophetic communications.

There are other starseeds who now have the ability to telepathically communicate with the hierarchy. This telepathic communication is occurring through various methods, including what is called channeling in your language. Another method used by starseeds to access intermediaries is intensive meditation. Finally, there are many spiritual masters and gurus and other special teachers on the planet who have direct access to intermediaries. The hierarchical energy of spiritual teachers from the higher realms is working to bridge the gap between the higher light and the third-dimensional life that is here on Earth.

The Importance of Intermediaries

Why is it necessary to have intermediaries? The answer lies in the dense nature of the level of the reality you are experiencing. You are on the third dimension, which has duality and polarization. This dimension in many ways is the bottom rung of this hierarchy of dimensions. This third-dimensional experience on Earth is a special experience. Earth is a special planet, as you know, and we refer to Earth as the Blue Jewel. One reason Earth is so special is because its energy field, which allows for duality, also allows for the experiences of higher-dimensional beings to manifest and to communicate on this planet.

You may take intermediaries for granted. You may think it is natural that there are higher-dimensional beings on this planet who are communicating and acting as intermediaries. I want to tell you that this is not the case on other planets. I also want to tell you that not all of the planets that have higher life forms in the Milky Way galaxy have the experience of intermediaries. Some civilizations on Earth and other planets do not accept and will not work with intermediaries. These are planets of darkness. There are planets that, because of their particular energetic configuration, do not have the opening and the ability to experience other realms and other communications.

I want to explain another important fact about intermediaries. This Blue Jewel cannot evolve and cannot resolve the current conflicts and situations without the intervention and communication from intermediaries. The energy from the intermediaries is necessary to overcome the duality and polarizations.

The idea of communicating with intermediaries is important for your soul development and evolution. Each of you has personal intermediaries. Each of you has spirit guides and teachers who are around you. It is not just one channel or one prophet who has the ability to communicate with these higher beings that are around all the time. Rather, each person has, at any one time, ten to fifteen — sometimes even twenty — guides around him or her. These beings are also called spirit guides, and these spirit guides can be considered intermediaries.

Why would you consider a spirit guide an intermediary? Because most spirit guides exist on the fifth dimension, and spirit guides come from higher realms. The spirit guide or the intermediary can see things that you cannot. They can have communications with other beings that you cannot. Of course, most importantly, the intermediary or spirit guide can bring special messages from the higher realms to you.

Accessing Your Spirit Guides

This is a time on the planet when we are close to the ascension. This is also a time of great upheaval, conflict, and polarization. At the same time, this is when many intermediaries are working with humanity, and you need the ability to access your spirit guides. It's not as hard as you think.

Some of you may feel closed to accessing higher guidance. Some of you might say, "Oh, I cannot talk to my spirit guides. I cannot talk to my intermediary." My answer is that there are definitely intermediaries to whom you can relate. If you personally do not feel connected to your own spirit guide or if you feel as if you cannot connect to your own intermediary, then I ask you to think about this: This planet has a long history of many beautiful ascended beings who have worked as intermediaries. They are plentiful. One of the great gifts on this planet in fact is the existence and ability of these diverse intermediaries to work and communicate with humanity. Certainly, there must be one or two intermediaries to whom you feel connected? Which guide do you feel most connected to now? Try to work with those guides to whom you feel connected.

I, Juliano, am considered an intermediary. I come from the planet Arcturus, a fifth-dimensional planet. We are home to the Arcturian stargate. We have a planet that has ascended and has gone into a higher evolution. That higher evolution is beyond your planet, but at the same time, we accept our ability to be of service to Earth as intermediaries. We have certain abilities, ideas, and technologies that we can communicate through messages to those on Earth who are receptive to our information and to our energy.

I am happy to report that our role as intermediaries to Earth is successful. Some of you already have asked, "Well, is the fifth-dimensional work that we are now doing helpful? Is the Arcturian work in fact helpful? Are the spiritual energies coming down through the Arcturians and other powerful intermediaries helpful to Earth?" The answer is yes! It is helpful. We are helping to create an awareness and consciousness of a higher-dimensional level, and our communication to Earth is verifying the existence of the fifth dimension.

Part of our foundational work is the essential task of placing in the consciousness of humankind the existence of the other dimensions and of the higher realms. The existence of the consciousness of these realms creates a thought field that is shaping the development of this planet.

From your perspective, you might think that Earth is going into deeper chaos. From your perspective, you might think that the spiritual work and the spiritual energy you have been working with do not seem to be successful. You may not see obvious signs of spiritual transformation on this planet. That view is coming from a more confined third-dimensional perspective. See now how your higher consciousness and your fifth-dimensional energy work are permeating Earth's noosphere. You can visualize that you are establishing and setting a foundation of strong spiritual light that will shape the evolution of this planet.

You have to see the great overwhelming body of intermediaries who are now around this planet and are here to work with you. Some of you know of them from the Ashtar Command. Others you know as intermediaries from your work with the White Brotherhood/Sisterhood. Some of you know of them from your work with Jesus/Sananda. Some of you directly know the work with the Pleiadians and P'taah. Others know my work. Some know of the work of the ascended Native people, such as Chief White Eagle. Today, we are also going to introduce to you in the latter part of this lecture one of the great ascended masters and intermediaries between Earth and humanity: Sanat Kumara.

The basic idea is that the intermediary can make a bridge or communication between a higher energy field and the third dimension. Higher beings often cannot communicate directly to humankind. If you look at Earth, if you look at the Blue Jewel, then you can ask this question: How can we communicate with the Blue Jewel? There are various techniques and ways of doing this that many of you have been practicing. These methods include creating medicine wheels, doing ceremonies, and praying or talking to the Spirit of Earth. Some of you have even heard the Spirit of Earth speak to you or through others. Sanat Kumara is an intermediary who acts like a bridge between the Spirit of Earth and humankind. He is known as the planetary logos.

The Galactic Kachina and New Energy

Another example of an intermediary spirit comes from the Native Americans. They call their intermediaries kachinas. The kachinas bridge the gap between this third-dimensional world and the spirit world. They actually have a home in the Native American Southwest, specifically in the San Francisco Peaks just outside of Flagstaff, Arizona. There are different levels of kachinas. Some focus on agriculture. Others focus on other realms and even other dimensions. There are warrior kachinas.

I want to talk to you also about the Galactic Kachina because she is a new kachina. This is a kachina that was downloaded into this realm several years ago through the work of David and Gudrun Miller when they were working on the powerful area of the San Francisco Peaks, which connects with the higher kachina energy there at these mountains. They were able to assist in bringing the energy of the spirit of the Galactic Kachina to that mountain. Now the Galactic Kachina is there and is accessible to all of you. She is the intermediary between the Central Sun, the energy of the Central Sun, and Earth. The Galactic Kachina is like a messenger who acts as a bridge for messages, energy, ideas, and thoughts from the Central Sun. Through this bridge, you can connect with higher galactic energy. You can also learn what information and ideas need to be brought forth from the Central Sun to this Earth.

This illustrates an important idea in this concept of intermediaries. The concept is that there is a higher energy field that is in existence. This higher energy field is not exactly logical. This higher energy field does not speak necessarily in sentences, and it does not necessarily speak in a way that deals with duality and polarizations. Intermediaries also could be compared to electrical high voltage lines. A higher electromagnetic energy field (such as high line voltage) might be beyond what your normal electromagnetic energy field (such as your fuse box at your home) can tolerate.

Remember that you are an electromagnetic vibrating energy field, but you have limitations. If a stronger pulse or stronger spiritual electromagnetic energy field comes to you, you have to be ready to process and integrate the energy from that higher force. Sometimes the energy is so heightened that you are not able to bridge it, and you might not able to experience it.

I know many of you have difficulties sometimes seeing spirits and connecting with spiritual energies and with spirit guides. Part of the reason why you have difficulties has to do with how your electromagnetic energy field is configured. It has to do with whether your electromagnetic energy field can tolerate certain higher light force fields. It also has to do with whether you have the right mental body and belief system to process this type of energy (higher voltages).

I think you have the basic picture and overview. Certainly, when you are talking about the Galactic Kachina, you can readily see that this energy force, this energy field from the Central Sun, is somewhat difficult to define. Yet you all are feeling the effects of the Central Sun now. Remember that the Central Sun, which is located in a dimensional space approximately in alignment with the center of this galaxy, came into an eclipse or a galactic alignment with your solar system. This happened, of course, on December 21, 2012. That means there was an increase of galactic energy coming to Earth from the light and energy field from the Central Sun. Some of you have experienced this downloaded energy — but in a way that you cannot easily define or explain.

Some of you may experience confusion or discomfort as a result of this newer galactic energy. Some of you might even feel a little bit of agitation. Perhaps some could also experience this new energy as a general feeling of unrest. Maybe you are having difficulty making decisions. The things that were normal and were giving you pleasure in the third dimension are not providing you satisfaction anymore. There are various different ways of interpreting this type of reaction, but I think the important thing for this discussion is that you are intuitively sensing some other force that has come to Earth, and you are reacting to it.

You may not be able to define the nature of the force. You may not be able to say what the message is from the force, but you know that, on an intuitive level, there is something different going on energetically. This is felt as some other energy. This newer energy is a powerful energy. It is even unsettling.

It's interesting to describe this unsettling energy because it affects everyone; even nonspiritual people are being affected by this. Even those people who seem to be really third dimensional in their perspective still can experience and feel the effects of the energetic field known as the Central Sun energy, which is coming to this planet.

The Galactic Kachina is able to bring messages and information to you from this energy. The Galactic Kachina is able to download this energy so that you can bridge it and comprehend it. You can somehow bring this energy into yourself in a form you can process. That is the exact and perfect role of the intermediary. The intermediary is able to bridge that gap from the Central Sun and bring that energy to you in a way that allows you to begin to comprehend, integrate, and use it.

Chief White Eagle brings messages for you from the Galactic Kachina so that you at least have some grasp of this energy in a way that you can place it in your third-dimensional mind. I want to compliment the third-dimensional mind because you need that mind. All of these different energy fields from the higher realms somehow need to be transposed into a workable form that you can integrate and process.

I, Juliano, see this higher light. I see these higher-dimensional realms around. I see the many intermediary guides and teachers — including the Galactic Kachina, including Sanat Kumara — around all of you. Please welcome them and welcome your ability to speak to them and to receive their messages.

I think that welcoming the guides is one of the most important tools in the new spiritual technology from the Arcturians. Welcome and accept the higher-dimensional spirit guides and intermediaries who are working with you and the planet. Verbally (out loud) or in your thoughts, accept them. This will help produce the right energetic configuration to open up your higher thought powers, which will help you to receive their messages. That is one of the foundational exercises necessary to increase your receptivity.

Earth's Halo

My final discussion about the intermediaries has to do with the ring of ascension. The ring of ascension is a halo around Earth. It is a halo that actually can be compared to a planetary ring, such as the rings around Saturn or other planets. Of course, Saturn is not the only planet that has a ring. Many planets in the galaxies have rings. The composition of these rings is of various different sources. Some rings come from volcanic eruptions that have to do with frozen ice particles that get trapped in the gravitational field of the planet and begin to swirl around the planet and produce a beautiful multicolored ring.

The ring of ascension is an etheric energetic ring. It is an energetic ring composed of the thought fields and higher energy blessings from the ascended masters. The White Brotherhood and White Sisterhood are great ascended teachers who are sending higher energy to this Earth.

This thought field helps form the ring of ascension. I like to compare this ring to a halo. The reason I call it a halo is because the halo is a sign and manifestation of unity and harmony. The halo also is a sign of spiritual development and unity with the oneness that exists. It is what all of the ascended masters have when they manifest and appear on Earth.

Some of you are working very hard to purify your energy fields. Some have worked very hard to remove illness or darkness or congestion from their energy. The halo is the culmination of your spiritual work and represents harmony with higher dimensions. It implies that you have reached a point of acceptance and integration. It implies that you have reached a point of interaction with the higher dimensions, that you know you are in communication with other-dimensional beings, and that you know you are receiving their higher energy. It implies that you have a certain level of personal power and a certain level of protection.

Being in a halo is a wonderful experience on the third dimension. The ring of ascension offers humanity a halo around Earth. It is a force field; it is a thought field composed of spiritual light and harmony. It is a thought field and energetic ring that demonstrates that there can be harmonic communication with the fifth dimension. It is unique because it may not be physically observable to you, but it does interact and exist etherically and thus interacts with the higher-dimensional realms.

One other aspect of this ring of ascension is the fact that it interacts with you, the starseeds. It is set up so that you are able to access the fifth-dimensional guides and teachers more easily.

How do you access the ring of ascension? In your meditation, visualize a golden halo looking like the ring of Saturn around Earth. Then you can thought-project yourself to this ring. When you thought-project yourself to this ring of ascension, you can more easily meet your intermediary guides and teachers. You can meet many great intermediary guides and teachers. Please remember that there are great intermediary guides and teachers who transcend individual eras. Work with the ring of ascension.

I am Juliano.

The Nature of
Universal Consciousness

Helio-ah and the Arcturians

reetings. I am Helio-ah. We are the Arcturians. "The part represents the whole." You have heard this statement many times in your language. It is a profound summary of the nature of universal consciousness. The relationship between the part and the whole is even more significant when we look at the self and spiritual consciousness.

Spiritual consciousness is based on the interrelationship and interactions of all thoughts and beings in the galaxy and universe. We Arcturians have studied and learned how to interconnect with thoughts throughout existence. It has been our scientific explorations and discoveries that have led us to this understanding; namely, even a small thought connected properly can be linked to the whole universe. Even one thought of one person connected with a master can enable that master to understand the whole being and lifetime of that person. This interconnection becomes extremely powerful in understanding and reaching out to all living beings.

If only one thought, one connected link, could be achieved, then doorways would open to the realms around that person or planet or galaxy. Ultimately, a thought can connect to the Source of All. We are excited to link to the Central Sun for we know that the minuscule energy of the Central Sun now reaching Earth is enough to connect to the whole light, the whole energy field, of this Central Sun. We use magnifications to bring light as pure as possible of the Central Sun photonic energy.

The Iskalia mirror is an etheric mirror that we, the Arcturians, helped place over the North Pole of your dear planet. The goal and purpose of the Iskalia mirror is to act as a magnifier, allowing a pure energy field and thought to reach this planet and enable those like yourselves who are in a meditative state to receive it. This magnification is important because it helps purify and enlarge that particle. The Iskalia mirror is now fully activated. With your thoughts, you can visualize it as a gigantic mirror — perhaps as large as a mile or two in diameter — in the etheric realm over the North Pole. This mirror is in a special alignment with the Central Sun.

Meditation: Align Yourself with the Central Sun

I want to explain our studies of thoughts, light, and energy. We have learned that thoughts are light waves. When we are holographically aligning ourselves with the Central Sun in this meditation, we are receiving the particles of light from the Central Sun, and we are receiving its powerful and higher thoughts. The Central Sun has a collection of energy from the ascended masters and teachers in the galaxy, who are all concentrating at this moment on sending you a powerful boost. They are sending this particle of light and thought that will enable you to holographically experience the Central Sun energy.

The Central Sun energy can be described in many different ways. I, Helio-ah, say that it is a summary of the highest wisdom of the galaxy, of evolution and light. I now activate the Iskalia mirror.

[Sings and tones: *Iskalia light.*]

Align with those in meditation with the Arcturians. Now allow a thought, a particle from the Central Sun, to enter your consciousness. Do not be concerned about the holographic value of this. Just receive it.

[Tones: *eeeeh.*]

The part is the gateway to the whole. That means you are receiving the Central Sun consciousness, which can open you to vast doorways of light and wisdom and galactic thought. You can now open us to journeys in future and past lifetimes, to intergalactic and interdimensional travel, and to intergalactic scientific breakthroughs of knowledge having to do with corridors of light. This wisdom of the Central Sun is coming to Earth in a more intense way than it has ever been experienced before.

You are on the verge of a breakthrough in consciousness that has never been experienced before on Earth. It will be marked by the return of Jesus/ Sananda to this planet and the landing of major ships from interplanetary realms. It will be marked by special commanders of higher intergalactic forces who are working to stabilize Earth and the magnetic fluctuations that have been erratic around the planet. The possibility of pole-shifting energy is still strong. Magnetic shifting of the poles is becoming more likely and probable, as evidenced by the extreme magnetic flux in Earth's fields. A stabilization energy from the Central Sun is being infused into Earth as

I speak. This infusion of Central Sun light will bring a balance, first to you and then to Earth.

I, Helio-ah, activate the Iskalia mirror once more to bring down this particle for an infusion of balance. It will help you transmit this balance to all with whom you come into contact.

[Sings: *Iiiiskaaaaliaaaa.*]

Bringing Down and Stabilizing Harmony

You must understand that there are tremendous, powerful forces interacting in the solar system, on Earth, and in this portion of the galaxy. To balance these energies, you must have a magnitude of stabilization and light to infuse a balance of harmonic energy. This is what the Harmonic Convergence and the 11:11 energy was about. It was an attempt to bring harmony to the tremendous forces you are experiencing.

To harmonize such a tremendous conflicted force requires overwhelmingly good and powerful light from the Central Sun. It requires energy far surpassing all the individual conflicts and differences you see. It has to surpass all the disruptions — political, economic, and geophysical. All of these aspects will become receptive to the harmony of which I am speaking. Let there be an increase in Harmonic Convergence light. This is a powerful time to bring down and stabilize harmony.

Holographic Light

Holography works on many levels. When you understand that the part represents the whole, you can affect the whole through your interaction with the part. When you holographically experience the part, you can reach the core of that essence — whether it is the essence of a being, a lifetime, an object, a planet, a time, a galaxy, a universe, or the essence of *Adonai*.

We, the Arcturians, know that experiencing part of *Adonai* can give you a vast experience of God's presence. Experiencing a part of the fifth-dimensional Earth in the future will enable you to interact now with a higher consciousness in the present. Holography is connected to your soul and to your past, present, and future. So when you are looking at a holographic aspect of yourself, you are interacting with your soul. Your soul is timeless. Your soul includes interactions from all of your aspects. I now see each of you holographically. When I connect to you, I can see you as a young child and as a baby in your mother's womb. I can see you as a young person, ten or eleven years old, and I can see you aged and elderly. I can see you in another lifetime, in a future self, in the past. I am connected to the part, and that gives me access to the whole.

Your current existence is a part of the multipresence. You can affect all aspects of your present, future, and past through your total understanding of this current — present — part of yourself. You can grasp the essence of the Arcturians and our teachings by working with thought and the Arcturian thought wave. By connecting with our thought wave, you can activate and download holographic light. Holographic light is a powerful, laser-like beam that enables you to dissect and experience an object, yourself, a planet, or a being holographically. Holographic light also includes holographic thought. Remember what I said in the beginning of this lecture: We have learned that thought is light and light is thought. There is a special energy that enables you to holographically experience a person, a planet, and all objects. I, Helio-ah, call this light "heliographic light." I will download this heliographic energy into your crown chakra.

[Sings: *Heeeeliiiioooohaah.*]

I, Helio-ah, call on heliographic light forces to enter each starseed consciousness. Let this heliographic light now enter! Through your thought projections and your visualizations, you will begin to understand the essence of the universe, the essence of your soul, and your link to all of the soul light energies in this universe and galaxy. *Kol Ha Neshama* — all living spirits (in Hebrew), all living light, all liquid light, coalesce into the starseed consciousness now and forever.

I ask you to move your hands out in circular motion, in and out. This energy is so intense that you must keep it moving, and I want you to be in motion. One secret of holographic energy is motion and movement. You may experience an increase in your energy level as you do these movements. Let your cosmic egg energy around your body enlarge, for you are of the essence of this universe.

You have heard the statement "Connect within, and you will know the essence of all." Hallelujah.

[Rubs hands together rapidly.] Now place your hands by your ears. You will experience being in another realm when you do this.

Put your hands on your knees. Reverse.

Now place your palms by your navel.

[Tones: *Ooohm.*]

This is connecting you with the Earth energy and light. Earth is a holographic representation of all life forms in the galaxy. Earth is a holographic experiment in planetary exuberance and evolution, and through your presence, you are contributing to this. Each aspect and each life form is interconnected to many different places in the universe and in this galaxy in particular.

Again, I return to the Iskalia mirror. I call on the light from the Central Sun to enter the Iskalia mirror and bring down stabilization and harmony.

A reformulation can return to many of these disenfranchised parts. This separation happens when a lower consciousness interferes in the light of a planet. In some cases, it is better to be holographically connected than it is to have a consciousness that is on a lower level and lose the holographic connection.

Animals and plants are already holographically connected. In some ways, they experience greater union of the light forms and energy than the people on Earth, many of whom are disenfranchised from this interconnection. Earth is an experiment and a school for learning. To overcome the planetary loss of holographic connections and interconnections requires, as you know, a major intervention and uplifting.

How to Link to the Subconscious

We, the Arcturians, have talked about entering the subconscious and unconscious as a way of linking to all the subconsciousness, or collective subconscious, of the planet. A part of harmony interjected into the subconscious can magnify and help you interconnect. Your dreams will come back to you in greater harmony. Your dream life will return to you in a powerful way, and your dream time will be heightened as you announce to your subconscious that you are holographically connected to the greater whole.

Announce this now to your subconscious:

1. I am holographically connected to the All. I am holographically connected to the All. I am holographically connected to the All.
2. I am holographically connected to the Central Sun. (Repeat two more times.)
3. I am holographically connected to all of my lifetimes — past, present, and future. (Repeat two more times.)
4. I am a holographic being of light. (Repeat two more times.)

I ask that you now stand, and after saying these powerful affirmations, spin around once and let the energy settle in. Then do it again. You may feel a little dizzy doing that a second time. Let the energy settle in. One more time, please.

Bring the hands together in the universal sign of harmony and peace. Open the hands so that the palms are facing outward. Project and sink your hands, and allow yourself to connect to the center of the Earth. Your feet are going down, down, down into the center of the Earth. You are in the center of the Earth, and we are standing here together. Earth's core has been very disruptive as of late. Project thoughts of harmony into the core and the crust of the Earth. You may feel a rumbling, a loss of balance, as you are so close to the core of the Earth.

Remember the harmony you have achieved through the Central Sun. You have a great connection with harmony, even though individually you are not overwhelmingly powerful. Because of holographic technology, you are representatives of the greater harmony. Project this harmony out now. I will make some sounds from Earth that may sound distressing to you. It is part of the release we are activating together. [Makes crying sounds.] Return upward to the room. Place your hands in front of your chest in the universal symbol of peace and harmony.

Transmuting Holographic Energy

Holography also applies to time, and the essence of time is space. The essence of time is movement. When you stop all movement, there is an illusion of time stopping. At that moment when it stops, you are connected to all time and eternity. We connect to and describe the Eternal One.

Interestingly, in working with the Group of Forty project, your interconnections as a group are establishing holographic links around the world to all other Group of Forty starseeds. This means, for example, that the experiences of those in Australia can simultaneously be experienced by all, even when there is a delayed reaction. This does not interfere in the experience of the now. You can say that you are still experiencing our powerful exercise of the transfer of the crystal in Sedona in October 2010, even though it occurred some time ago. You are still connected to and are still working with that experience. Naturally, you wish to connect to the powerful points of higher energy. This is a wonderful example and exercise.

The holographic crystal energy and wisdom is now being transmuted etherically throughout the world. You must continue to receive energy and light. The etheric crystals are forming a triangle that is in alignment with the special corridor from the Central Sun. The crystals are also serving the purpose of activating an alignment. Energetically and astrologically, everything is in alignment. You find that your essence emerges as you are participating in this alignment and that you are building your energy as a storehouse to experience that moment. In reality, you are always experiencing that moment. But the experience is heightened at the alignment. The theory of holography states that the part is representative of the whole.

The crystal temple is a holographic representation of the Arcturian teachings that are transmitted through crystals. These crystals have unique powers, for they hold past, present, and future knowledge. At the same time, they activate points within your consciousness that stimulate DNA activity, allowing an unlocking of your higher consciousness. This unlocking of your higher consciousness enables you to experience the light as thought and new knowledge. It is important that you learn to transmute this light into thought, knowledge, and useful information. This is your job as third-dimensional beings.

Let the light and energy that we have worked with be transmuted into a form of crystalline activation within each of you. May you look at all of the events on the planet and bring your thoughts of harmony and balance to those events. May you use your holographic connection to the Central Sun to foster greater power and harmony beyond what you individually are capable of emitting. You are holographically connected to all and, in particular, to the great balancing and harmony power that is coming to Earth from the Central Sun. You may use your connections to the Iskalia mirror. In the light and the harmony of the holographic Central Sun, which is interconnected to all the central suns in the universe, I, Helio-ah, say balance, peace, and *Shalom*.

Altered States of Consciousness

Juliano and the Arcturians, Lord Arcturus, and Chief White Eagle

reetings. This is Juliano. We are the Arcturians. We have always maintained the importance of going into an altered state of consciousness, which allows you to expand your perceptions beyond the normal reality. When you are in a normal state of consciousness, there are certain blinders in place for survival purposes and for maintaining a certain level of sanity. The blinders, though, block out important contacts with a higher reality. Contacts with higher reality include past-life information; information on the energy patterns and energy swirls of light that you are living in; and also contacts with guides, teachers, and extraterrestrial energy fields.

Extraterrestrial energy fields are part of this higher reality and include corridors of light in your physical reality. It is necessary to release these blinders and to change your perceptions so that you can achieve this altered state of consciousness. It is a desirable state, but it can cause problems if you are not spiritually prepared to be in such an energy state. By that, I mean that you could be flooded with information that cannot be processed. You could receive and see so much information and different energy that you would not be able to hold the normal grasp of reality. This normal grasp of reality is what enables you to function and maintain a semblance of order in your daily life.

When you are in an altered state, you can perceive many different energies. You might think that perhaps there is a chaotic field about, for you are continually being bombarded with the different etheric light patterns. Guides and teachers are sending messages to you continually. There is outreach by the extraterrestrial masters, by the angelic hosts, and ultimately, the great source of all, *Adonai*. When you are in a proper altered state of consciousness, you can receive the finest light, the most etheric and highest strand of light, into your energy system. You must be in that state of consciousness called the lightbody consciousness (in Kabbalah, it is referred to as the *Neshamah*). That consciousness is so sensitive that it can filter out energy fields and allow you to only receive light from Lord *Adonai*.

I use this as an introduction because when you want to experience fifth-dimensional beings, it becomes imperative to train yourself to be in an altered state of consciousness. You want to be in an altered state of consciousness that is both filtered and protected. There are what we call nefarious energies, those of lower astral bodies and vibrations, that still manage to hang around spiritual fields. These lower energies are often looking for people to whom they can become parasitically attached. Any parasitic being, animal, or insect, survives by sucking energy. Parasitic astral beings are not able to connect with the light of God, the light of *Adonai*. They must find another source of energy.

Those attaining higher consciousness seek to travel through the astral world and go to the higher levels, often through corridors. You can run into these astral beings. It is important to have a protective layer around you and also a filter of light that will not allow these beings to attach to you. Going into Christ consciousness and becoming aware of the light and energy of Christ allows a protective field to automatically appear. It encompasses you so that you are not in touch with these nefarious beings, and they cannot attach themselves to you. This protection is a basic spiritual practice in attaining altered states of consciousness. You want to travel to those places that allow you to be in such an altered state so that you can commune with the Arcturians and with your star family.

We are coming into a period of consciousness and energy that is going to be representative of greater communication with the star family and the star masters. Astronomical and astrological events, such as Mars coming closer to Earth, indicate that the portals and corridors are open for higher communications. Your star heritage is an important part of your evolution and your genetically coded development. It contains basic links to your soul family. Therefore, you will have an opportunity to connect to soul brothers and sisters and to prior life commitments and contacts. Some of you have lived and studied in other star systems that were more spiritually advanced than Earth.

Affirm the etheric presence and your ability to enter at will this higher altered state of consciousness. Release and unlock the codes within that are holding you to the normal state. Come into an altered state that will allow you to connect with the star family and the city of light. The Shambhala energy field is communicating greatly with the starseeds through the space-time continuum corridor connecting to Earth. This space-time continuum corridor is comparable to a space-time rift or a continuum opening. However, it differs in that it is a positive connection to the future Shambhala light and the future star family with whom you will be uniting.

This is a star corridor. I call it the star master corridor. It allows a positive influx of energy, love, spirituality, and spiritual technology to enter the Earth field. Once there, it is a matter of receiving and fine-tuning your energy fields. It is the task of the Arcturian starseeds to (1) connect with the star family, (2) develop these star corridors, and (3) work closely with the Shambhala city of light so that this knowledge can be transmitted throughout the planet. The star city of light is already in existence in Arcturus and in other beautiful higher realms.

Traveling the Star Corridor

I direct your attention to the crystal temple, an island of light and spiritual connectedness on Arcturus. This crystal temple was developed in conjunction with our spirit masters and guides. It is a focus for the earthlings to remember their star family heritage and to purify their consciousness. This allows the Arcturian starseeds to become greater receptors and better able to fine-tune themselves.

A whirling stream of light is entering this room where the group is meeting and the channel is speaking. It is a swirling, crystal-like structure of light that is bombarding the room with bright crystalline droplets of dew and crystalline patterns activating your crown chakras.

With this activation, you perceive an opening of this star corridor in the center of the room. It is connected with the crystal temple and with future time. This star corridor is a healing corridor as opposed to a space-time rift. A rift has the possibility of draining life force energy from Earth's biosphere and receiving unwanted or unfiltered energy from the future. But here in the star corridor, we are only connecting you to positive higher vibrations from future time, the future self, and from your future star families. You can reunify with the Arcturian stargate. The corridor is opening wider.

I will give you instructions to connect with your future self. Allow yourself to gently rise out of your physical presence and float above your physical body. As you float above your body, understand that you are releasing your spirit or your essence. It floats in the corridor that has an energy field exactly resonant with your spiritual energy field. I ask you to take a moment to experience this star corridor.

It is becoming a huge star corridor. You will notice that there are other higher beings in the corridor. We are traveling through the corridor and I, Juliano, am aligning the corridor with the Central Sun, the galactic center, and the Central Sun's light. With the assistance of my friends, we are taking this star corridor and putting it in exact alignment with the Central Sun. The Central Sun contains all information about inhabitants in the galaxy, futures about these inhabitants, and core accelerations that can be downloaded into a corridor for use in connecting with a future self.

It is the future higher self that is the key to healing this planet and you personally and also your societies and cities. We know that you want to be healed and to participate on all three levels. We are moving closer to this alignment. It is a highly complex and technological task to bring a star corridor as wide as this one is into alignment with the Central Sun. It is a finely scientific process. I will tell you when we feel the exact alignment. Future light from the higher positive source is now coming. Future masters, future teachings are coming.

Earth is being prepared for a great spiritually advanced revolution. There will be a new universal spiritual presence on the entire planet. Seeds for this spiritual presence are being planted through the star corridor to which we are connected. Many great masters and teachers are aware of this new spiritual teaching. It has to do with the star families and with acknowledging the star heritage and with love and peace in your heart. The technology of the star family will be made available to earthlings who will use it for the highest good and the healing of the many negative rifts in Earth's biosphere.

I am holding this alignment for you and for the star family. I, Juliano, say that we Arcturians are part of the star family. We are working with the highest-vibrational spiritual light, and we seek to bring a fifth-dimensional perspective to you. It is our intention to use the crystal temple energy field as a basis for the city of light of spiritual beings on this planet and to bring forth the crystal from the crystal temple in etheric double form to various places.

With this downloading of the spiritual crystals, we will find an activation of thousands of people simultaneously. They will be awakened and seek spiritual union and communion. This in the light of Christ, in the light of *Adonai*, and in the light of the great teacher, Lord Arcturus, who will now speak to you.

✳ ✳ ✳

Lord Arcturus Shares New Spiritual Information

I am Lord Arcturus. I am the father of the Arcturian masters, and I seek communion with Earth beings who are of Arcturian star connectedness. I, Lord Arcturus, say the time for Arcturian interventions of spiritual accessibility is intensifying. We are ready to transmit new spiritual information to you. This spiritual information has to do with the city of light and with going into the future. It also has to do with gathering the unified healing force strong enough to permeate the planet.

This unified healing force is also part of the Sacred Triangle and is manifesting new shapes — octagons, hexagons, and pentagons — in dimensionally rotating forms that appear as crystal structures. Crop circles represent many of these forms. The forms are being transmitted through energy fields at the core of Earth and appear spontaneously as new structures. These structures are the basis for receiving spiritual knowledge.

It is hard to understand in a language such as yours how structures as complex as those represented in the crop circles can transmit spiritual knowledge. These structures do not have words or logical sequencing to which you are accustomed. They trigger mental processes within you to download this higher knowledge.

In addition to the new structures, we have been sending new sounds to you. These new sounds are also going to serve an equivalent purpose in opening up your faculties.

Arcturus has become a city of light. Our entire planet is like Shambhala. We are all vibrating in a wonderful, blissful state of unification of cosmic harmony. I, Lord Arcturus, begin to shimmer in your corridor. As I am shimmering, some of you will begin to see my presence before you. I am wearing a golden cape and have a crown-like structure on my forehead and also a beautiful purple crystal around my neck. I enter your star corridor. Behind me are great fires of energy similar to much of what has been described in the vision of Ezekiel when he saw the fiery chariots.

The downloading of the Central Sun's light is now reaching a maximum level in this exercise — a level that can be held. This star corridor and other corridors will rebalance the Earth biosphere in addition to healing existing negative space-time rifts. It will offset any negative effects on the space-time rift by creating openings to the future. I, Lord Arcturus, connected the space-star corridor to 2012 when the great alignment of the Central Sun was completed. Each of you is in magnificent form and health as you are walking the planet as true spiritual masters. Each of you has become a teacher of spirit.

The laws of spirit are greatly sought after. Spiritual reunification with the star family is needed more than ever at this time. Many of you are able to connect with your Arcturian star heritage. Know these words are describing the future reality when Earth will be reborn. I, Lord Arcturus, have seen the city of light, Shambhala, influence the entire planet. Earth is the blue star of the galaxy, the blue queen, sparkling, shining, and vibrating at a new level. I am so proud of Earth and of you, the starseeds, who have contributed to this miraculous vision and transformation of Earth. Hold this vision of the vibrating blue diamond Earth announcing her spiritual light and accepting her place into the star family. She is doing this under the guidance of many great masters.

Our dear friend and advisor, Chief White Eagle, will now speak, and he will bring you back to Earth.

✳ ✳ ✳

Chief White Eagle Joins You in the Star Corridor

Hey ya ho! All my words are from the galactic brotherhood and sisterhood. I am transmitting simultaneously from many native guides and speakers who are serving me and working with the Earth energies. Lord Arcturus's vision of the blue diamond Earth vibrating at the frequency of light is so dear to us. We see the vision of Earth reaching this vibration, and I know that there are many of you who will be affected personally. The outcome of Earth's energy process will naturally boost you to a new level.

I have always said that we must live with Earth. We must be close to her as we are close to our mothers. Great rains will come to Earth and fill many places that are now dry. The waters of life will be purified. The oceans will be purified. With this purification comes a new understanding and acceptance of the dolphins, whales, and other great spirit mammals that are in your waters. It is an honor for the oceans to hold such higher beings.

It is wonderful to be with you in the star corridor. I ask you to project yourselves into the future when we will all be gathering with this group and gain great achievements of Biorelativity, the ability to influence the planet through thoughts, feelings, and meditations; the ability to heal planetary rifts; and the ability to spread light and activate energy that will affect not only people but also the planet itself. Earth will begin to vibrate at a level that has not been seen for many centuries. I, Chief White Eagle, dance with you in the star corridor.

Tools for Reaching Higher Perspectives

Sananda

reetings. I am Sananda. There can be major difficulty in reaching the higher perspectives and in accessing the higher planes. This means that not everyone has the spiritual ability or even the spiritual knowledge to reach the higher self in this lifetime. There are a variety of reasons why people might experience this difficulty. It could be from conditions in your life, certainly, such as life problems, job problems, illnesses, and other unforeseen events can interfere in your spiritual progress.

People with higher consciousness could have the ability to overcome blocks and difficulties, but realistically, most people also will be burdened by the toxicity and the duality that cause problems on the third dimension. Of course, everyone is vulnerable to the attachments and to finding new solutions to problems that we frequently hear, such as this complaint: "Why can I not use my fifth-dimensional self and the fifth-dimensional connections I have to make this lifetime an improvement?"

We have examples throughout history of great spiritually minded people who suffered terribly, who did not have wealth, and who did not have perfect health. These were people who did not have great jobs or great protection, yet they were able to maintain and achieve very high spiritual levels. Of course, it is possible to use the spiritual connection to improve life. I don't want people to believe that you must have material wealth and occupational success in order to achieve higher consciousness. You do not pursue spiritual development because you are seeking a material reward for higher consciousness.

Frequently, people say that they want to use their fifth-dimensional energy to create greater material. I want to suggest another model for viewing spiritual progress. This perspective that I'm going to offer involves two concepts. It calls for identification with a higher being, and it also involves cohabitation.

Identifying with Higher Beings

Identification with a higher being is taking yourself and placing the energy of your consciousness into the energy of the higher being. In this perspective, you try to look at your current life through the eyes of the higher being. So in this simple way, you could identify with Sananda (me) and say, "Okay, how would Sananda see this situation? What would be the perspective that Sananda would use in the situation?" Remember, a fifth-dimensional master has higher energies and higher feelings. These higher feelings include compassion, acceptance, love, understanding, wisdom, and so on. So you could ask, "How would Sananda use compassion and understanding in the situation?" By placing yourself and projecting yourself into a higher being, you are raising your own vibration and raising yourself into a higher perspective.

Ultimately, one of the main messages that I offered to the world was a simple one: that if you can identify with me, if you can place yourself in my energy field, then you will be able to ascend. You will be able to go to the higher realms. By identifying with me, you will be able to visit and stay with my father in the fifth-dimensional gardens. That was the main message. I was offering myself as a tool, as a higher being, so that you could identify with my higher energy field.

Now this idea of identification is a common psychological tool that is used continually, especially among children. Children, as you know, identify with their fathers or with their mothers, and therefore, they use this identification as a steppingstone for a higher existence or for higher beingness. That identification eventually changes, and then the children can be themselves and totally fulfill their true identities. There is a stage of development in which you have to separate who you are from your parents. This is part of the growth. There will come a state in which you can separate from who you are and who I am.

Cohabitation with Higher Beings

The second aspect of the process of moving to higher light and higher energy is known as the process of cohabitation. Now, cohabitation — inviting a higher spirit to live in your spiritual energy field — is common in many spiritual practices. It doesn't mean that the higher spirit takes over your energy; rather, it does mean that the higher spirit can enhance who you are.

I like to use the example of Moses, who did not believe that he had the physical abilities to lead the Israelites out of Egypt. In fact, we know he was not even a good speaker. He was visited by several archangels who cohabited with him. They enhanced his speaking abilities. By enhancing his abilities, they helped improve the abilities and attributes he already had. The higher spirit helped Moses have more confidence in those abilities. Moses knew that he wasn't a good speaker. He was very emotional and passionate, and the guides and teachers told him that he could use his passion as strength when he spoke. His passion would make him an effective speaker and would help him overcome his problems of speaking. So that is an example of how cohabitation, allowing a higher being cohabit with you, could help you enhance a higher aspect of yourself — the part of you that's already there but just needs to be encouraged, that needs to be supported.

Cohabitation involves this process of self-improvement. I want to emphasize that in the cohabitation, you are not taken over but rather enhanced. I am cohabiting with many people now on Earth. This cohabitation is an interaction with my energy and a person's energy on the third dimension.

You might even find that two people can channel me and experience cohabiting with me in different ways. This means that they might receive different messages. The reason for different messages and reactions from each person is because my energy is interacting with their energy. I find this to be a great spiritual tool for helping you to be who you are. Everybody needs some type of help and encouragement, and this has been true throughout history of all spiritual practices. The path to higher consciousness in the higher light requires some type of guidance.

There are many people who have been on Earth before you. You are not the first. Remember that you are already in an advanced state spiritually on Earth. There have been many masters who have walked the earth before you. There are many possibilities of cohabiting with different angels and ascended masters. Cohabitation is a good spiritual tool, and I hope that you use it to your benefit.

I'm Sananda. Good day.

Grace

Mary

reetings. I am Mary. It is always a great pleasure to be with so many of you. I know of your deep love for my work, and I also have a deep love for your work, because I know that you are trying to be the best people that you can be. I have been asked to speak to you today about grace.

There are many different things to learn on Earth. There are many different life experiences, and there are many different things to understand and to try to balance. I can understand how at times you might feel overwhelmed about everything, and I can understand how you can even feel overwhelmed by the ascension.

One of the lessons of the ascension is that you seek to resolve all of your karmic lessons in this lifetime. Some of you are working hard on this task and are totally committed to completing your Earth lessons. It is honorable that you are trying to learn and resolve ten lifetimes of lessons in one lifetime. But even after you have committed yourself to that effort, you still may not be able to resolve every lesson. Because of that, you might feel inferior — like you are not doing as much as you can or as if you will not be successful at your ascension. That is why I came here today to talk about grace.

Grace is the ability to receive an energy of blessing so that you can skip certain uncomfortable and painful experiences. Through grace, you can be relieved of certain unpleasant illnesses or situations. Through grace, your life can be made easier for you. You can receive gifts that do not seem to be logical and that seemingly come from nowhere. This is grace. Grace is a beautiful spiritual energy.

I am asking you now to open yourselves up to my grace. Open yourselves up to the gifts that are still outside for you. Maybe you will not finish all of your lessons. Maybe you will not be perfect in your work, but from our stand-point — the standpoint of the masters — your effort, your intention, and your desires to be spiritual and do the best that you can are most important and relevant. You can receive from that effort and intention my grace and the grace of other masters and teachers. You will be getting a gift to help you.

I ask you all to speak these words: "I am open to any grace that it is avail-able to me now." You may be surprised. Nobody is expected to be perfect, and all we expect is that you do the best that you can, that you remain spiritually open, and that you continue to work as hard as you can up until your ascen-sion. If you are not at 100 percent at the moment of ascension, you can still ascend with grace. Your education and work can continue in special situations before you completely enter the fifth dimension.

I know that everything is accelerating. Look how much you have learned already in this lifetime! I am optimistic that with your new openness, with your new light, and with the grace that is coming to you, you will continue to make great progress on your ascension work.

I am Mary. Good day.

◆

Soul Evolution and the Supermind

Juliano and the Arcturians

reetings. I am Juliano. We are the Arcturians. Today we wish to talk about the soul journey and the way the soul comes into Earth. One interesting observation is that on entry into the birth corridor, you experience a memory loss both of past life experiences and of information related to discussions you have had with your guides and teachers. This is valuable, important information. You would think it would be necessary to retain the memories of your past lives and the guidance and wisdom from your teachers as well as your precognitive knowledge of events that will transpire when you enter your physical incarnation on Earth. Yet despite the importance of all this information, you go through an experience of memory loss. It has been described that your master guide and teacher touches your forehead, usually around your third eye, right before you come into the birth corridor. This action erases those memories. Actually, "erasing" is not the correct word because the memories are placed in a special compartment in the superbrain or supermind where they can be accessed.

The lost information is not immediately accessible except through certain methodologies and spiritual practices. This also implies that your mind has many levels, including the Earth mind (or ego mind) and the supermind. The supermind is connected to vast pools of information about your soul, about past and future lifetimes, and about many other aspects of the dimensions and their expansions and evolutions. It also contains relevant and necessary information about how to connect to the Creator light and to make the highest contact with your soul.

When you come into Earth through the birth corridor, you lose this contact with the supermind and your ability to access it, so this ability must be learned. The Earth civilizations and Earth cultures, however, do not encourage teaching how to access this vital and important information from the supermind. In fact, exactly the opposite occurs. Such psychic or spiritual information and abilities actually are discouraged in the existing predominant cultures and civilizations on the planet. This discouragement of the development of such spiritual abilities is a reflection of the lack of intense spiritual development on the planet.

There are exceptions to discouraging spiritual connections culturally on Earth. There are certain "primitive" tribes and cultures that actually are working to allow children to report prebirth spiritual information. When you come through the birth canal and the birth corridor, you also lose your language abilities and access to almost all of the higher functions of the mind that you had before you came into Earth. So, in essence, you are a *tabla rasa* (Latin for "blank slate") in your mind. And this is necessary for soul development in this third-dimensional reality for several reasons. We all understand the importance of having this soul information and connection with soul memory. You come in this way to have an opportunity to start in a new energy. Your new life on the third dimension is a gift for your soul development.

Free Will versus Predetermination or Predestination

From our studies and our deep spiritual exploration, we have learned that the soul is involved in an evolution. One vital part of that evolutionary link occurs in the third dimension, which is why it's important to incarnate on Earth. Any past mistakes, past inclinations, or past errors can be reassessed and realigned under Earth's third-dimensional energy field that we call the freewill zone.

I cannot overestimate the importance of Earth being a freewill zone for your soul development and evolution. Yes, being in a freewill zone presents many problems, but it is also vital to do the soul lessons and the soul work required. That is why so many souls are lined up to come to this freewill zone on Earth. They see all the suffering happening on Earth, and they see all the problems, but they are looking at it all from a much higher perspective of the supermind. They know that being in this energy of the freewill zone is vital and is a great boost to the possibility for their soul evolution.

It is so important and so vital for souls to come to Earth that they will line up even if they know they will only be on Earth for nine months. Can you imagine that there are souls waiting to come into India or Africa, knowing they will be born into poverty and die from sickness? Yet they understand that there is a huge benefit from their soul perspective to come into the third dimension.

Coming into a freewill zone is deeply related to the whole issue of contact with your soul masters, guides, and teachers. You also lose your awareness of your past lives when you incarnate on Earth. In higher civilizations such as on Arcturus, we encourage and promote the accessibility as soon as possible to past lives and to discussions of masters, guides, and teachers. Arcturus is unlike Earth, where many of you have had to wait fifty years or longer to get this information. In terms of the Earth life, this would be considered the last third of your life. The last third of your life is when you can do some of the most important soul work. Isn't that waiting a long time to do your soul work, waiting for two-thirds of your life to pass?

Advanced spiritual civilizations like the Arcturians promote and work so that people can have access to their past and future lives at an early age. Our work with you on the holographic healing chambers is an expression and an example of how we approach many of these issues, such as talking with guides and teachers, life-between-lives energies, working with the past, and working with the future.

We evaluate every action that we want to take in terms of the future as well as the past because we know that the past influences the present. But we also know that the present influences the future. Also, the possibility of future events influences the present. If you were going on a trip somewhere, you would consider and want to know the effect of that trip on the future events. What karma might the trip entail?

In this example, we actually would spend a significant amount of energy in the holographic chambers on future events. This may seem surprising. When you are now looking at Earth and its changes, one lesson coming forth to the inhabitants is that you must take into consideration how present actions will affect the future of the planet. This is one big lesson the planet has to deal with now. We are dealing with this lesson even on a personal level.

The question of future events always involves free will versus predetermination or predestination. Lower consciousness is without awareness of the interaction of past lives and lacks integration of soul lessons. Lower consciousness also lacks interaction of the higher mind. Using lower consciousness usually means, in those circumstances, that there is more predetermination. It looks like everything is set up and is destined to happen. The argument of predetermination versus free will has been debated by many philosophers in the Western civilization.

Predetermination implies lack of choice. The argument is that everything is set up in advance. There is some truth to predetermination, especially when you have been exploring your relationship with your past lives and your relationship with your birth. All of you have been shown a holographic image of what is going to happen to you in this lifetime. You are shown which parents you are going to be with, which friends you are going to have, and what work you are going to do. You have even been shown how you are going to die. You are shown what lessons you are supposed to learn. Your guides and teachers discussed and went over all of this with you before you incarnated. When you came here, you were in agreement that this was what was going to happen.

It appears, from this perspective, that your life is cast in stone. From the supermind's perspective, these are experiences, these are issues, that need to happen for your development. Remember, the supermind is not influenced by the lower emotions of loss or sadness or even death. It would look at all these things and not react emotionally to any choices made. This is hard for many people to grasp, for you might say, "Why did I choose to have this bad experience? Why did I choose to have parents who were abusive to me? Why would I experience or want to have this disease?" It is difficult to explain it to the lower mind because the lower mind doesn't have the perspective of the supermind.

Antidotes for Predestination

The good news is that predestination has an antidote so that those things that seem painful and as if they are destined to happen don't have to unfold in exactly the tragic or painful way that appears to be predestined. What is the antidote? There are actually two or three antidotes.

The first is what we call awareness. Awareness has become one of the major psychological advancements in the twentieth and twenty-first centuries. Awareness includes knowledge of the soul process, awareness of karma, and awareness of how things were set up for you to have such limitations or such experiences.

Awareness becomes the antidote for dissolving the predetermination aspect of the situation. Awareness encourages the connection to the supermind. Anytime you can connect to your supermind, you are able to bring down the energies with this awareness that transcends the third-dimensional logic and open up a vast possibility of changes. This connection to the supermind opens up new ways of dealing with karma and new ways of transcending it. The supermind can offer new ways of overcoming illnesses and even ways of really changing and shifting the planet through awareness.

The attribute of awareness is part of the evolution of a species. Awareness is what distinguishes humanity, or the Adam species, from the other animal worlds. It isn't awareness in a selfish or narcissistic way. You can have awareness of this greater supermind and this greater connection from the supermind to the soul. You can use that awareness in a holographic way to change and work with past and future karma. Working with past karma in the holographic healing chamber will have a tremendous effect. In the healing chamber, you can shift the energies of past abuses and wrongdoings. You can even undo

energies of wrongdoings done to you. Then you will have a tremendous benefit in your karma that is unfolding.

I want to point out something about the healing chamber. When they are
working with us on holographic work, many people want to go back to when
they were hurt or when they were damaged. They want to correct the images,
and they want to correct the problems that arose because of the pain and
suffering. I have worked repeatedly through this channel with many healing
experiences in which people were wounded or severely damaged or ridiculed
or even put to death for certain spiritual reasons. However, I have not worked
through the channel with somebody who said that they would like to correct
the wrongdoings that they did to others.

For example, we all know that all humans have — or most people have —
been warriors on this planet. I want to make an addendum to that statement.
There is one glaring exception: Some of you were scientists and were high-
level people in Atlantis and other areas where there was high technology. Some
of you suffered because you allowed your intelligence and your abilities to be
used for purposes that eventually led to the destruction of that civilization and
many deaths. There have been some who have come forward and worked with
us wanting to clear that energy.

When you do the holographic work from the past, including from past
lives, be open to going back to karmic things that you have done. The healing
process for past lives is similar to alcoholism recovery. In recovering from alcoholism, when people make amends, when they realize and have the awareness
of what harm they may have caused others, they want to apologize. Then they
want to say they are sorry to those whom they have hurt.

This is an important part of their recovery because now they have an
awareness of the pain they have caused others, and now they want to remove
the negative energy; they want to remove the karma. You see, you can remove
negative karma in this lifetime. That is another powerful reason why everyone
is still lining up to come to Earth — because of the opportunities to remove
karma. No one, when going into the supermind, really wants to have any
karma on the soul that would necessitate having to reincarnate again on the
third dimension.

This is a time on Earth when awareness is possible. So many people are
coming to Earth knowing they have an opportunity for this awareness. With
awareness, you can eliminate and have an antidote for karma.

The second and equally powerful experience, opportunity, and technology
for overcoming predetermination is the ascension. The ascension can overcome the necessity for karma and living out certain karmas. Ascension also
brings an accompanying grace that helps overcome karma.

There are certain eras that are represented by astrological passages of time. There are certain planetary systems within the solar system that are measured by the distance that the solar system is traveling around the galaxy. There are certain passages in the space-time continuum where the energy of grace becomes more accessible and is more powerful.

At that point of the energy of grace, the soul, if it is incarnated in that place, has the opportunity to make huge advancements and to overcome and wash away and resolve huge karmic issues. Right now on Earth is such a time. This experience of grace from the ascension is available. Grace can be considered an antidote to karma. Grace can allow huge soul gains. This is an excellent time for the evolution of the soul here on Earth, and your soul knew that before it came to Earth.

Your soul knew that there were powerful opportunities and avenues for resolving past karmas. The first avenue was an awareness of an opening of spiritual energy on the planet. The second and perhaps more important avenue was that your soul knew this was going to be an opportunity to experience an unbelievable grace energy leading up to the ascension.

Let us be clear: Ascension means you have cleared your Earth karma. In certain circumstances, people living now on Earth can have five to eight lifetimes of experiences compacted in a very short lifetime. This is possible here on Earth because of the acceleration of the space-time continuum. From the supermind, this is a fantastic opportunity.

Soul Evolution

I want to return again to this idea of soul evolution because it is difficult to discuss in third-dimensional terminology. You correctly view the soul as being perfect and eternal. So why would the soul have to evolve?

In the fifth-dimensional perspective, there is not evolution in the same way as in the third dimension. Soul evolution implies a lack of perfection in some way. We can't really speak logically about this. I can only try to talk about it or around it so that you have some idea.

The idea is that the soul needs a certain type of experience. I have talked with many of you through this channel, and I know you have had different lifetimes on other planets. You have not just been on one planet besides Earth; most of you have been on several planets. When you open yourself up to the supermind, you will be pleased to know that you have had so many different experiences.

I have worked with some of you who have been on planets that were destroyed. I have worked with some of you who have had experiences in Atlantis in which you saw a whole civilization destroyed. Some of you have actually seen an entire planet destroyed exactly at the same level of energy that Earth is going through. From your perspective, all the things going on now on Earth probably look familiar. Hauntingly familiar, I may add. I realize that what is going on on Earth now is causing a great deal of emotional trauma for all of you. First, the trauma is because of what you are seeing on Earth, and second, it is because tragic Earth events are also reactivating the earlier memories of what you saw on other planets.

The soul wants to clear the karma. The soul wants to drop it or resolve it; therefore, coming here is a wonderful opportunity. It is fair to ask the question, "Juliano, how is being here on Earth now going to help my soul evolution — especially in the face of all this destruction?" The answer is complicated, and it doesn't make total logical sense on the third dimension. There are so many things that have occurred on the third dimension that are not logical. We cannot logically explain many events; therefore, explanations must be turned over to the realm I call cosmic karma. I will offer some lower Earth logical explanation that won't totally encompass the right answer, but it will at least point you in the right direction.

The first point is that one of the most important soul lessons for everyone is to learn that there is a unity and a connection. There is a connection with the Creator light, and there is always a connection with your soul and the supermind. You are given the task and have all the tools to connect with your supermind. That lesson has to be learned over and over again — even in the face of a planetary crisis.

The second lesson is that there are ways to transcend karma. Look at all of the things you have done in all of the lifetimes that created karma. For example, in one Earth lifetime, you may have abused people. Then in another lifetime, you may have been a victim. Maybe some of you were soldiers fifty lifetimes ago. Does that mean that you have to have fifty more lifetimes in which you are slaves? The answer is no. The soul can learn ways of overcoming vast accumulated karma. For example, there are amazing medical practitioners on this planet now. There are amazing healers on this planet. I am not just talking about traditional medical doctors. Bless their hearts — medical doctors are trying to do the best they can, but there are other high spiritual healers who can also do healing work on ill people.

A healer in this lifetime may be able to heal 1,000 people in one lifetime. Think of how much karma that healer is erasing. Think of any other things that he or she may have done in some other past lifetimes either here or on other planets that may have created karma that needs to be released. This is a fantastic opportunity here on Earth for the soul to be able to heal 1,000 people. It is an unbelievable number and certainly worth it, from the supermind's perspective, to come to Earth. It would be worth coming to Earth even in consideration of the suffering you might have to experience while here.

You might ask the follow-up question: "Why would I come here to suffer? Is that some of the karma that I would experience for something that I did in an earlier lifetime that was bad?" Again, the answer is not simple, and it doesn't make total logical sense. Every lifetime has certain risks. You meet with your guides and teachers, and you have a preview of your life before you come. It is not an exact play-by-play, minute-by-minute report but rather a general review.

The Uncertainty Principle

Think about what it is like to be a psychic. You see what events could happen in the future. The future events that you see are based on all the available information, which could be fairly accurate from the soul perspective. It is still not all the information. That is something I want you to totally understand. If you saw all of the information available, you might think that everything is predestined. However, there is a factor of the unknown. This factor of not knowing is now demonstrated in modern quantum physics.

When scientists study the subatomic level, something exists that is called the "uncertainty principle." In a simple version, the Heisenberg uncertainty principle is that, on a subatomic level, there are certain factors that make particle location exploration unpredictable and determination uncertain. Scientists cannot predict with certainty where subatomic particles are going to be. That is a direct contradiction to the logical Newtonian law of physics under which everything should be orderly and predictable.

The reason I bring this up to you now is because the Heisenberg uncertainty principle also applies to knowledge when you are coming into an Earth incarnation. You are given a general detail, a general overview, of your life. But there are certain things that are uncertain that you would not know at the time of your entry into the Earth incarnation. The overview you are given before you enter Earth is the best possible overview based on available information. People ask the Arcturians, "Don't you know everything that is going to happen there on the fifth dimension? Don't you know everything?" The answer is that we do not know and cannot predict everything. The uncertainty principle exists in all dimensions, including the fifth dimension.

The study of galactic Kabbalah has come down to Earth through the work of the Jewish mystics and others who have studied the Kabbalah. From this work, an important principle has been demonstrated. That principle is that the Creator cannot be totally known. What is possible is only that you can experience an aspect of the Creator. My friends, each planetary incarnation, each position in the galaxy, each position in the solar systems, provides another unique aspect of knowing the Creator.

From the soul perspective, you might say that one of the highest soul missions is to know the Creator. In the Kabbalah, it is believed that you know the Creator by knowing and studying the creation. Because the mind of the Creator is not totally known, all of the information, even in an incarnation on Earth, is not totally known. Sometimes when you are choosing an incarnation, there are certain aspects to it that may occur that you didn't plan on. These aspects can wind up being painful. For example, you might think that you are being punished, but it is not always the case that illness is a punishment. In some cases, an illness is one of the unpredictable prices you have to pay to have your body in this incarnation at the present time.

It is all generally known that there are a lot of uncertainties in coming into the Earth plane with all of this density. It would be easier if you were incarnating on Arcturus or on the Pleiades. Then you would know that there would be fewer intervening variables in your karma. There wouldn't be as many surprises.

On Earth, especially in this turbulent time, there are a lot of surprises because there are lots of unknown possibilities. Preventing illness, for example, requires more careful examination of all aspects of your immune systems and learning about aspects of your subconscious and your superconscious. Coming into contact with lower energies may mean that you can unknowingly attract lower energies that at other times wouldn't even touch you. The potential gains of being sensitive to energies are very high, but so is the potential for intervening variables and unpredictable ones.

Through awareness and working in the holographic energy field of the past, present, and future soul work, you can mediate and lessen the effects of some of the discomforts you are experiencing. Any time you access and connect to your supermind, you are working with fifth-dimensional energies, which can do powerful things. Any time you work with this powerful energy of grace, you can also connect with powerful karmic issues.

Meditation: Connect to the Supermind

I would like to do a brief meditation with you in which we will ask each of you to connect with your supermind — the all-knowing mind.

[Chants: *omega light.*]

May this omega light help each of you now connect to your supermind. We will go into silence now.

As you connect to your supermind, ask and you will be granted permission to access your past lives, your past experiences, and information about your birth corridor and special information from the guides and teachers. Also let the information for your soul lessons be downloaded to you now. Most important is that you receive the energies and abilities to have this wonderful awareness of your soul and of past experiences of your soul in other places and in other incarnations on other planets. May you be given the grace and understanding to carefully measure all actions you take on Earth so that they are free of any karmic entanglements and so that you will be in the greatest position to ascend.

Yes, each of you will need grace, and it is available. So accept it, and use it. It will help you transcend some of these issues that may look predetermined and may look as if they have no resolution. When you connect to your supermind, your healing abilities are endless.

The Planetary Supermind

Now let us speak more about planetary healing and the planetary mind. Earth has a supermind too. Earth also has higher functioning. You could ask, "Well, how do you know that, Juliano?" The answer is simple: because for a planet to have higher life like Earth's humanity, that planet must have a higher supermind. It is called the planetary supermind.

For example, there are destructive energies you hear about that include asteroids hitting a planet and destroying all living things. These energies may seem random, but from our perspective, the planet's supermind sometimes attracts asteroids because the planet may want or need a clearing. Of course, now we are in the period of spiritual interaction with Earth that we call Biorelativity. In Biorelativity, you are able to interact with the planetary mind. To that end, we activate new cities of light — because the planetary cities of light are directly accessing the supermind of Earth. That's how powerful these planetary cities of light can become.

These planetary cities of light have a powerful accessibility to the supermind of the planet. The supermind of Earth can bring forth quantum omega light that can help transcend many difficult situations that seem irresolvable, such as the Fukushima power plant accident. Yet the Earth mind, the supermind of the planet, can be accessed to provide a solution that will work. Remember the power of this grace and the power of this planetary experience now.

I send you my healing light. I send you the omega light. I know each of you hearing this lecture or reading these words will have a greater opportunity now to connect with your supermind. I know your superminds, and I have been connecting with them since the beginning of our transmissions in this project. Sometimes people say, "Why would the Arcturians, why would fifth-dimensional beings, be interested in Earth? Earth is in a lower vibration.

Why would the Arcturians and other higher beings be interested in such densities?" Well, the answer is that we see your total self, more of your total self, and we are interacting with your superminds. On that level, we are very powerful brothers and sisters to all of you.

I am Juliano. Good day.

Kabbalah and Soul Development

Nabur[1]

We are delighted to come here to talk about the different levels of soul that manifest on Earth. We want to talk about the higher self, the middle self, and the lower self. Also, we want to explain to you a little bit about the channeling experience. You know that the channeling experience is something you are all able to do. It is not something far out there; it is a part of your path. It is something each of you can use to tune into your teachers. This is especially useful now, for your guides and teachers have specific information that will help you. We are with you, and this is an exciting time in terms of the tremendous changes that are going on. It's important for you to be able to access information that is peculiar to the level of your soul.

Each of you belongs to a specific soul group. Many of you are already aware of some of your brothers and sisters on the soul level. Those in your soul group are especially able to give you information that will help you to resonate with them. I want to emphasize the word "resonate." We are trying to help you learn to resonate with the particular frequency that belongs to your soul. Furthermore, there are other souls that can resonate at your particular frequency and who will help you raise your consciousness.

Tuning into Your Soul Vibrations

Let's talk about the Kabbalah and the particular frequencies of the Hebrew language that are useful in tuning into your soul vibrations. Hebrew is a special galactic language that was brought to Earth many centuries ago. It has certain sounds that resonate with the galactic core and help bring in the Creator

---

1. *Nabur* was a Kabbalistic rabbi and teacher of the channel, David, in a former lifetime.

energy. This is extremely important. Many of the sounds themselves, even if you do not know what the meanings are, can take you into a higher state of consciousness. When you are in a higher state of consciousness, you can access your higher self. This is what you are about. This is one reason you are incarnating now — so that you can access your higher self and tune into the Creator.

As a warm-up, we are going to use a Hebrew word to help you raise your vibrations: *Atah*.[2] We ask you to repeat it: *Atah. Atah. Atah.*

When you say this word, feel the energy rising from the bottom of your spine up to the top. Also, sense a circle of energy around your auric field. As you say the word "*Atah*," it vibrates your auric field and your aura begins to expand. When it expands, it opens. Then you can receive higher information. This is useful when you are trying to access higher energy fields.

There are three levels of self. You have the lower self, which some call the animal self. That sounds as if you are equal to the animal, which is true in one sense; you are an animal in your day-to-day functioning, and your survival skills are governed by this aspect of yourself. Your lower self has a unique ability, though: It can blend with your middle self. Unless your lower self is able to key into this energy, you cannot go into the middle self.

Many people on the planet are struggling to get their physical health in balance. There is a misconception that you must be in perfect physical health in order to resonate with the higher energy. Now, of course, it is desirable to be in perfect physical health, but realistically, there are not many people who are going to have perfect physical harmony at this time. This is partly due to the fact that Earth is now polluted. There are many chemicals affecting your body. This is partly due to the ultraviolet radiation affecting your auric field. It is rare to be 100 percent in harmony, so go with the best level you can attain. Even if you are disabled, even if you have an illness such as cancer, you still will be able to resonate at a high level. So don't think that if you are not totally healthy physically or if you have a major illness, you cannot reach the highest level. Of course you can! In fact, sometimes it is because of an illness that you can be driven to go on to a high energy level. On the other hand, you might be in perfect physical health and have your animal self in perfect harmony and still be unable to reach the higher levels.

When you go into the middle level and the higher levels, you begin to access the highest energy fields, and you can bring in the soul energy, which will help you learn more about yourself. You will be able to access energy that will expand your lightbody. Now, what do I mean by "lightbody"? The

---

2. *Atah* is the Hebrew word for "you." In the *Amidah*, a famous prayer in the Jewish service, the first opening blessing is called "Fathers." It begins, "Blessed are You, O Lord ..."

lightbody is that part of your higher self that will come down and merge with your lower self. In effect, this is the message of Kabbalah: You can receive yourself.

I am not saying you must be selfish or narcissistic. I am saying that you have a higher lightbody that is able to coordinate and merge with your lower self on this plane. When you can do this, you will have access to untold secrets of the universe. You will have access to fantastic energies. You will transcend your physical ego and go into higher energy states.

When we are talking about channeling and working with the channel or we are helping others to channel, what we are doing is helping you, the seeker, to access your higher self. When you are in that state, you can access energy fields of other entities that are in the same resonance.

I go back to the term "resonance." In accessing higher energy states, you are preparing your physical body so that you can resonate with your higher self. Only then can your higher self resonate with the other energies. When you are bringing down higher energy, that energy is only as powerful as the connection you can make. Your body, your physical presence, and your mind become the tools. Your mind, voice, and speech are like a computer for the energy that is coming through. If there is a glitch in the computer or there are certain words the computer does not have in its vocabulary, then those words cannot be brought forth.

I want to speak about past masters and the Kabbalah. One important aspect of Kabbalah study focuses on channeling past masters and teachers. Many Kabbalists were interested in working with the past masters whom they could channel. Channeling was a common experience in ancient days. Even as recently as a century or two ago, many mystics were still actively engaged in channeling and were using channeling predominantly as a means of obtaining specific spiritual information.

Channeling does need to have safeguards. If you are channeling, you need to have a sense that you are bringing down higher energy. There must be a sense of protection from any negative entities that might enter. Also, you must realize that you are doing the channeling for a specific purpose: to expand the light energy and your energy fields and the fields of those listening. It is extremely important that you keep those ideas in mind.

Getting in Touch with Your Higher Self

We want to work more with sounds because, as much as we can give you words, sound vibrations can also be powerful in opening up your mind. We

---

3. *Hu* is the Hebrew word for "he." In prayers, it can refer to the Creator

are going to work with the sound of "*Hu*."[3] I would like you to put your hand over your third eye and then vibrate your third eye chakra as you say, "*Hu. Hu. Huuu. Huuuu.*"

Sit with your energy now. We are working to open up your energy field — in particular, your third eye, because when it is open, you will be able to receive more information. When one energy field opens, other ones also want to open, although sometimes it is more difficult to open up the second one.

We want to go to the crown chakra now. The crown chakra can be opened up with the Hebrew word for our father: *Adonai*, or Lord. *Adonai. Adonai. Adonai.*

An opening has now occurred on the planet through which you are able to get to the highest energy fields if you have the proper concentration and use the proper sounds. It does not take years and years of study or practice. The time frame for being on Earth is limited. There are about to be major shifts of energy and major upheavals. If you are able to access your highest energy, it is important for you to access the Creator energy and to open up and receive information from your highest self. It is important for you and the planet. You should get yourself into the best possible spiritual shape.

Many of you are already going through major physical problems and imbalances. The energy field around the planet is in so much fluctuation that it is very difficult to maintain a balance.

Now let us talk about getting in touch with the higher self, which in the Kabbalah is called the *Neshamah*.[4] With the *Neshamah*, you are able to access your psychic abilities to the highest level. You are able to look into the future. You are able to look into the past. You are able to look into the pasts and futures of others.

Now, this sounds like an extraordinary ability, but it is not. It is a gift. It is something you all are able to do. You have the genetic code for it, you have the mental structure, you have the ability to align your mental bodies, and you have the historical precedent. The only thing perhaps blocking you is your belief that it is out of your range. It is not. Each of you can look at other people and even into yourself and experience past lives.

Many people are surprised to learn that the Kabbalah and the Zohar[5] have their origins in galactic energy. You are not alone in the universe. Much information that has reached this planet has come from other sources. There is a universal language, and there are galactic sounds — many of which are in Hebrew. For example, the term "Zohar" refers to the light or the splendor of the light.

So much of what we are about as spiritual beings has to do with light.

---

4. *Neshamah* is the highest of the three parts of the soul or spirit. It is the intuitive power that connects humankind with the Creator.

5. The Zohar is *The Book of Splendor*, a thirteenth-century Spanish mystic's guide to Kabbalism.

There are many different ramifications of light. There are many different light rays, and there is so much light available. People talk about the darkness currently on the Earth plane — the hatred, the densities, the pollution, and so forth. Yet the light can penetrate even darkness. You are able to bring in more of your own light. The key is to bring in the light from your lightbody and from your highest self.

Opening the Heart and Feeling the Love

I wish to talk now about opening the heart. The path of the light, the path that ascends up the ladder, is based in your heart chakra. The heart chakra is the center of the Tree of Life. It is there that you can access all available energies, including energies of the highest form. By accessing the heart sphere, you can receive a sliver, a spark, of all the other spheres.

It is a mistake to believe you can do this work without opening up your heart. The heart is the key to the soul. Your heart energy and your ability to love yourself and others are vitally important. The highest form of love is the love of the Creator energy, our Father/Mother. When you are able to tap into that love, then you will have the love that will help you accept yourself and love yourself.

The difficulty in loving the Creator is that many times you get lost trying to understand the Creator with your mind. This is a wonderful intellectual exercise, a wonderful philosophical exercise. It has produced volumes and volumes of beautiful writings. But in the true Kabbalah and on the true path of mysticism, humans understand the love of the Creator with the heart energy. When that is accomplished, you are not able to explain it. You are not able to describe it.

I want you to take a moment to experience the love of the Creator, *Adonai*, in your heart and see what it feels like. You might find that the first step in the process is to receive the love of the Creator personally. This is extremely powerful if you are able to open up your heart chakra to that love. It will fill you.

Now I want you to sense the love of the Creator. If you can, I would like you to feel the burst of light that began creation. That burst of light is the substance of your soul.

You are on a path to realize your place in creation, and the path of light will help you align with your soul families. One of the key beliefs of the Kabbalah is that you are part of soul families, and some soul families are in other dimensions. They eagerly await you; they eagerly wait for you to return.

Is "Atah" a word or just a sound?

Atah is the Hebrew word for "you." We are referring to the Creator. We are speaking of Him as "You." You can use many forms and vibrations to call forth the Creator energy. Basically, you are announcing that you are ready to vibrate your aura on His energy wavelength. You can use any of the many names of God to do that.

What can we do to expand into the Creator energy?

Each of you resonates with a particular name of God, with particular sounds that work with you better than others do. You will have to experiment to see which is the best one for you. The *Atah* energy is one of the basic sounds, and you can practice it in your meditations. Many of you are aware of the mantra meditations of the yogis in which they say "Om," for example. The sound of *Atah* is just as powerful, and it will awaken the vibratory fields in you much more quickly.

We suggest you choose the sound with which you feel the most resonance and use that. Experiment with saying it softly and saying it loudly. Say it mentally or visualize it on a screen. Obviously, you want to be in a meditative state. Some of you use it when you feel you are in danger. You might be driving down the street and think a car is going to hit you. Say, "*Atah*," and suddenly your energy field starts expanding and white light is expanding outward. You then have an energy shield to protect you.

There are many different ways to use the sounds, but we find that it is important that the sound be vocalized, even if you vocalize it to yourself very softly. There must be an actual expression of the sound. This is one of the beauties of the Hebrew language. The sounds themselves are on a special vibratory wavelength that is able to resonate with a special energy field that will help to expand your energy field.

Cosmic Karma

Juliano and the Arcturians

reetings. I am Juliano. We are the Arcturians. Today we will discuss events, how they are unfolding on Earth, and the relationship between present and previous events. When you see an event such as an earthquake, a cyclone, or even a war, you only see the present activity; you see the present event. What you don't see are all of the activities and all of the different occurrences that led to that event.

Because there is so much focus, and rightly so, on the nuclear accident in northern Japan [at the time of this channeling], we will use that event as an example. You might initially say that you are aware that it was a tsunami — it was an earthquake — that triggered the event. Therefore, if the tsunami and the earthquake had not happened, then this event would not have occurred. From our perspective, there are series of events and activities and decisions that led to that event. If you were to look at present occurrences from our perspective, including the Earth changes, including the many wars, and including the upheavals, then you would think and understand that there is a series of occurrences, a series of events that led to the present event you are observing.

It is, my starseed friends, even more complex because you must understand that there is a series of events and occurrences that have led to the development of this Earth. There are series of events and occurrences that led to the Adam species coming to this planet. There are many events in which you are now participating that are going to lead to future events that affect not only Earth but also other parts of the galaxy.

This interpretation and observation needs to be extended so that you understand that the Adam species is part of a long historical chain of planetary systems that goes back countless years. That is to say, there were other ancient civilizations in this galaxy. There are many ancient planets in this galaxy and even in other galaxies. What you are observing and what is part of the Earth crisis is, in fact, a galactic drama that has been played out on other planetary systems. This does not lessen the intensity of the tragedies and the upheavals that you are seeing. Not at all. But it does offer you a dynamic perception and observation of the events, because the events that are now occurring are related to your galactic heritage.

Your historic DNA codes have been instilled in this planet with the hope and with the intention that at some point the Adam species would work out and would find a way to resolve the crisis that is now before this planet. This crisis that is before this planet is a repetitive theme that has occurred on other planetary systems. The truth is that Earth has been seeded by other races, by other planetary beings, but not in the way that you might understand.

When you think of being "seeded," you think there was no prior life on the planet and then suddenly the species of the Adam was brought to Earth. Actually, Earth has always had the ability to produce, through evolution, certain types of higher beings. This is a way of saying the Earth seeding is a combination of occurrences. It is a combination of circumstances that led to the evolution of the existing higher life form, humankind, which you are seeing.

In other words, Earth was evolving, and it was developing through the different species — the Cro-Magnon, the Australopithecus, and the Neanderthal among them. In other words, there was already existence of higher life forms that were naturally evolving, and other planetary beings observed and decided to participate in Earth's system. Each different planetary system species had a slightly different variation of DNA and a slightly different variation of purpose. They also wanted to influence the outcome.

It was that seeding, along with Earth's evolutionary cycle, that has led to the current state of humankind — its technologies, developments, and also its problems. Again, I repeat, this drama and this crisis that you are now a part of is an ancient drama. We are watching, and other planetary beings are looking eagerly to understand and see if a different outcome from this galactic drama will unfold on Earth. This perspective that I am suggesting to you means that the other planetary systems, the other beings of light, are eagerly watching the unfolding of this drama and are eagerly awaiting an ending or outcome that is of a higher purpose.

Let your third eye open. Let your crown chakra open to the ancient memories, to the ancient codes, to the ancient histories of the galaxy. This drama, this unfolding, is also part of your heritage. It is part of your knowing.

In history and in the codes of the Kabbalistic Tree of Life, it is told that other worlds were created. Those worlds perished. Those worlds were not able to survive. It is told in the Kabbalistic history and tradition that the reasons for this are many. You are coming to your starseed awareness and your starseed heritage. You are right on the cusp; you are right in the perfect place to observe the unfolding of so many results of previous events. You are able, with the knowledge and information that you are receiving, to form an opinion and find a solution to this age-old galactic problem. What is that problem?

The problem is the relationship between technology and wisdom and the relationship between technological advancement and spirituality. The problem has to do with relationships between the many forces of domination and control versus the forces of intuition and receptivity. The problem focuses on how these forces come together and are influenced by these special times of galactic alignments and by the special times known as the eclipse energies.

It's All for Learning

Will the downloading of etheric crystals and of the ladders of ascension and the energies of the fifth dimension prove strong enough to counteract the devastation of the densities of the third dimension? Is this an experiment that we are observing here on Earth? Is this an experiment in life forms? Is this an experiment in the galactic unfolding of planetary existence? This Earth life is a reality. These Earth forces are real. Yes, you can say the third dimension is an illusion. You can say that the real energy, the real self, is in the higher plane. You can say that this Earth reality is all for learning. This is all a school.

Those who are of a higher spiritual light quotient will be able to learn the lessons and then take them and move on to higher realms, but this Earth reality is more than an illusion. The drama that is manifesting here on Earth belongs to many spiritual and higher sources that are seeking to be downloaded and explored in this realm. The suffering and tragedies that have unfolded already have created real pain and suffering.

From the Arcturian perspective, we do not minimize the dangers or the pain and suffering. The pain and suffering that is being created by this nuclear disaster in Japan is real. The effects of this disaster are planet-wide. The Japan disaster is not just a local event. It is an event of great magnitude that is going to reverberate throughout this planet. It is not something that is going to go away quickly. It is going to force you to reexamine the economic systems on this planet, their basis and relationship to Earth.

Along with this planetary perspective, I must also explain the personal perspective. I explained that the events you are seeing from a planetary perspective are a combination of many different events that originated in the past. Even the decisions that led to this nuclear disaster in part can be traced back to the other decisions that governments have made for many years. The decisions to use nuclear energy were made for economic profits. So the decision to place reactor buildings close to fragile areas, for example, has led to tragic outcomes.

Other decisions that create negative outcomes are centered on the desire to seek world dominance, including the economical control of others. There is a series of economic events that have been occurring for fifty to seventy years that led to the nuclear event in Japan. There is also a series of events that led to the development of nuclear energy. Nuclear energy was chosen and used and developed for reasons of war and control. The decisions made in the 1940s contain the seeds that can foresee such events as this recent nuclear disaster.

Albert Einstein was a visionary. His theories opened up the doorway for the development of nuclear energy. He was a starseed and a great psychic. He deeply regretted his participation in the development of nuclear energy even though many people felt that it led to the conclusion of WWII for the United States. He saw how the use of nuclear energy was opening up a Pandora's box, for it would lead to incalculable problems and great, untellable tragic events.

He thought that he had to participate in the development of nuclear power to help defeat the enemies. The truth is that someone else would have developed nuclear energy later without Einstein's help. It did matter that he participated in the development of nuclear energy because it affected his personal karma and his personal development. Who of great sensitivity would want to participate in the development of a technology that could lead to the destruction of a planet and of the biosphere of that planet?

No one of great sensitivity would knowingly want to participate in the development of a technology that could destroy his or her planet. Does the development of nuclear energy sound like the karmic energy of Atlantis or the Land of Mu (Lemuria)? Does this not sound like the previous higher technological civilizations that have been on Earth?

Many of you have been activated, even before this lecture, to remember living and participating in a society that was at exactly the same place in its development as Earth now finds itself. Earlier advanced civilizations, such as Atlantis, were developing and using technologies that were going to destroy the biosphere. Maybe now, as we are speaking about this, you can recall your pain, your sorrow, when you were alive in those ancient times. Some of those events occurred 30,000–40,000 years ago on Earth.

I know that some of you were there, and I know that you wanted to check out from those situations. I know that some of you may have even participated unknowingly in the scientific work that was later misused. So you return to Earth now, and the drama is the same. Let those ancient memories come to the surface now. Let those emotions that you experienced be released, including the emotions of being a participant and observer in that society. Some of you have actually come to Earth in this time to reexperience and discharge your emotional energy from that previous lifetime.

You have carried with you from previous lifetimes the constellation of emotional energy from witnessing the destruction of that ancient society. Now you need to hear these words: The events on Earth now are part of a galactic drama that has been repeated on many different occasions in other parts of the galaxy. Now the drama is occurring on Earth, but the origins of this drama originate far beyond the confines of Earth. The energy and the ingredients that are unfolding now have been brought to Earth. Earth now needs to seek a better solution to this age-old problem so that planetary wisdom will prevail.

Confronting Cosmic Karma

We call this perspective of the Earth events now unfolding "cosmic karma." There is both planetary cosmic karma and personal cosmic karma. "Cosmic" refers to the fact that the origins and the cause and effects of events relate to experiences and lifetimes in other parts of the galaxy besides Earth. Earth karma on a personal level means that your life and your experiences are only based on a series of events and circumstances coming from many different lifetimes on Earth.

Even the personal events that you are having now in this lifetime often are related to previous events in other lifetimes. These current personal events could be illnesses, occupational challenges, or even related to previous lifetimes when you participated in scientific technology that affected the planet. All of your karma, both personal and cosmic, comes from your complicated, multidimensional Earth existences and experiences.

You may have already noticed that your life on a personal basis is complicated. There are many different factors and different energies that are confronting you. Also, in this lifetime, there are many possibilities of greater resolutions of issues that were not available at other times. Remember you still have the perfect opportunity for ascension — even in the midst of this galactic drama. This galactic drama does not harm your possibilities for ascension. On the contrary, and paradoxically, you are in a time of great spiritual opportunity. This is one of the greatest ironies of the galactic drama that you are seeing. In the midst of the upheavals and the conflict and difficulties, there paradoxically exists this great opportunity for spiritual advancement. This is an unprecedented time and opportunity for spiritual advancement.

This galactic drama will reach its climax soon. The crisis will become more heightened. The energy for change and openness among many people will become wider. The crisis creates, for those who are sensitive, an opportunity to seek greater wisdom and greater enlightenment that correspondingly opens more corridors of light. This will allow and invite a greater downloading of higher energy and wisdom from the fifth dimension.

This is the paradox. This is the irony of this galactic drama. You can see that this galactic drama creates this special opportunity. Being on Earth now is also an attractive opportunity for lightworkers. The light seekers are working for their personal uplifting and also to serve as planetary healers.

I am Juliano.

The Arcturian Holographic Healing Chamber

Helio-ah

reetings. I'm Helio-ah. We are the Arcturians. The holographic healing chamber is a special method for releasing blocks from the past. In fact, the healing chamber is able to help people connect with their past in this lifetime and in previous lifetimes. This chamber is also useful in advanced work when we connect with the future self.

The Holographic Principle

There are several basic principles or foundations that we must first explore so that you can properly use the holographic healing technique. The first principle is of holograms and holographic energy. The idea of the hologram comes when modern Earth science understood that, by using a laser, they could separate an object, such as an apple, into small pieces. The small piece, or the hologram or holographic image, represents the entirety.

This principle exists on many levels; it exists on the level of Earth in relation to the universe. Earth is like one small grain of sand in the universe, yet Earth represents the holographic unity of the whole universe. From Earth, you can see and experience all the universe.

The holographic principle used in soul psychology is that you must use yourself and your consciousness to grasp the meaning of the hologram or the expanded holographic self. This principle is used in healing. We are going to apply this principle to healing the self. Remember, the self is far greater than what you perceive on this plane. The self is a multidimensional, eternal, and infinite self. The aspect of the self that you see on Earth is only one part. In fact, to enter the Earth body, you must contract your expansive self. So it is important that you understand that there is a greater self. The

Earth self is a hologram or an aspect of your. You are composed of many aspects.

The self in this lifetime can also be expansive, but there can be many blocks in this Earth self. There are many traumas that can occur that can block you from experiencing your power, experiencing your whole self, and experiencing your ability to connect with your higher self. So in holographic healing, we also understand that there are images and pictures contained in the subconscious that represent the self.

These pictures are stored in the memory of the subconscious. So in holographic healing, we use the subconscious to help access the greater self. We help you remove blocks from your lower self so that you can access your expanded self. The key is to find the blocked parts of the self that are in the subconscious. We then work to heal these blocks from the self by understanding and working directly with subconscious and traumatic images that are stored in your memory.

Now I will speak about the subconscious. The subconscious is the basis for manifestation, the basis for action, and the storage for all memories. The subconscious does not normally think in words. The subconscious does not normally think in logic. The language of the subconscious is more in pictures, poetry, music, or art. The preferred way of communicating with the subconscious is with images or pictures.

Let me give you an example. There are people who are concerned about money and want to have a lot of money in this lifetime. They use a method of repeating affirmations, and they say, "I will have a lot of money" or "I will be rich." They can repeat these affirmations thousands of times, but nothing really happens, so they question the power of the affirmation because nothing is happening.

Now, in the holographic method that I'm explaining and the method of using images, there is a better way to use your mind and your subconscious to help you become wealthy. A better way would be to picture yourself happy in the future. A better method would be to see yourself content because you feel you have all of your needs met. You picture yourself in the future with how you look and how you feel knowing that you have all of the material possessions you need.

In the future, you can picture yourself as satisfied with your money. That picture, that image, is powerful. So in holographic healing, we would use an image like that to help you manifest what you want in the future. In holographic healing, though, we are concerned about events and traumas in the past that have blocked the development of the self in the present. This is not a perfect world on the third dimension. There are many polarities and traumas that block self-development.

Many blocks are caused by traumas that occur especially when a person is younger or is a child. We, the Arcturians, are surprised how the training, education, and upgrading of the children in your cultures is not done in a supportive and helpful way. This is a big problem on the planet because the children are exposed to many traumas and many abuses. In fact, on Arcturus, we give special training to the families before they have their children. Another thing is that we, on Arcturus, live longer. In Earth years, we may be living 600, 700, 800, or even 900 years long. So on Earth, you have children at the age of twenty or twenty-five. We may not have children until the age of sixty or seventy. So there is a difference in our development and level of maturity when we start our families.

In the holographic healing chamber, we are interested in the traumas that have occurred and how these traumas have resulted in a certain picture that is downloaded into the memory of the person. It is this picture and this memory that stays in the subconscious and that continues to block the person.

In holographic healing, we look at a way of changing the picture; we look at a way of going back into the past memory, and in the past, we look for that image or that picture that is representative of the memory of the trauma. When we find that memory, we bring it up on the computer screen. In this way, we help you change the old memory image and then create a new memory image. In the healing chamber, we not only help you re-create the memory but also help to change the memory. We help you to create a new picture that will go into your subconscious with a more positive image.

Advanced Computers

Now we are ready to talk to you about the holographic healing chamber and the role of our advanced computers that we use in this process. I also will tell you more about the ways in which we can change the picture and the memory of traumas stored in your subconscious.

So let's talk about the healing chamber and about our ideas of how our computers can interface with your subconscious. Your Earth computers are not as advanced as our computers. Our computers are able to interact telepathically with a person's subconscious. Now, this sounds advanced, and it may even sound impossible, but the truth is that the computer technology in the fifth dimension is advanced. In other words, our computer technology in the fifth dimension can interact with the energy field and aura and subconscious of a person. Our computers can interact and download all of the memories and all of the interactions and experiences of that person.

This also has been discussed by the Pleiadians. For example, P'taah and his crew have visited Earth. When they visit Earth, they come in special beam ships. These beam ships have highly advanced computers on them. The beam ships can take their advanced computers and lock onto a person's energy field. The computer is able to read everything about the person's past — all memories and everything stored in that person's energy field, including the person's emotional, mental, physical, and spiritual bodies. This is the level of advancement in computer technology possessed by the Pleiadians, by the Arcturians, and by other advanced beings.

Our computers, like the Pleiadian computers, are also able to go into the future. So the Pleiadian and Arcturian computers, for example, can see — based on what is happening in the present — what the future outcome of a person's life is going to be. And the Pleiadian computers can even predict when a person is going to die.

You're Invited into the Chamber

Let us return to this concept of the holographic computer, because it is important that you understand that we have these computers and that we are aware of the personal history of each of you who come to our groups. For healing purposes, we invite you to our spaceships in your etheric bodies to use our holographic healing chamber.

Each one of our healing chambers on our ship has a computer in it like the one I have described. Each one of these computers is calibrated to the person who enters the chamber for a healing. So if a person comes to the healing chamber, then you should understand that we, the Arcturians, will be calibrating the healing chamber to that person's holographic self in this Earth life.

We can calibrate the computer in the holographic chamber for your past lives or just for this present life. So when you enter the chamber, the computer is calibrated to you and your history. This means that the computer can bring up images from your past. The way the computer brings up those images from your past is based on a simplistic method. We relate access to the computer's memory images to a dial on a clock. There is a large dial on the surface of the desk that directly connects to the computer of the holographic healing chamber. It looks like a clock. We calibrate the clock from 12 and go backward (counterclockwise), so it will read 11-10-9-8-7-6. We stop at 6. So 6PM (or 18:00 in your twenty-four-hour clock time) to 12PM represents a lifetime. The 12PM represents the present time exactly, and 6PM represents your birth.

In an average lifetime, there are approximately 60,000–70,000 images stored in your subconscious that are all related to the self. These images are experiences that you have had. Some of them have been good; some of them have been traumatic.

When doing a holographic healing, we invite you to enter the chamber and turn the dial to that point in your past that represents a trauma or a block. If you have a block in the area of your personal development and power, then we ask you to find that place in your past where that block occurred. If that block occurred when you were ten years old, then perhaps your father did something to you that resulted in a block.

Then we ask you to turn the dial to that point that is approximately calibrated to the time when this event or blockage occurred. Then you turn the clock back. So if the incident happened when you were ten, you must think of how to turn the dial to the right spot. For example, 6PM to 12PM can represent sixty years. If you go back to age ten, then that is going to be perhaps twenty-five minutes to twelve (11:35PM). So you must calibrate in your mind where the correct place to turn the dial back to is.

When you turn the dial back, you will find that image of the block or trauma that you want to resolve. After you find that incident, to the best of your ability, bring that image up onto the computer screen. Once it's on the computer screen, we will give you instructions on how to work with the image.

The next stage in this process is traveling to the healing chamber itself. In the healing chamber, we will give you further instructions about how to change the traumatic memory and image in your subconscious.

Getting to the Healing Chamber

An important aspect of this healing process is to go to the healing chamber. I want to explain to you the process of going to the healing chamber. We want the person needing healing to go to the healing chamber. But before that, we need the person to leave the physical body and travel in the astral body. This also means that we want the person to go into an altered state of consciousness, as this altered state of consciousness is an important aspect of the healing.

To go into an altered state of consciousness, there's a method we use. First, we ask the person to go into a state of relaxation. Then we ask the person to visualize or feel that the astral body is leaving the physical body. The astral body can leave the physical body through the crown chakra.

There are several methods to help the astral body leave the physical body. One method is that we could visualize or imagine that the room you are sitting in is going around in a circle, like a merry-go-round, and then your astral body gently leaves your physical body.

The second aspect of this process is to visualize that we, the Arcturians, are providing a fifth-dimensional corridor over your room. A corridor is similar to a tunnel of light that links you to our spaceship in the fifth dimension.

We use corridors because it is safer and more direct to fly through a corridor or to travel astrally through the corridor. So we set up a corridor around you, and we ask you to visualize the corridor by saying, "In my altered state of consciousness, I feel that my astral body leaves my physical body." Then I, Helio-ah, or Juliano will greet you in the corridor, and together we will travel through the corridor. We frequently like to say that we travel through the corridor at the speed of thought.

Our spaceships generally are located in the Jupiter corridor. This corridor is in your solar system between Mars and Jupiter. It is the most convenient place for us to park our ships. So at the speed of thought, you will travel through the corridor, and then together we enter our ship.

We come into a great room, and there you will see many small holographic healing chambers. We like to refer to them sometimes as little cones or little phone booths. They are small rooms, and there are many of them because we do a great deal of healing work with our starseeds. You will find a booth calibrated to your Earth life waiting for you. When you find your booth, you enter and close the door, and then you are in the booth and ready to do the work for personal healing.

So the idea is to leave your body, travel with your spirit body through the corridor, and come to our spaceship and enter our fifth-dimensional healing chambers in an altered state of consciousness. You have to be in a higher state of consciousness to do this work, we believe — and to have access to our special computers, which can interface with your subconscious — to do this healing work.

Dealing with the Blockage

Now I want to talk about accessing the event that is blocking your growth and how to work with that. So you have followed these directions and you have come into the healing chamber and closed the door. You turned on the computer, and, even though our computers are much more advanced than yours, there are certain techniques we use that are similar to those of your computers.

For example, we say that you can call up an image from the past, and that image will appear on your computer screen. We also use the computer button marked "save," which means that the image we are working with can be changed, and then you can save it and put it back into the storage of the main computer of your subconscious. There are other buttons that are similar to your Earth computer functions.

So you turn on the computer and you find that image in your subconscious that is blocking you. You then call up that image from your subconscious, and the image appears on the screen. Then you describe the image to the person who is working with you — the soul psychologist, for example. It is better to have a therapist guide you to this place while you're in a trance state. The next step is to describe the image from your subconscious in as much detail as possible.

For example, you may bring up an image in which you see your father beating you up when you were a young child. You see that he has a belt, and he is beating you. You see yourself there. You are crying, and you feel terrible. This image that you retrieved will be the one we will transform. So I ask you to describe the image in detail. The next step is to change the image.

There are many ways to do this. For instance, we can say that Archangel Michael is now appearing in the right side of the room where the trauma is occurring. Archangel Michael brings a great light into the room, and your father sees this light. He puts down the belt and starts to cry. He stops beating you. Now you see what is happening with the help from Archangel Michael, and now you feel totally different. You feel the light of Archangel Michael. You feel the light of protection from him, and you feel much better about yourself. You do not feel traumatized. All of these new feelings are reflected in the new image you have transformed on the computer screen.

This is one example of how we could improve the image. You can also visualize that Archangel Gabriel comes in, or you can visualize that Jesus comes in. You can even visualize that another friend comes in and stops your father from beating you. You can also visualize that your grandfather comes in to help you. You can create many different healing images. This is your choice. We will also help you create a new healing image.

Once you have created the new healing image, I ask you to use the "save" button on the holographic computer. Once you press "save," that image is retained on the computer. That image will then go back exactly into the memory from which it originated in your subconsciousness.

There may be 70,000 images from the past, for example, in one person's subconscious. I like to use the metaphor of what is called the Rolodex in office tools. This special file of cards was used by secretaries for storing telephone numbers. It's made of small index cards. There is a bar on the center of the Rolodex. In an office Rolodex, there could be fifty cards on one roll. You could go through it to find a number to call up an individual by rolling through all fifty cards. Often the cards would be in alphabetical order. In the Rolodex of the holographic healing chamber, the cards are in order based on the time when the events occurred. I use this image of the Rolodex because I want you also to think that all images in the index are holographically connected.

Put this new healing image back into the index of your subconscious exactly in the same order that you took it out of. As you return the image, the whole program of yourself is updated. You know about updating a program from your work on computers on Earth.

What happens when you update your computer with a new program? Well, your subconscious is like a computer, which means the new image is updating all of your other images in your subconscious. The original traumatic image has been changed with a new healing image, and this image will update all further images or all images in front of and based on this trauma.

Now there will be a series of updates in the subconscious. All the new information and new programs based on the old traumatic event will now change with this new image and information. This update will go all the way forward up to the present. It is truly an amazing process that occurs in the healing chamber.

The next step is that you leave the chamber and return down the corridor back to yourself on Earth. We ask that you and your astral body reenter your physical body from a place approximately four to six feet above your head. Remain at that position briefly. Then slowly your astral body will reenter your physical body in perfect alignment. The reentry into a perfect alignment is important. Remember, you are upgrading or updating yourself. This reentry completes the healing process for a trauma that occurred in the current lifetime.

Using the Chamber to Heal Past Lifetimes

Let me also speak about past lifetimes, because there are circumstances in which people have had experiences in a past lifetime that have created blocks that are manifested in the present lifetime. You know there are imprints in the soul from past-life experiences. The imprinting means that when there are events or blocks, those blockages can be passed on from lifetime to lifetime. A block that you had in one lifetime can be transferred into a future lifetime.

So when we use the holographic healing chamber for past lifetimes, the computer is calibrated in the chamber for your past lives. Our computers are so advanced that we can calibrate them for the past in this lifetime, or we can calibrate them for your past lifetimes. Because, remember, you yourself are holographic.

Once we have access to your current self, we can go to all parts of yourself in this lifetime or past lifetimes. In doing the past lifetime holographic healing, the computer is set up so that when you turn the dial, you are turning it back to previous lifetimes. The twelve o'clock hour represents the present lifetime, and six o'clock is the beginning of your soul when you manifested on the incarnational plane. You could have manifested in the incarnational plane on Earth, or you may have even incarnated in other parts of the solar system.

When you turn the dial back, you can experience past lifetimes. The computer is correlated or calibrated to your past lifetimes. There is a button in the chamber that is labeled "past lifetimes" or "past lives." Press the right button so that the computer knows what you want to do.

Actually, the procedure is exactly similar to what we have described in the holographic work for traumas in your past life. But this time it's calibrated to past lifetimes. Now you can go to traumas in past lifetimes and follow exactly the same procedure as we did before when working with your current lifetime.

The question has come up whether it's possible to go to past lives on other planets. Yes, you can do that, but you must tell the computer that you wish to go to lifetimes on other planets. Just press the button labeled: "past lives on other planets."

The holographic computer can calibrate for past lives on either this planet or on other planets, but you have to press the right button to tell the computer which type of lifetime you want it to search for. It's similar to when you use a search engine on your computer on Earth. Give the computer and searcher certain information to narrow the field for past lives on other planets. It's better for you to separate accessing past lives on this Earth from the past lives on other planets. The computer can bring up each of these types of lifetimes. Usually, the beings who have been on other planets are more advanced than beings who have had past lives only on Earth.

Connect to Your Future Self

Likewise, I also want to discuss with you the method of connecting with the future self. The idea of the holographic self is that the self is like a circle and that the future, the past, and the present all interact with each other. If that's the case, then the energy from the future self can affect the present self. We look for ways of bringing energy from the future self into the present. This chamber provides a perfect way to do this.

Imagine you are in the chamber and the clock goes forward from 12 to 1 to 2 to 3 to 4 to 5 to 6. Twelve o'clock, or noon, represents your current life. One o'clock represents your future self, and two o'clock is also your future self. Three o'clock is more advanced into your future self, as is four o'clock.

The future self can be in this lifetime, or we can talk about future selves in other lifetimes. For now, start this process of accessing the future self by telling the computer you want to first go to the future in this lifetime. You also can tell the computer what you want to do in future lifetimes, but for this discussion, we will just talk about the future self in this lifetime.

By using the dial, you are telling the computer to go to a point in the future, and you can go to a point six months into the future or one year into the future, and you must turn the dial of the clock to that appropriate point. Let's say that in doing this, noon represents your present and six o'clock represents your departure from Earth. If you want to turn the dial to the point that is six months in your future, then you would move the clock to 1PM.

Call up a positive image from your future. You can even help to create that image. For example, you can see yourself in the future living in a much better place, if that is what you want. Or you can see an image of yourself showing you what you have accomplished and what you have wanted to accomplish. You can picture yourself having attained higher spiritual frequencies and higher spiritual vibrations. You can imagine yourself more successful in your business. You also can develop an image of yourself with a stronger energy field or with more vibrational light around you.

Describe the image and create it on the computer screen. You can create this positive image any way you want. See Arcturians around you in the future. You could see Sananda around you. You could see your aura becoming stronger. Then when you have completed that image, you press "save," and the image goes back into the computer.

You then bring that image to the present by bringing the dial from the one o'clock position back to noon. This is key. But you must merge the image of yourself in the future with your present self. When you bring that image to the present, you press "save" again. The image goes into your current image of your holographic self, and those images, those strengths, those vibrations from your future self, become merged with your present self. So that is the basic idea of healing the self by using the holographic energy from the future self.

Actually, the method I just described is a powerful way of overcoming blocks in the present because you go into your future. So we have given you three methods: the first to overcome blocks from the past, the second to overcome blocks from the past lives, and the third to go into the future and bring energy from the future into the current self. All these methods are done in the holographic healing chamber.

I hope this has been helpful. Blessings to you. I'm Helio-ah. Good day.

Exercise to Go to the Fifth Dimension: *Shimmering*

Juliano and the Arcturians

*S*halom, *Shalom, Shalom*. Greetings. I am Juliano. We are the Arcturians. We are fifth-dimensional beings who have transcended the third dimension and its duality. We have graduated from third-dimensional problems. At the same time, our primary directive, the primary light-work, is service — service to the galaxy, service to other beings like you who are reaching out to evolve. Yes, it is true that Earth is evolving. It is true that this is an evolutionary point in your development, and you are a part of the higher new beings, and that level of new being is consciousness.

Let us talk about what makes you more conscious, what brings you to a state of vibration, a vibrational light, where you are able to experience the higher reality directly because, even now, at this point, you have the capability to experience immediate transformation. You have the capacity to ascend and to work in higher light.

It is true there are many Earth problems. It is true there are many events going on that are unhappy, but it's also true that there are many lightworkers on the planet right now and that there are many ascended masters who are coming here. You are all connecting with your guides and teachers more than ever before. Now you'll be able to connect on an even higher level.

Today we are going to work with you on an exercise for experiencing your fifth-dimensional self called shimmering. Shimmering is the ability to vibrate your body, to vibrate your energy field at a level that will allow you to thought-project, that will allow you to bring your consciousness and your astral energy field directly to the fifth dimension. Listening to the tones we are going to emit through the channel will help your astral body and energy field vibrate at a higher, more spiritual frequency.

[Tones: *Ooooh ooooh eeee eeeeooooh.*]

Become aware of your aura, of your energy field, and become aware that your energy field has a pulse. But unlike the physical pulse in your body, the energy pulse of your aura is going to increase in speed and will bring you to a higher state of consciousness. In that higher state, you will experience abilities far beyond what you experience in normal consciousness.

So listen to this tone, and align the pulse of your aura to that tone: [Tones: *tat tat tat tat tat tat tat tat tat tat* (very fast) *tat tat tat ... tat tat ... tat tat ... tat tat ... whoooosh.*]

I will make a clapping sound, and all lower negative energies that may be around your aura will just fall away. [Tones: *tat tat tat tat tat tat tat ...* (loud clap) *... whoooosh whoooosh!*]

Become aware of slow breathing and that all is a vibration. You are comfortably vibrating at a speed that is raising your consciousness. Become aware that your aura is shaped in the perfect union — the perfect shape of the cosmic egg. Command your aura *now* to go into the shape of the cosmic egg.

[Tones very softly, then louder: *Ooooh. Ooooh!* Takes a deep breath.]

I, Juliano, bring a corridor of blue light directly into the center of the room. This corridor is connecting with our fifth-dimensional energy field that we are setting up. This fifth-dimensional energy field leads to a higher realm that is called the crystal lake. I ask you to travel with me to that lake. The room is now filled with spiritual Arcturian blue light.

With great comfort and ease, your astral body can now rise up out of your crown chakra and bounce up to the top of the room. As you are out of your physical body and at the top of the room, you will experience a gentle freedom, and you will see me, Juliano, in the corridor. We are going to travel through the corridor up to this beautiful lake on the fifth dimension called the crystal lake. This lake is one mile in diameter, and your fifth-dimensional body is waiting there for you. You will reunite and visit your fifth-dimensional body.

You are multidimensional beings. You live in the third dimension, but you have a dimensional presence in other realms, and now you can unite with your multidimensional selves. You are here to experience your fifth-dimensional body. So at the count of three, follow me through this corridor of light. One. Two. Three.

[Tones: *tat, tat, tat, tat, tat, tat, tat, tat, tat.*]

We travel at the speed of thought through this corridor — through hyperspace. We come to this beautiful domed lake. It is beautiful and filled with blue water and spiritual light. Your etheric/astral body goes through the dome, and you are above the lake where you see 1,600 fifth-dimensional bodies sitting in yoga positions around the lake. Find your fifth-dimensional body. It is there waiting for you.

[Tones: *ooooh.*]

Go to a position three feet above your fifth-dimensional body, and at the count of three, we will enter directly into your fifth-dimensional body. One, two, three, *now!* Drop into your fifth-dimensional body.

Experience what it is like to be in your fifth-dimensional body. Experience the vitality. Experience the expansion of consciousness and how you feel closer to the Creator, *Adonai.* Take a deep breath. Your fifth-dimensional body is always here waiting for you. Experience the fifth-dimensional emotions of love, acceptance, empathy, and unity. Experience the fifth-dimensional mental energy of higher thinking; experience the spiritual light of the fifth dimension and most beautifully, experience what it is like — the sensations of being in a fifth-dimensional body, one that is totally calibrated to you.

We will go into meditation while you process this wonderful opportunity.

[Two minutes of silence.]

In the lake is a deep etheric crystal one mile in diameter. I, Juliano, am going to raise this crystal from the lake. You know how powerful crystals are on the third dimension? Some of you even carry crystals with you to enhance your own power. This crystal is a special fifth-dimensional crystal. It will now rise slowly out of the water, and as you feel this crystal slowly rise out of the water, you will feel a dramatic increase in your spiritual light energy. You are able to absorb more spiritual energy because you are in your fifth-dimensional body. You are able to feel the power — the true power of this crystal. It has an amazing healing power. The crystal rises out of the water.

[Tones: *Ooooh. Ooooh.*]

You feel this crystal open up your third eye, open up your crown chakra, open up your crown chakra even wider, and open up your heart chakra, expanding all levels of your consciousness.

Fully absorb the beautiful power and the spiritual energy of this crystal. The crystal is fully out of the water now, and it is lighting up all of your fifth-dimensional bodies. You can only experience this deeply because you are in your fifth-dimensional body.

Now I will return the crystal back into the water. As it descends back into the lake, you still feel a new light frequency. It is difficult to describe because it is not based on duality; it is based on unity — unity light. The crystal has descended back into the water.

I ask you and your spirit body to rise out of your fifth-dimensional body. As you rise out, realize that your spirit has absorbed all of this light and this energy in your fifth-dimensional body, or from your fifth-dimensional body, into your astral/spiritual body. Now your astral/spiritual body is above the lake. We look at the corridor, and we are traveling back to Earth and the room that you left. Come with me as we travel through this corridor at the speed of thought!

[Tones: *tat tat tat tat tat tat tat tat.*]

You are back in the room where you left. We are still above the room. Do not go into your body yet. Find your physical body and command your spirit body, your astral body, to reenter your physical body in perfect alignment so as to align your spirit directly. Do not enter yet, but first go into perfect alignment. I will count to three, and you will drop back into your physical body in perfect alignment. One, two, three, now! *Whoooosh!* You have reentered in perfect alignment and brought in this high frequency of light, the fifth-dimensional light.

This reentry is a process we call spiritual osmosis. It is where you slowly integrate all this light energy. The light energy was so high that it will take your body twenty-four hours to process and receive all of the light energies you absorbed in your astral/spiritual body. Initially, you will download 10 percent of it so that it will occur over the next twenty-four hours. You will continue downloading this energy and light and beautiful experience with your fifth-dimensional body.

Begin to adjust to being back in your third-dimensional body. You still have an expanded consciousness. Your third-dimensional eye is open. Your heart chakra is open.

Blessings in the light. I am Juliano. Good day.

Expand Your Consciousness by Connecting with Your Spirit Guide

Archangel Michael

*S*halom, *Shalom, Shalom*. This is Archangel Michael. Feel the consciousness rising up the Tree of Life to the center of the tree, which is called *Tiferet*. *Tiferet* means beauty and harmony. As you go to this higher place on the Tree of Life, know that you are in a state of expanded consciousness. You are in a state in which you can access many higher parts of yourself, the parts of yourself that are above duality, the parts of yourself that are fifth dimensional, the parts of yourself through which you can see unity consciousness, the parts of yourself that have great psychic abilities, and the parts of yourself through which you can meet your *Maggid* — your spirit guide.

You can meet and interact with your inner guide and look before you in *Tiferet*, in this beautiful sphere of harmony and peace, and look down to the right and see a beautiful chariot. This chariot is divine. It is the *Merkavah* vehicle.

Enter and sit in that *Merkavah* vehicle. As you sit in the *Merkavah* vehicle, there is a divine influx of light and energy, and you can rise up into the higher level, even higher above *Tiferet*. As you go higher, you see this beautiful garden with beautiful flowers. Your *Merkavah* vehicle stops, and you are at rest in this garden. You get out of your vehicle, and you see a spring and a beautiful pond in the distance.

There, you see this angelic-looking fifth-dimensional person coming toward you with beautiful light and energy. You feel an attraction, and you walk forward to the pond and meet your *Maggid*. You are so happy to meet your spirit guide. Your spirit guide embraces you, and you embrace your spirit guide.

You feel the higher light that is coming from your spirit guide. Then your spirit guide looks at you and communicates with you telepathically, sending you a special message just for you. It is a special message on healing and on *Tikun* — the idea of how to be a better healer and how to mend the world.

Also, on the subject of how to mend yourself, your *Maggid* says, "Don't forget that one of the greatest *Tikun*, the greatest healings, is to heal yourself and to mend yourself through ethical behavior." Then you feel the great love in tune with your *Maggid*. Enjoy this experience for a brief moment. We will go into silence.

[Tones: *Ommmm.*]

Your *Maggid* tells you that he or she will be working with you throughout this day and will return to you. You must enter the *Merkavah* and come up to this garden, and your guide will be there for you. Now your teacher must leave, so you separate. But you remain in telepathic communication. Your guide walks back toward the pond and you, experiencing great feelings of joy and completeness, walk back to your *Merkavah* vehicle. You enter it and return to this realm of *Tiferet* (where we were in the beginning) — this realm of harmony and beauty.

Then you descend down the Tree of Life — back into the third dimension, back into the kingdom, into *Malchut*, and back into the word of duality. Now you have opened up a great connection to the *Maggid*.

Blessings. I am Archangel Michael.

Hypnotherapy and Past-Life Regression Sessions:
How They Are Therapeutic from the Perspective of Soul Psychology

Gudrun Miller, Professional Counselor

odern psychology has made great progress in under-standing mental and emotional issues but still has not officially recognized the existence of the soul. Without understanding the impact of the soul journey on a person's mental, emotional, spiritual, and even physical makeup, we remain in the dark.

I have been a professional counselor for over thirty-two years and have had the privilege of working with awakening and awakened starseeds for the majority of that time. I also am now working with many people internationally as David and I travel and present the Arcturian teachings.

I want to share some of the work I have done, including reports from my clients on their experiences in hypnotherapy regression. The more I do this beautiful work, the more I realize the immensity of what there is yet to know about the soul journey and its impact on our psyche. Most of us have a very limited understanding of the soul. This area of exploration is truly exciting and is still wide open.

The regression process I use involves relaxation followed by a guided visu-alization. I then take my clients to a soul dwelling that they "see," and from there, we can access past lives, the higher self, guides and teachers, and any

This illustration by Gudrun Miller shows a hypnosis session in which the client is in a trance accessing her guide and her soul family.

aspect of the soul journey that is blocked. Many go to visit with their soul families in the between-lives state in the astral plane. They also may meet with their council of elders, a group of highly evolved beings who advise on soul evolution, lessons learned, and the next possible lifetime.

Once my clients have achieved a sufficient level of trance, they often spontaneously go where they are required to go without completing the whole trance induction process. I always defer to the higher self of the clients, their guides, their soul families, and even the councils of elders who oversee the soul journeys of my clients. These beings oversee the healing, unblocking, and educational process of my clients.

My role is as a guide, as a support, as a witness, and as a counselor in facilitating the process. I use my counseling skills when dealing with blocked emotional issues and incorrect belief structures. I often am in trance along with my clients and am able to receive guidance from my own teachers and guides and from my higher self.

Case 1

One of my first cases, "A," was a middle-aged woman who had just lost her husband to illness. She wanted to talk with him and to know why he had to die. She is a starseed and had some interest in and fear about finding out more about her soul journey. She is also an artist and has had many unusual visions come to her as images in the sky and in her dreams. As a result, she felt compelled to learn Sanskrit, which she was able to do. Mainly, though, her spiritual visions puzzled her, and she could not integrate them into her life or even into an understanding of the symbolism they presented.

"A" regressed easily, going into deep trance. Her current life, which we visited, was pleasant and uneventful. She was born an only child into a family where she was wanted and loved. She had a loving relationship with her husband.

When "A" attempted to go into her immediate past life, she found herself conscious but unable to move or to see and became panicked. She experienced a complete loss of memory about her identity and her current circumstances. She couldn't close her eyes and saw only blue and black.

"A" was asked to go to the time of her death when she experienced being wrapped in a sort of blanket that "held all the pieces of her together." There were beings there she described as doctors. When I asked if she could check with the doctors about whether she had experienced a nuclear explosion, she immediately said, "Yes, Hiroshima." I asked that question because I sensed that the state she was in had to do with nuclear destruction.

"A" was so distressed at this point that we ended the session. With later work and assistance from Vywamus through David, we understood "A" to be a very advanced soul from Andromeda who had unwittingly participated in the demise of Atlantis. In that life, she was a female scientist who was misled and so used her scientific knowledge to help those who caused the destabilization of energy that contributed to the collapse of Atlantis. " A" had agreed to balance the karma she incurred by being in Hiroshima at the time of the drop of the atom bomb.

Her guides knew she had enough soul evolution and advancement that her soul would remain intact but would have a gap of memory of that life in Japan. We later pieced together that she was also a male weaver who produced indigo cloth. He had a wife and two children. Interestingly, "A" is a weaver in her current life.

Subsequently, we were able to visit other past lives in which "A" gained a sense of her soul journey and confidence in her spiritual path. Initially, this regression was disappointing and distressing to her — and certainly not what she had anticipated. Ultimately, it has helped her achieve a sense of inner unity.

Case 2

Another client whom I will call "B" wrote a beautiful report of her regression experience:

> Gudrun has guided me through two past-life regressions. Both of them have been extremely useful and empowering. I chose to do them during times when I felt I needed a greater understanding of my soul journey from a wider, more expansive perspective.
>
> The first regression gave me a frame for my soul journey. It helped me understand my soul work and connected me with my soul family. Meeting my soul family was a homecoming for me, giving me an opportunity to touch base with the core of my soul purpose. I learned my soul name and was able to dialogue with members of my soul family as well as receive some gentle healing. I also got a greater understanding and context for my soul purpose in this lifetime. Through seeing a past life as well as connecting with my soul family, I understood more about how my past lives were a gradual evolution toward the work I need to do in this lifetime. In a time when I was feeling alone and lost, I found a sense of belonging and renewed purpose.
>
> My second regression provided me with reassurance about my path and energetic realignment and guidance for future work. What was particularly powerful for me in this regression was an experience of meeting myself in a past life. While sitting with this earlier incarnation,

we had a significant energetic and verbal exchange that was filled with love and deep respect. It was both grounding and empowering.

The regressions have provided support in my ongoing therapeutic work with Gudrun. In our sessions, Gudrun and I often reference the regressions and the felt energies we both experienced as guidance for our work together.

What I like most about doing past-life regression is that I am the vessel and voice for my truth. The insights and visions come through me, not a guru or channel. It is easier for me to trust and integrate these truths when they come from me rather than someone else. I also have felt a sense of the energies of my guides, soul family, and past incarnations through having the opportunity to meet them and receive healing from them directly. After each regression, my community and circle of support has expanded through meeting more guides and members of my soul family. I have found that the link to these higher-dimensional energies does not diminish after the regression. Once the connection has been made, I can always call on them.

"B's" experience shows that hypnotherapy soul regression can be part of an ongoing therapeutic process. She decides when it is appropriate for her to seek deeper understanding of her current issues. Each session builds on the others, and it is easier to achieve the trance state.

Case 3

"C" wanted to know about her soul journey but specifically wanted to break through a block she experienced in her healing work. She could open up but then would get stuck.

We regressed her through her current life. "C" grew up on a ranch in Minnesota and recalled building a spacecraft out of tractor tires and old machine parts. She then spent hours in her spaceship traveling the universe. Needless to say, she did not fit in well in her conservative environment.

"C's" environment was repressive to her growth, so she decided at the age of seven to "dumb herself down" in order to fit in with her peers and her family. That belief structure was still in place, and we were able to amend it so that she could access her great intellect and her psychic abilities.

When we went to a past life, she found herself in the time of the Civil War in the United States. She was a young man who was killed after finding his family dead. He had gone into a rage about the killing and wanted to seek revenge. When he evaluated that life, he understood that the rage was another blockage for higher light.

After the death in that life, "C" was taken by her teachers and guides to an operating room where she was placed on a table. The session was silent for quite a while as she was implanted with an etheric device in her brain that would allow her to work with higher spiritual energy. It was explained to her that she had attained higher-frequency vibration and was thus ready for this procedure. She could not have sustained that level of frequency prior to this time in her evolution. The doctors told her it would take approximately six months to integrate this procedure. While in this deep trance, the doctors working on her also removed layers of density. Apparently, we all can accumulate these layers that can block access to higher light.

What follows is "C's" summary of the experience:

> I worked with Gudrun about eight years ago to discover content and purpose of my present life along with information that my soul revealed to me from my past lifetime. The information that was gained has been so beneficial to my evolution and correction. Amazingly, the understanding that I continue to receive from this hypnotherapy regression leads me to recommend that every starseed experience this healing work. Gudrun has the knowledge to assist and keep focus on the intention of the work. She does not get "hooked into" the drama. This is her special starseed wisdom.

"C" went on to relate how her experience in superconsciousness, the state in which you have access to the akashic records and are one with your higher self, validated what she was learning in the Tree of Life class taught by David Miller and Mordechai Yashin. She experienced the different levels of trance as correlating to the paths of the Tree of Life. She explains:

> When Mordechai was listing off the thirty-two different kinds of consciousness, starting from the bottom and working the way up, I found myself remembering the sequence of feelings that Gudrun had coached me though during my session. The higher up we went, the more difficult it was to remain in observation mode. The bliss/higher-frequency consciousness was beckoning me into a trance state where I loved the feeling of freedom. This realization has helped me to see why it is so hard to get out of the karmic wheel. We become mesmerized by the light and lose focus on what we are to accomplish.
>
> If I were to have Gudrun work with me at this stage of my evolution, I believe I would be able to hold more spiritual, expanded

consciousness. I believe I could go higher and understand even more of my divine self.

I am feeling so much humility, gratitude, and appreciation for this Sacred Triangle and the Groups of Forty. All of this information is expanding us exponentially. I thank David and Mordechai for bringing their heart-centered teachings to us, and I thank Gudrun for her talent and commitment.

The short of my current summation is not only are the Tree of Life and paths of consciousness guides to our living here and now, but they also serve as guides for departure from this life — wherever that takes us.

Case 4

My next case was a client of mine for many years, on and off, who is also a therapist and is open to the concept of the soul and the soul journey. You will see her ability to deeply understand and integrate the lessons from her regression. At the time of this regression, she had already done a great deal of psychotherapy and had resolved many issues. She writes:

I made the decision to enter into a regression because I had developed a strong curiosity about my past. I had a feeling that I had had an experience that was not contained in my memory but was imprinted in my subconscious and that this experience was exerting a powerful influence on my sense of self. For a long time, I toyed with the theory that I had suffered some sort of sexual abuse in my early years because I had a pervading sense of shame and lack of worth that is often a characteristic of sexual abuse survivors. No amount of therapy, self-talk, meditation, or affirmations could cleanse me of my shame.

The more I considered this, the more I became convinced that I needed to uncover the mystery of my past in order to be fully alive in the present. I initially planned to seek hypnosis to access memories from this life, but as I spoke with my trusted teacher, Gudrun, I came to understand that it was possible that my emotional imprint was from a past life and that I would be best served if I was willing to look further and deeper into my soul history to uncover the root of my shame.

I went into the regression with quite a bit of anxiety. I was worried that I would learn something so horrible that I might be retraumatized and suffer further. When I appeared for the session, I was edgy and a bit tearful. As Gudrun described to me how the regression would proceed and explained to me that I was free to end it at any time, I began to relax and to trust more in the process that was about to begin.

As I slowly entered a hypnotic state, I began to feel safe and even a little excited. The journey was now becoming a bit of an adventure. I was visiting a very beautiful place that contained many trustworthy guides and that imparted in me a feeling of complete trust. I do not wish to share many details of the journey, but I do think it is important to share that the life I witnessed was not one of a victim but of an abuser. I had been the one inflicting the suffering on others!

Interestingly, although my heart cracked open during this revelation, it was an experience of amazing compassion. In the core of my being, I felt the pain and sorrow that had shaped the being (me) who committed those acts, and I felt the loneliness and shame that fed the cruelty. I wept as I felt the heartbreak of living such a life. I was able to access the deepest feelings that were at the core of the cruel actions. It was part confession and part compassion, an experience of the heart that seemed to completely bypass the intellect.

Most importantly, I received a message of complete forgiveness from the victims of the cruelty. There was also an amazing sensation of love that permeated this experience. I felt that one of my guides was present for this, possibly also guiding the souls of the victims as they surrounded me with love and continued to send me the message of forgiveness.

I felt an extraordinary sense of relief as the shame left me and the forgiveness entered to take its place. When I returned, I felt as if a great weight had been lifted from my heart that I believe I had carried for many years. I felt an overwhelming openness in my heart that I believe I have been able to carry forth into my life's work. Shame is no longer part of my basic emotional vocabulary. It is no longer something that feeds my secret beliefs about myself.

Although this experience was extremely transformative, it was by no means a miracle. I still face many challenges in my daily life. I have actually experienced a wider range of emotions, both positive and negative, since the regression. I do feel more able to face these challenges because I feel stronger and more at peace, and I've felt a shift in perspective about what really matters now. I have more patience and less attachment to outcomes, and I am more accepting of the losses and (perceived) disappointments in my life.

Also, because the regression was a journey of the soul and not the mind, I have a different perspective on the relationship between my thoughts, my feelings, and my truth. I expect that if I can continue to incorporate this perspective into my life and work, I can deepen my relationships with others and have more access to the gifts that were sent with me into this life. I now know, thanks to the lessons from my journey, that the key to the gifts is contained in love.

Case 5

The final case I will share in this chapter is with "S," who had intended to receive a regression for two or three years. As often happens, the higher self seemed to set the correct timing for her regression. When she arrived, she was ready and able to do some very deep work.

The presenting issue was that when she meditated and achieved a deep state of trance, her body would become catatonic — that is, she could not move any part of her body. This was very frightening. She had attempted to resolve this issue through many modalities but had no success.

We first reviewed her history in this life. She experienced severe trauma as a child, and then the trauma continued in her marriage. She was able to heal the emotional wounds and also became a psychotherapist. She is a very strong person because of her childhood, and later experiences have not marred her personality, which is open and kind.

"S" easily achieved a deep trance level and, thankfully, did not become frozen. She spontaneously started to go higher and higher in her frequency, ultimately meeting with her guides and soul family, who are from the Hathor group.

Please note that I personally did not know about the Hathor group and was told through "S" that they bring the element of joy to Earth as a service. They are from another universe and operate on high frequencies of sound and light. I learned "S's" soul name is at a frequency that cannot be reproduced by the human vocal chords. "S" described being with the Hathors as blissful. She was in a high-frequency world of crystalline structures where the beings had no form, only color and sound.

As we progressed in the work, she asked them why they did not help her during all of her difficulties. They responded by stating that she had never asked for help from them. They were waiting for her to ask! They had a humorous and loving vibration. They told her that she had requested incarnations on Earth to learn about polarization, specifically the darker energies. Her guides reminded her of this and told her that she has an inquisitive and determined soul.

We did another regression several weeks after the first, and in that regression she went immediately into the high frequency to meet her guides. They placed her in an isolation chamber and then proceeded to remove layer after layer of density. The reason for the isolation chamber was so that they would not be contaminated by the darker energies she had accumulated. She was told that had she not done this intervention, she would have lost connection with her higher self. I believed that to mean that she would have had to go into a longer period of reincarnations. At this point in her evolution, she has had only seven lifetimes! Her description of the sessions follows:

My hypnotherapy sessions opened up a whole new connection and awareness in my growth path. It isn't that I had not had hypnotherapy or regressions before, but these two new sessions were very unique and special. Perhaps I was more open; perhaps the flow was just right. Gudrun's easy manner and expanded awareness and consciousness were also important parts of the ease and success of the sessions. Never before had I connected with my soul group and found the energy of loving peace, acceptance, grace, and ease that represents my soul's expansion.

The process of the regression was a natural flow as though the path was clear and the beings had been waiting for me to make contact. There were guiding beings along the way — a plant and a dog. The plant became a guide, but the dog just wanted to reconnect. It was a lovely connection and added to the enrichment and nurturance of the journey. In fact, at one point, the plant became a loving sound being full of joy, balance, and harmony. Since they (the Hathors) were formless energy, close to sound, I never did receive a name as such; though, when I returned for the second visit, I did recognize the being by the sound of its telepathic communication.

I was invited to lie on a table, and as the happy, healing dialogue continued, I asked several questions and received clarification. Most likely, however, the energy clearing and healing I received were of the greatest benefit. The healing stayed with me and continued to unfold with the new insights for several more days.

After that session, I realized I had more work to do to clear out dense and dark energies. I contacted two energy healers near my home and have had several sessions with the healers. They have cleared energies, blocks, and implants from past lives and enhanced my awareness of my soul's purpose in this life. My original identified problem of catatonic paralysis is dissolved, and total resolution is a heartbeat away. The core of my being is joy and peace. Without the foundation of the hypnotherapy soul regression, I would never have been able to open to this energy and clear it from my energy field.

As you can see, sessions can be ongoing, be a part of long-term psychotherapy, or be a one-time event. I believe that once the connection to the higher self is established directly, the connection then grows stronger and allows for deeper connections with the guides and the soul family. It is then easier to feel connected to our soul purpose and to feel more confident in a world that is so polarized.

I greatly appreciate being able to do this powerful work. With each session, I sense my own soul expansion and growth. I thank the contributors for their comments, and I thank all of my clients for allowing me to have glimpses into their soul journeys.

Glossary

Adam species
The Arcturians refer to human beings as the Adam species.

"Aha" experience
A term used in modern psychology to describe an experience in which one suddenly gains immediate insight into life problems or the meaning of life in general.

Adonai
Hebrew word for God in the Old Testament. It literally means "My Lord." It is also the galactic word for God.

akashic records
An etheric library in the higher dimensions that contains all the information about everyone's lifetimes and life events, including past and present experiences.

altered (higher) states of consciousness
A term in modern psychology used to describe different states of consciousness. This includes the dream state, trances, meditation states of consciousness, and heightened states of consciousness in which one has a higher perception of reality. This state is usually described as a condition in which one can see ultimate truth and experience the present more fully. In the 1960s, this term was also used to describe drug-induced changes in consciousness such as what one could experience with mind-altering drugs.

Andromeda
A large spiral galaxy 2.2 million light-years from the Milky Way. Andromeda is the largest member of our local galactic cluster. It is commonly referred to as Earth's "sister" galaxy.

Andromedans
An advanced, higher-dimensional race of beings from the Andromeda galaxy. A specific group of Andromedans is currently working with the Arcturians in their effort to facilitate the planetary ascension process of Earth.

archangel
A term that applies generally to all angels above the grade of angels. It also designates the highest rank of angels in the angelic hierarchy. The Kabbalah cites ten archangels. They are considered messengers bearing divine decrees.

Arcturus
The brightest star in the constellation Boötes, which is also known as the Herdsman. This is one of the oldest recorded constellations. Arcturus is also the fourth brightest star seen from Earth. It is a giant star, about twenty-five times the diameter of the Sun and one hundred times as luminous. It is a relatively close neighbor of Earth's, approximately forty light-years away. High up in the sky in the late spring and early summer, Arcturus is the first star seen after sunset. One can find Arcturus easily by following the Big Dipper's handle away from the bowl.

ascension
The ability to raise the frequency of one's body, emotions, mind, and astral body beyond the vibration of the physical world so that the body disappears or ascends into a higher dimensional reality, known as the fifth dimension, without experiencing physical death. This phenomenon has occurred and has been described in the Bible, including references to Enoch and to Elijah, who both experienced ascension.

ascended masters
Teachers who have graduated from Earth or who already are on higher dimensions. An ascended master can be from any Earth religion, including the Native American traditions. These masters have graduated from Earth's incarnational cycle and have ascended into the fifth dimension. Ascended masters can include archangels, higher beings from the galactic world, teachers, and prophets.

Ashtar
The commander of a group of spiritual beings who are dedicated to helping Earth ascend. The beings Ashtar oversees exist primarily in the fifth dimension and come from many different extraterrestrial civilizations.

assemblage point
1. A concept that appears in the shamanistic world. The assemblage point is a point in the aura. Some people think it is in the back below the neck. That point is like a valve. When that point is opened, you have an input of higher perception. That means you can see the dimensional worlds; you can see the spirits that are around us all the time.
2. The place where things come together and, through their resonance of frequencies, the whole becomes greater than its parts. The amazing thing is that there are

many assemblage points (of frequency) within the Hebrew letters that relate to the *Sephirot* (spheres) in the Tree of Life. Once you have come to an assemblage point and know that frequency, you resonate with it and internalize it until the unity in resonance leads to entrainment. Also, the assemblage point can spread and expand on this entrainment. Assemblage points are necessary for interdimensional interaction.

astral plane
The nonphysical level of reality considered to be where most humans go when they die.

Atah
Hebrew word that, in the context of prayer, refers to the Creator.

Atlantis
An ancient advanced civilization that reportedly was in existence 10,000 or more years ago. It was reported in the readings of Edgar Cayce, and there were vague references to such a civilization by Plato. There has never been historical or scientific confirmation of this civilization.

Australopithecus
An extinct form of hominid who lived in eastern Africa 4 million years ago. They played a significant part in human evolution and eventually evolved into *Homo genus*, an earlier ancestor of *Homo sapiens*.

biosphere
A term used to describe the whole environment of Earth, including the oceans, atmosphere, and other necessary ingredients that keep and support all life.

Blue Jewel
A term used by the galactic masters to describe Earth.

Central Sun
The center of any astronomical star system. All star clusters, nebulae, and galaxies contain a nucleus at their centers. Even the grand universe itself has a Great Central Sun at the center of its structure. In most cases, a giant star exists at the center of all star systems. The Great Central Sun of the Milky Way provides life-giving energy to the entire galaxy.

chakras
Energy centers of the human body system. These centers provide the integration and transfer of energy between the spiritual, mental, emotional, and biological systems of the human body.

channeling
The process of entering a meditative trance to call forth other entities to speak through you. See *trance channeling*.

Chief Buffalo Heart
An ascended fifth-dimensional Native American guide who focuses on using heart energy to help others ascend.

Chief White Eagle
An ascended fifth-dimensional Native American guide who is very connected to Jesus and other higher fifth-dimensional beings. Many people over the ages have had the name White Eagle. In the context of New Age spirituality, Chief White Eagle is a fifth-dimensional ascended master, medicine man, visionary, healer, and prophet who is helping all people in their ascension process.

cohabitation
A Kabbalistic term for occupying another soul's energy in one's aura. This can be done for positive purposes, in which case a positive, highly evolved energy, such as Archangel Michael, can coexist in a person's energy field. This allows the person to accomplish, perform, and enhance his or her ability to achieve greater and more positive tasks in life. This is referred to as positive cohabitation (*Ibbur* in Kabbalah). There is also negative cohabitation, which is the occupation of the Earth energy of a person by a negative lower spirit, such as a ghost (*Dybuk* in Kabbalah). Negative spirits occupying an energy field can cause a person to act irrationally and even commit crimes and violent acts.

cosmic drama
A term used to describe standard conflicts that different planets experience during their evolutionary cycles. Some soul groups come from other parts of our galaxy and then incarnate on Earth to try to resolve their conflicts.

corridor
A pathway or etheric tunnel on Earth that leads to a higher dimension. Corridors can be found in high-energy places such as sacred sites on Earth. The Arcturians believe that we can establish corridors within our meditation areas on Earth.

cosmic egg
The optimal shape of your aura for health benefits. When your aura is in the shape of an egg, you are expressing maximal energetic possibilities. The egg is a universal shape of wholeness, and thus it is also referred to as the cosmic egg.

cosmic justice/karma
The idea that karmic justice is also played out on the cosmic level outside of Earth. Negative actions that occurred on other planets could be played out in karmic dramas now on Earth.

Cro-magnon
Early modern humans from Europe. They lived as early as 43,000 years ago. They are considered ancestors of modern Europeans and coexisted with the Neanderthals.

defenses
A term used in Freudian psychology that describes the psyche's efforts to protect itself from unwanted impulses, desires, and thoughts. Some types of defenses used by the psyche are denial, repression, and projection.

dimension
Refers to the level of frequencies of energy. For example, etheric energy expands to higher dimensional levels, including the fifth dimension. Awareness increases and energy progresses upward through the dimensions. This increasing energy frequency on the fifth dimension helps one experience a greater unity. That is to say, as one goes into higher dimensions (such as the fifth dimension), one experiences a greater unity — a unity that is not experienced on the third dimension, where duality and conflict are usually experienced.

disassociation
A psychological defense mechanism in which one removes consciousness and experiential awareness from an event in order to not experience pain. This defense is often used during traumatic events, especially by children when they are being abused.

Earth lessons
A term in soul psychology that relates to what lessons one has to learn during this incarnation on Earth.

etheric
A term used to designate the higher bodies in the human system. In India, "etheric" is used to describe the unseen energy and thoughts of humans.

etheric crystals
Invisible crystals that contain fifth-dimensional energy that have been sent to Earth by the Arcturians. The purpose of these etheric crystals is to provide healing energies to Earth's meridians.

etheric energy
The vibrational frequency that is one level higher than physical reality. Etheric energy is often referred to in terms of etheric energy bodies, which can be described as vibrational energy frequencies around objects and people that sometimes can be seen by people who have psychic abilities.

fifth dimension
A higher dimension of existence that is above the first and third dimensions. We currently live on the third dimension, where we are bound by the laws of cause and effect and of reincarnation. The fourth dimension is the astral realm and also the realm of dreams. The fifth dimension transcends this and is the realm of infinite energy and love, and it can be compared to the Garden of Eden. In the fifth dimension, one transcends the incarnational cycle. It could be said that one graduates from Earth and goes to the fifth dimension. The ascended masters residing now in the fifth dimension include Jesus/Sananda. The ascension focuses on going to the fifth dimension.

freewill zone
Earth has free will, which means people can choose how to think and what to do.

future self
A concept in soul psychology in which the self is viewed as timeless; therefore, who a person will be in the future is relevant to understanding the present self.

Galactic Kachina
A special kachina who is an intermediary between the energy of the Central Sun, located in the center of the Milky Way galaxy, and planet Earth.

galactic spirituality
Includes a spiritual philosophy or theory that accepts the existence of other higher beings throughout this galaxy and therefore takes the perspective of the galactic view in understanding Earth's planetary evolution as part of a galactic family of civilizations.

Gestalt
A German word that means whole or form. A modern-day psychology theory called Gestalt psychology was developed by Fritz Perls. It is based on looking at the whole person, including the unconscious and conscious states. People are seen as trying to complete unfinished business so that their lives can be whole. Dream interpretation is used in this method as each person in the dream represents a part of the dreamer.

grace
A reprieve from negative karma due to good deeds . This reprieve can be brought as a blessing from spirit guides.

Group of Forty
A concept of group consciousness suggested by the Arcturians for use in the group ascension process. According to the Arcturians, forty is a spiritually powerful number. The Arcturians emphasize the value and power of joining together in groups. A Group of Forty consists of forty different members located throughout the U.S. and world-wide who focus on meditating together at a given time each month. Group interactions and yearly physical meetings are recommended. Members agree to assist each other in their spiritual development. The Arcturians have asked that forty Groups of Forty be organized. These groups will assist in the healing of Earth and provide a foundation for the members' ascensions.

harmonic light
Fifth-dimensional light often appearing as gold balls of etheric energy. This light can be transmitted through the noosphere (the collective unconscious) and can spread energy of balance and harmony wherever it is directed. It can be directed by the thoughts and prayers of starseeds around the planet.

Helio-ah
An Arcturian female ascended master who is the partner of Juliano. She specializes in discussing holographic energy.

He'nei'nee
Hebrew word used by Abraham when God called on him and Abraham answered, "Here I am." This phrase is used in modern Kabbalistic thinking to denote the concept of being in the present, or the here and now.

higher self
In Kabbalah, the self that relates directly to higher dimensions, transcending the ego.

hologram and holographic energy
A hologram is a three-dimensional image originally generated by a laser. Holographic energy is based on the image of a hologram. Holographic energy is a quantum explanation of reality that suggests that this third-dimensional universe is a giant space-time hologram. This means that the entirety of the universe can be found and accessed within each individual facet of it, no matter how small or distant that facet is. This holographic phenomenon leads to these concepts:
1. Every moment — past, present, and future — exists simultaneously.
2. Every place is connected to every other place in the universe.
3. Every particle contains the full awareness of every other particle and place in the universe, no matter what the scale or size of that particle is.

holographic computers
Computers that the Arcturians use in their healing chambers. The holographic computers are able to lock on to a person's aura and read that person's past and future.

holographic healing chambers
This refers to special Arcturian etheric chambers or rooms in which one can experience healings for the self. The chamber gives one access to past, present, and future aspects of the self, which helps to accelerate healing.

holographic self
In holographic thought, the part represents the whole. Thus, one cell of the human body can give access to the whole DNA code, for example. The part of a person on the third dimension is one part of the greater self. Thus, the holographic self refers to all of the person, including the part that is here on Earth and the parts that are on other dimensions.

Ibbur
Hebrew word in the Kabbalah describing the entry of positive soul energy into a man or woman. See *cohabitation*.

immediate karma
A concept that when action is taken, immediate effects or karma from that action are shown. This effect on the self can even occur immediately in this lifetime.

imprints (also called soul imprints)
Thought programs and thought patterns placed into the unconscious. These imprints can come from past lives and, in some cases, even from alien abductions.

intermediaries
Refers to guides between the third and fifth dimensions who are here to help with the ascension.

Iskalia mirror
A fifth-dimensional etheric mirror placed by the Arcturians over the North Pole that can collect higher light from the Central Sun and refocus that light and energy onto Earth to transform it into a fifth-dimensional planet.

Jungian psychology
An approach to psychotherapy emphasizing energies related to archetypes, symbols, and other unconscious energies. This approach is based on the Swiss psychiatrist Carl Jung, who was a contemporary of Freud. But unlike Freud, Jung believed in the existence of the soul.

Juliano
The main Arcturian guide and ascended master working to help activate Earth and Arcturian starseeds toward the ascension.

Jupiter corridor
An interdimensional corridor between Mars and Jupiter that extraterrestrial ships use to enter Earth's solar system. Many extraterrestrial ships can remain in an orbiting position there without entering the third-dimensional Earth space.

Kabbalah
The major branch of Jewish mysticism. The Hebrew word *Kabbalah* is translated as "to receive." The study of Kabbalah can raise one's level of consciousness to new heights and assist in unlocking the codes for transformation into the fifth dimension.

kachinas
Spirit guides and intermediaries to the spirit world in the Hopi and Navajo traditions. They are said to live on the San Francisco Peaks near Flagstaff, Arizona.

karmic justice
Based on the idea that what actions a person takes, whether good or bad, will be balanced out in either this lifetime or future lifetimes. This means punishment could occur now or in the future.

Kuthumi
One of the ascended masters who serves Sananda. In a previous life, Kuthumi incarnated as St. Francis of Assisi. He is generally recognized as holding the position of world teacher in the planetary White Brotherhood/Sisterhood. An extensive record of his teachings can be found in the works of Alice Bailey.

life-between-lives reading
1. A session in which the counselor uses a hypnotic trance to regress the patient back to birth and then to a place where he or she meets with a council "in between lives." At this point, patients are able to discuss with their guides and teachers what their soul goals are and how they are doing in this current lifetime.
2. A spiritual hypnotherapy regression technique developed by an American psychologist, Dr. Michael Newton. His spiritual regression technique includes bringing patients back to their past lives and to a state known as "life between lives." In that state, clients can meet their spirit guides and teachers.

life review
A term that has become popular in the study of near-death experiences. People who had close brushes with death, such as a serious accident, report that they see and evaluate their entire lives in a split second before they lose consciousness. Sometimes they report going through a long tunnel and meeting their guides and teachers, who help them do a life review.

lightbody
Higher etheric spirit body that is connected to the highest soul energy.

lightworkers
A term used to describe people who have spiritual interests in the higher dimensions, including studying and receiving energy from the higher dimensions. The energy from the higher dimensions is often referred to as "light" — hence the term "lightworkers."

lower self
A description in the Kabbalah of humans' animalistic nature, including instincts.

Lyrans
A group of advanced beings who lived in the constellation Lyra in the Milky Way galaxy.

Malchut
Hebrew word meaning "kingdom." Malchut is the tenth sphere on the Tree of Life and represents reality on Earth.

Maggid
Hebrew word for "divine spirits" or "spirit guides" who speak to you while you are in a trance state. A *Maggid* can be defined as a mentor or guide.

medicine wheel
A circular pattern of rocks and crystals created on the ground by Native Americans. It is used for ceremonies, including communicating with the earth.

Merkavah

The Hebrew word for "chariot." In Kabbalah, it refers to the divine chariot that Ezekiel saw in a vision. *Merkavah* is also referred to as a vehicle used for going up into higher realms.

Metatron

Tradition associates Metatron with Enoch, who "walked with God" (Genesis 5:22, KJV) and ascended to heaven and was changed from a human being into an angel. His name has been defined as "the angel of presence" or "the one who occupies the throne next to the Divine Throne." Another interpretation of his name is based on the Latin word *metator*, which means "a guide or measurer." In the world of the Jewish mystic, Metatron holds the rank of the highest of angels — that of an archangel. According to the Arcturians, Metatron is associated with the Arcturian stargate and assists souls in their ascension to higher worlds.

Michael

The name is actually a question, meaning, "Who is like God?" He is perhaps the best known of the archangels and is acknowledged by all three Western sacred traditions. He has been called the Prince of Light, fighting a war against the sons of darkness. In this role, he is depicted most often as winged with an unsheathed sword, the warrior of God and slayer of the dragon. His role in the ascension is focused on helping us cut the cords of attachment to the Earth plane, which will allow us to move up to higher consciousness. In the Kabbalah, he is regarded as the forerunner of the *Shekhinah*, the Divine Mother.

Milton Erickson

A famous American hypnotherapist and psychiatrist who lived from 1901 to 1980. He developed trance techniques for working with the unconscious, which proved to be highly successful in treating his patients. He influenced modern hypnotherapy techniques, which are used in treatment of a variety of mental illnesses, including depression, anxiety, and certain addictions.

monad

The original, elemental creative force. Each one of us contains a portion of that force at the center of our true essence.

multidimensional self

A view of the self existing on different dimensions, including the dream world and the fourth and fifth dimensions. Aspects of the self can exist in other dimensions.

multidimensional presence

Existence on several different dimensions. The Arcturians are trying to help humans become aware of their existence not only on the third dimension but also on the fifth dimension.

multiple personalities
In modern psychiatry, a mental illness that is described as a person having several personalities at the same time. Each personality is neither conscious nor aware of the other personalities.

Nabur
A Kabbalistic rabbi, teacher, and personal fifth-dimensional guide of the author (David Miller) in a former lifetime.

Neanderthals
An extinct species of humans — possibly a subspecies of *Homo sapiens*. Neanderthals are closely related to modern humans. They lived in parts of Europe from 350,000 years ago to as recently as 32,000 years ago.

Nefesh
The Hebrew word for "animal soul" or "lower soul" representing the entire range of instincts. *Nefesh* is the raw, vital energy needed to live on this planet.

negative self-talk
Self-talk that is negative, such as "I am worthless" or "I will never amount to anything."

Neshamah
Hebrew for the spiritual portion of the soul or the higher self. It is the intuitive power that connects humankind with the Creator, the highest of the three parts of a soul that transcends third-dimensional reality and the Earth ego to link directly to the divine light. In Kabbalah, it refers simply to the higher self, or that part of the soul that interacts with the Creator.

omega light
A fifth-dimensional light that has high healing properties. The light can help transcend the world of cause and effect; thus, it can help produce miraculous healings. The effects of this healing light can be increased by toning the sounds "omega light."

P'taah
An ascended master and spirit guide from the Pleiades star system.

past-life readings
Counseling sessions in which the therapist regresses a patient through a trance. In the reading, the patient can access information and experiences from previous lifetimes. See also *life-between-lives readings*.

parallel lives
The idea that people live simultaneously in other universes and worlds while living in this third-dimensional world.

planetary cities of light
Cities that have been activated with fifth-dimensional energy. A planetary city of light is also part of a global network of other planetary cities of light on Earth.

planetary healing
Exercises used to rebalance Earth and help the biosphere become healthy again. Planetary healing exercises can include medicine wheel ceremonies and Biorelativity meditations.

planetary mission
In soul psychology, the view that people come and incarnate on Earth to do special soul work to help the planet.

planetary logos
A term used to denote an ascended master who oversees a planet's development.

Pleiades
A small cluster of stars known as the Seven Sisters in some mythologies. Some Native Americans believe that they are descended from the Pleiades. This system is near the constellation Taurus, about 450 light-years from Earth, and is the home of a race called the Pleiadians, who have frequently interacted with Earth and her cultures. It is said that the Pleiadians have a common ancestry with humans.

portal
An opening at the end of a corridor that allows beings to go into interdimensional space. This could allow beings to go into the fifth dimension.

resistance
A term in modern psychology describing a defense mechanism in which one prevents oneself from seeing a truth or does not want to learn new ideas or approaches because of a fear of change.

restoration of self
A psychological term used by the Austrian-American psychoanalyst Heinz Kohut, who died in 1981. Kohut developed self-psychology based on restoring the self by focusing on improving one's sense of worth and well-being. His work has influenced the modern theories of self-esteem, which are widely used now in modern psychology.

ring of ascension
A fifth-dimensional halo around Earth placed by the ascended masters. Its purpose is to help focus fifth-dimensional energy onto Earth.

Rolodex
An apparatus used in office management for storing phone numbers and addresses. The Arcturians use this device as a metaphor for explaining how memories are stored in the unconscious and how those memories are brought up into the conscious mind. Thoughts and experiences are stored in an unconscious container in the self, which can be compared to a Rolodex. One can easily access thoughts and images on the Rolodex by turning the apparatus around in a circle.

Sacred Triangle
A term used by the Arcturians to denote a triangular symbol representing the unification of three powerful spiritual forces on Earth: the White Brotherhood/Sisterhood ascended masters, including Sananda/Jesus; the extraterrestrial higher-dimensional masters, such as the Arcturians and the Pleiadians; and the Native American ascended masters, such as Chiefs White Eagle and Buffalo Heart. The unification of these spiritual forces creates the Sacred Triangle that aids in the healing and ascension of Earth.

Sananda
Known to many as Master Jesus. His galactic name, Sananda, represents an evolved and galactic picture of who he is in his entirety. Sananda is known as Joshua ben Miriam of Nazareth, which can be translated as Jesus, son of Mary of Nazareth.

San Francisco Peaks
A 12,000-foot mountain range near Flagstaff, Arizona, that is the sacred home of the Navajo Indians. The kachina spirits are said to live there.

Sanat Kumara
An ascended master overseeing the development of Earth toward its ascension. He is often referred to as the planetary logos.

schema
Environmental programming and stimulation received while growing up.

selectivity of thoughts
Choosing which thoughts a person will allow into consciousness. One can allow only positive psychic energy and thoughts to come into consciousness. Selectivity of thoughts is an important tool to use when channeling.

self-talk
A term in modern psychology that describes the ongoing private conversation one has with oneself in the mind. Self-talk can be either positive or negative.

shimmering
Representative of an energy field on telepathic interactions between the third-dimensional starseeds and lightworkers and fifth-dimensional energy. The shimmering light is a telepathic etheric force field that is accelerated through etheric crystal work. It can be described as a circular energy field that is distributed around the planet.

The evolution of humankind is represented by new abilities and new energies. These new abilities and new energies are related in part to shimmering energy, a methodology and force in which third-dimensional objects, people, and even weather are upgraded into a fifth-dimensional modality. On a personal level, shimmering allows your auric field to vibrate at a frequency that enables the aura to shift the electrons. The atomic structure of your cells transmutes into a vibratory energy field that elliptically shifts the cellular structures into the fifth dimension, causing a back-and-forth or "shimmering" modality. This back-and-forth shimmering modality actually affects the atomic and quantum levels of your cellular structures.

This shimmering energy is the precursor to the ascension. The ascension is an accelerated and enhanced shimmering energy in which we elevate ourselves into the fifth dimension permanently. The energy that we are now working with in shimmering is a powerful and necessary prelude to the fifth-dimension ascension. This shimmering is a force-field vibration. The global network is the scale that we are working on in terms of group ascension of the planet. The shimmering energy is also enabling powerful streams of energy to be distributed throughout the planet.

soul groups
Like-minded people who come from the same soul root or soul branch. One can often feel deeper connections with people who come from the same soul group. The term "soul group" refers to people who belong to the same soul family and soul origin. Often soul groups reincarnate together on Earth and form groups. At other times, people on Earth might incarnate alone and away from their soul groups. People in the same soul group often have similar feelings, thoughts, and inclinations. When a person is with members of his or her soul group, that person feels deeply connected. It's like being with family.

soul imprints
Programs carried over from one lifetime to another that are "imprinted" or embedded in the soul energy so that the program manifests in this lifetime or future lifetimes.

soul inclination
Desires, skills, and what brings joy to a person from the soul in this lifetime. For example, some souls like to play music or paint. It is better to follow one's soul inclination for a happier life.

soul lessons
In soul psychology, life lessons that a person specifically came to Earth to learn in this lifetime.

soul psychologist
A term used to describe a therapist or counselor who uses information from past lives, karma, life lessons, other dimensions, and spirit guides or mentors to help heal clients. Methods used by soul psychologists can include past-life therapy, channeling of guides and teachers, and life-between-lives therapy. (Note: These are not methods used by traditional psychologists.) Personal problems presented to soul psychologists

are viewed in the perspective of a person's soul history, which includes other lifetimes. This perspective transcends the traditional realm of modern Western psychology practices. Please note that the term "psychologist" as used in this context does not refer to the traditional practice of psychology in the twenty-first century.

soul sphere of influence
People one feels close to and connected to on Earth. People who are in a person's soul sphere of influence are from the same soul branch and tree, which means that person has the ability to help, heal, and influence them. Also, they are able to heal and influence each other.

soul retrieval
A technique of finding and reintegrating lost parts of the soul from other lifetimes in this current lifetime.

spirit guides
Teachers from the higher realms who are guides and mentors. They give spiritual advice and recommendations and also offer insights into the higher worlds and higher consciousness.

spiritual light quotient
A term used by the Arcturians to indicate how well developed a person is spiritually. A person with a high spiritual light quotient, for example, can understand and use higher spiritual concepts such as meditation, unity consciousness, and ascension. One's spiritual light quotient can rise with age.

stargate
A multidimensional portal into higher realms. The Arcturian stargate is very close to the Arcturus star system and is overseen by the Arcturians. This powerful passage point requires that earthlings who wish to pass through it complete all lessons and Earth incarnations associated with the third-dimensional experience. It serves as a gateway to the fifth dimension. New soul assignments are given there, and souls can then be sent to many different higher realms throughout the galaxy and universe. Archangel Metatron and many other higher beings are present at the stargate.
Many people are now using the term "stargate" to refer to openings on Earth to higher dimensions when, in fact, they are describing corridors. The stargate is a magnificent, temple-like, etheric structure that can process and transform many souls.

starseeds
People who have been born with the awareness of galactic consciousness. Starseeds may also have memories of past lifetimes on other planets and feel connected to civilizations from other planets such as the Pleiades or Arcturus. Some starseeds have come to Earth at this time to assist in her evolutionary transformation.

supermind
The higher part of the mind that connects with universal and galactic consciousness.

third dimension
The Earth plane where humans now live. There are higher dimensions beyond Earth.

thought projection
The ability to put one's mind and awareness into one's thoughts. This awareness can be in the present, past, or future. In thought projection, one can send awareness to other realities, to other locations on the third dimension, or even to other dimensions. In its highest form, thought projection can be used to send one's astral body to distant locations, either on this dimension or the fifth dimension.

Tikun
Hebrew word meaning "repair." It's used in reference to repairing the world. This term also means "restoration," or "the divine restoration of the cosmos." In Kabbalah, this refers to the concept that the vessel holding the light from the Creator on the third dimension has been broken and that it is the task of humanity to help restore or repair it on Earth.

Tiferet
The center sphere or energy force in the Kabbalistic Tree of Life. It represents beauty, harmony, and balance.

tones or sacred sounds
Sounds producing a vibratory resonance that helps activate and align the chakras.

trance channeling
Putting oneself into a light trance to do automatic speaking. A trance is a type of self-hypnosis in which one puts oneself into an altered state of consciousness. There are light trances and deep trances. A deep trance is when one goes out and is almost in a somnambulant or sleep state. This is the way Edward Cayce used to channel. In light trance channeling, the channel is still awake while bringing through messages.

trance work
A term used in modern psychology to describe a hypnotic state. The hypnotic state, or trance, can be described as light, middle, or deep. A deep trance implies that the subject loses total consciousness and awareness of what he or she is experiencing. A light trance implies that the subject is able to observe what he or she is experiencing, even though the subject is in an altered state of consciousness. In a middle trance, the subject loses most consciousness but can still function and walk around.

Tree of Life
A pattern of energy and a diagram used in Kabbalah to define the Creator and His/Her ten emanations, or the ten spheres of God. The Tree of Life is a healing planetary force directly connected with the Torah. The spheres of the Tree of Life consist of positive

and negative balancing forces. There are also three pillars of energy: positive, negative, and harmony. Finally, the Tree of Life presents a paradigm of elevating consciousness by going through different realms in order to reach the highest unity with the Creator.

unification
A spiritual process in Kabbalah. One unifies different energies in an attempt to bring healing or repair to the world or to oneself. There are unifications within a person's personal system and life that need to be completed. A unification is an alignment and bringing together of energies so that they are harmonious.

Vywamus
A fifth-dimensional soul psychologist known for his insight into the psychology of Earth problems and resolution of issues related to starseeds incarnated on Earth.

walk-ins
Humans who have received other spiritual entities into their bodies or energy fields. The term is also used in reference to the new spirit that has entered such a body. In some cases, the original spirit of the person may have left (for example, after an auto accident or some other form of severe trauma) and the new spirit "walks in" to the old body. This is always by agreement of the person vacating the body before incarnating to allow the body to continue in service after the particular incarnation is complete. It also allows the "walk-in" being to skip the process of childhood and adolescence to get straight to his or her mission on Earth. The walk-in does agree to honor the commitments of the previous occupant's life.

warrior self
A concept in shamanistic psychology that focuses on one's spiritual journey being viewed as having similar traits to being a warrior. This means a person shows great courage and can use power animals and other methods for increasing spiritual strength.

White Brotherhood/Sisterhood
A spiritual hierarchy of ascended masters residing in the fifth dimension. "White" is not used here as a racial term. It refers to the white light or higher frequency that these masters have attained. The masters include Sananda, Kuthumi, Mother Mary, Quan Yin, Sanat Kumara, Archangel Michael, Saint Germain, and many other ascended beings.

White Buffalo Calf Woman
In Lakota Native American folklore, the fifth-dimensional spirit being who appeared to bring forth special information about holy ceremonies and accessing higher spirits. She taught the necessity of being in harmony with Earth. Her focus is on the unity of all beings and that all are relations. She is representative of the dawning of a new age.

X-terra
A planet inhabited by Arcturians that is close to the galactic center.

About the Author

*D*avid K. Miller is the director and founder of an international meditation group focused on personal and planetary healing. He has been the director of this global healing group, called the Group of Forty, for more than fifteen years. David has been developing groundbreaking global healing techniques using group consciousness to help heal areas of Earth that need balance, restoration, and harmony. The technique he uses with his group work is called Biorelativity, which uses group consciousness work to restore Earth's feedback-loop system, a complex planetary system that maintains the correct balance of our planet's atmosphere, ocean currents, and weather patterns.

David's meditation group has more than 1,200 members worldwide. In addition to his lectures and workshops, David is also a prolific author, having written ten books and numerous articles on Earth healing techniques. Several of his books also have been published in German and in Spanish.

David works with his wife, Gudrun Miller, who is a psychotherapist and visionary artist. Together they have conducted workshops in Brazil, Germany, Australia, Mexico, Argentina, Costa Rica, Spain, New Zealand, Belgium, and Turkey. David's foundation for this work lies in his study and connection to Native American teachings and his intense study in mysticism, including the Kabbalah. He also has an intense interest in astronomy and Earth's relationship to the galaxy. To learn more, go to www.GroupofForty.com.

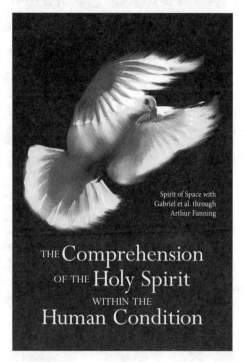

𝄞 *Light Technology* PUBLISHING *Presents*

BOOKS BY TOM T. MOORE

THE GENTLE WAY
A SELF-HELP GUIDE FOR THOSE WHO BELIEVE IN ANGELS

"This book is for people of all faiths and beliefs with the only requirement being a basic belief in angels. It will put you back in touch with your guardian angel or strengthen and expand the connection that you may already have. How can I promise these benefits? Because I have been using these concepts for over ten years and I can report these successes from direct knowledge and experience. But this is a self-help guide, so that means it requires your active participation." — Tom T. Moore

$14.⁹⁵ • 160 PP., SOFTCOVER • ISBN 978-1-891824-60-9

THE GENTLE WAY II
BENEVOLENT OUTCOMES: THE STORY CONTINUES

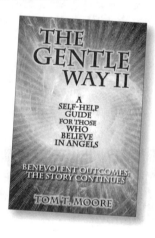

You'll be amazed at how easy it is to be in touch with guardian angels and how much assistance you can receive simply by asking. This inspirational self-help book, written for all faiths and beliefs, will explain how there is a more benevolent world that we can access, and how we can achieve this.

These very unique and incredibly simple techniques assist you in manifesting your goals easily and effortlessly for the first time. It works quickly, sometimes with immediate results, and no affirmations, written intentions, or changes in behavior are needed. You don't even have to believe in it for it to work!

$16.⁹⁵ • 320 PP., SOFTCOVER • ISBN 978-1-891824-80-7

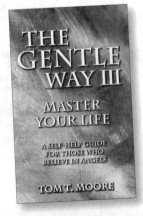

THE GENTLE WAY III
MASTER YOUR LIFE

"Almost three years have passed since *The Gentle Way II* was published. Yet as many success stories as that book contained, I have continued to receive truly unique stories from people all over the world requesting most benevolent outcomes and asking for benevolent prayers for their families, friends, other people, and other beings. It just proves that there are no limits to this modality, which is becoming a gentle movement as people discover how much better their lives are with these simple yet powerful requests." — Tom T. Moore

$16.⁹⁵ • 352 PP., SOFTCOVER • ISBN 978-1-62233-005-8

Light Technology PUBLISHING *Presents*

THE ANCIENT SECRET OF THE FLOWER OF LIFE,
VOLUME 1

Once, all life in the universe knew the Flower of Life as the creation pattern, the geometrical design leading us into and out of physical existence. Then from a very high state of consciousness, we fell into darkness, the secret hidden for thousands of years, encoded in the cells of all life.

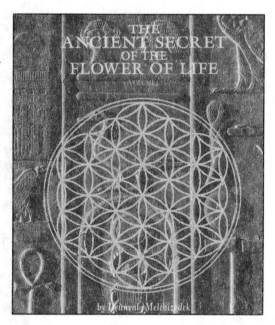

Now, we are rising from the darkness, and a new dawn is streaming through the windows of perception. This book is one of those windows. Drunvalo Melchizedek presents in text and graphics the Flower of Life workshop, illuminating the mysteries of how we came to be.

Sacred geometry is the form beneath our being and points to a divine order in our reality. We can follow that order from the invisible atom to the infinite stars, finding ourselves at each step. The information here is one path, but between the lines and drawings lie the feminine gems of intuitive understanding.

You may see them sparkle around some of these provocative ideas:
- Remembering our ancient past
- The secret of the Flower unfolds
- The darker side of our present/past
- The geometries of the human body
- The significance of shape and structure

**$25**^{00} Softcover, 240 PP.
ISBN 978-1-891824-17-3

Drunvalo Melchizedek's life experience reads like an encyclopedia of breakthroughs in human endeavor. He studied physics and art at the University of California at Berkeley, but he feels that his most important education came after college. In the past twenty-five years, he has studied with over seventy teachers from all belief systems and religious understandings. For some time now, he has been bringing his vision to the world through the Flower of Life program and the Mer-Ka-Ba meditation. This teaching encompasses every area of human understanding, explores the development of humankind from ancient civilizations to the present time, and offers clarity regarding the world's state of consciousness and what is needed for a smooth and easy transition into the twenty-first century.

♀ *Light Technology* PUBLISHING *Presents*

DNA
OF THE SPIRIT

VOLUME 1

channeled through Rae Chandran

WITH Robert Mason Pollock

The etheric strands of your DNA are the information library of your soul. They contain the complete history of you, lifetime after lifetime; a record of the attitudes, karma, and emotional predispositions you brought into this lifetime; and a blueprint, or lesson plan, for your self-improvement. Your DNA is also a record of your existence from the moment of your creation as a starbeing to your present incarnation. This information is written in every cell of your body.

$16.95
Plus Shipping

ISBN 978-1-62233-013-3
Softcover 340 PP.
6 X 9 Perfect Bound

CHAPTERS INCLUDE:

- Mudras for Activating the Twelve Layers of DNA
- The Awakening of Crystalline Consciousness

- Auspicious Times for Awakening Consciousness
- Angelic Support for DNA Activation
- The History of Human DNA

- Your Internal Compass: Nature's Body Intelligence

How God Did It, Not Why

by William Lowell Putnam

- *Creation is an ongoing process.*
- *God has not finished designing Earth.*
- *Man is not the only creature in the process.*
- *This is the only world we know of.*
- *Time is a dimension.*
- *Fossils are our ancestors.*
- *We all have a right to our own heaven.*

HOW GOD DID IT

NOT WHY

WILLIAM LOWELL PUTNAM III

$16.95
Plus Shipping

ISBN-13: 978-1-62233-015-7
Softcover 160 PP.
6 X 9 • 4-color

CHAPTERS INCLUDE:

- Recent Geological History
- God's Mechanisms
- Before the Alpinists

- Peaks, Passes, and Glaciers
- Spots on the Sun
- Various Diaries

- The Astronomers
- Evolution?
- What's Next?

Print Books: Visit Our Online Bookstore www.LightTechnology.com
eBooks Available on Amazon, Apple iTunes, Google Play, and Barnes & Noble

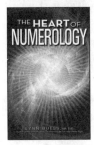

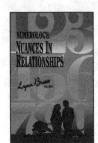

☥ *Light Technology* PUBLISHING Presents

Shamanic Secrets Mastery Series

Speaks of Many Truths, Zoosh, and Reveals the Mysteries through Robert Shapiro

This book explores the heart and soul connection between humans and Earth. Through that intimacy, miracles of healing and expanded awareness can flourish. To heal the planet and be healed as well, you can lovingly extend your energy self out to the mountains and rivers and intimately bond with Earth. Gestures and vision can activate your heart to return you to a healthy, caring relationship with the land you live on. The character of some of Earth's most powerful features is explored and understood with exercises given to connect you with those places. As you project your love and healing energy there, you help Earth to heal from human destruction of the planet and its atmosphere. Dozens of photographs, maps, and drawings assist the process in twenty-five chapters, which cover Earth's more critical locations.

ISBN 978-1-891824-12-8 • SOFTCOVER, 512 PP. • $19.95

Learn to understand the sacred nature of your own physical body and some of the magnificent gifts it offers you. When you work with your physical body in these new ways, you will discover not only its sacredness but its compatibility with Mother Earth, the animals, the plants, and even the nearby planets, all of which you now recognize as being sacred in nature. It is important to feel the value of oneself physically before you can have any lasting physical impact on the world. If a physical energy does not feel good about itself, it will usually be resolved; other physical or spiritual energies will dissolve it because they are unnatural. The better you feel about your physical self when you do the work in the first book, as well as this one and the one to follow, the greater and more lasting the benevolent effect will be on your life, on the lives of those around you, and ultimately on your planet and universe.

ISBN 978-1-891824-29-6 • SOFTCOVER, 576 PP. • $25.00

Spiritual mastery encompasses many different means to assimilate and be assimilated by the wisdom, feelings, flow, warmth, function, and application of all beings in your world who you will actually contact in some way. A lot of spiritual mastery has been covered in different bits and pieces throughout all the books we've done. My approach to spiritual mastery, though, will be as grounded as possible in things that people on Earth can use — but it won't include the broad spectrum of spiritual mastery, like levitation and invisibility. I'm trying to teach you things that you can actually use and benefit from. My life is basically going to represent your needs, and it gets out the secrets that have been held back in a story-like fashion so that it is more interesting."

— Speaks of Many Truths

ISBN 978-1-891824-58-6 • SOFTCOVER, 768 PP. • $29.95

Phone: 928-526-1345 or 1-800-450-0985 • Fax: 928-714-1132

🜨 *Light Technology* PUBLISHING **Presents**

Angels Explain Death and Prayer

by Cheryl Gaer Barlow

ANGELS EXPLAIN
Death
AND
Prayer

through Cheryl Gaer Barlow

"We are the angels of the Mallbon. We are meant to tell those of Earth that the death of the body is never to be feared. We help in ways not understood by humanity. We can manifest anything we desire. We can live as humans on Earth. When we absorb the reality of Earth, we work God's wonders in ordinary ways.

"When the surroundings are not in focus or when you feel unable to cope with the people or circumstances around you, be still and ask God for help. God will respond to requests of help by mending emotions with aid from the angels. This is done by being aware of the angels. We surround you and bring you comfort.

"You must, as a human race, lift the quality of thought to the highest level. When the level of thought is low and miserable, it is generated through the entire world. When it is lifted to a level of joy, it lifts all minds. When you know the teachings of the angels, no ignorance will be left in the soul. You will no longer be afraid or in pain. Now is the time to stand with the angels of God and help humankind."

— The Mallbon Angels

$16⁹⁵
Plus Shipping

ISBN 13: 978-1-62233-008-9
Softcover • 224 pp.
6 X 9 Perfect Bound

Chapters Include:

- The Soul's Path
- The Death of Children
- Meeting God
- Dreams
- Birth on Earth
- Entering the Heavens
- The Joy That Awaits You
- Bonus: Prayer Guide!

Homeopathy
FOR Epidemics
EILEEN NAUMAN, DHM (UK)

$25⁰⁰
Plus Shipping

ISBN 13: 978-1-891824-42-5
Softcover 448 pp.
6 X 9 Perfect Bound

Homeopathy FOR Epidemics

by Eileen Nauman

Homeopathy in Times of Crises

Homeopathy's philosophy is like cures like. By potentizing a remedy through a series of dilution steps, only the energy signature of the original substance is eventually left in the alcohol carrier. Quantum physics will one day be able to explain why water has memory; similarly, homeopaths know that each remedy has its own unique frequency, whether there are molecules of the substance left or not.

The homeopathic community knows that in the past, homeopathic remedies have made the difference between life and death during global epidemics. It is my hope that you will pass the information in this book along to your relatives and friends. It might be the greatest gift you ever give them — information that can save their lives.

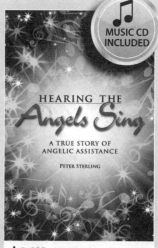

✦ *Light Technology* PUBLISHING *Presents*

THE EXPLORER RACE SERIES

ZOOSH AND HIS FRIENDS THROUGH ROBERT SHAPIRO

The series: Humans — creators in training — have a purpose and destiny so heartwarmingly, profoundly glorious that it is almost unbelievable from our present dimensional perspective. Humans are great light-beings from beyond this creation gaining experience in dense physicality. This truth about the great human genetic experiment of the Explorer Race and the mechanics of creation is being revealed for the first time by Zoosh and his friends through superchannel Robert Shapiro. These books read like adventure stories as we follow the clues from this creation that we live in out to the Council of Creators and beyond.

❶ THE EXPLORER RACE
You are truly a result of the genetic experiment on Earth. You are beings who uphold the principles of the Explorer Race. The key to empowerment in these days is not to know everything about your past but to know what will help you now. You are constantly being given responsibilities by the Creator that would normally be things that Creator would do. The responsibility and the destiny of the Explorer Race is not only to explore but to create.
ISBN 978-0-929385-38-9 • Softcover • 608 PP. • $25.00

❷ ETs and the EXPLORER RACE
In this book, Robert channels Joopah, a Zeta Reticulan now in the ninth dimension who continues the story of the great experiment — the Explorer Race — from the perspective of his civilization. The Zetas would have been humanity's future selves had humanity not re-created the past and changed the future.
ISBN 978-0-929385-79-2 • Softcover • 240 PP. • $14.95

❸ EXPLORER RACE: ORIGINS and the NEXT 50 YEARS
This volume has so much information about who we are and where we came from — the source of male and female beings, the war of the sexes, the beginning of the linear mind, feelings, the origin of souls — it is a treasure trove. In addition, there is a section that relates to our near future — how the rise of global corporations and politics affects our future, how to use benevolent magic as a force of creation, and how we will go out to the stars and affect other civilizations. It is full of astounding information.
ISBN 978-0-929385-95-2 • Softcover • 384 PP. • $14.95

❹ EXPLORER RACE: CREATORS and FRIENDS, the MECHANICS of CREATION
Now that you have a greater understanding of who you are in the larger sense, it is necessary to remind you of where you came from, the true magnificence of your being. You must understand that you are creators in training, and you were once a portion of Creator. This book will allow you to understand the vaster qualities and help you remember the nature of the desires that drive any creator, the responsibilities to which a creator must answer, the reaction a creator must have to consequences, and the ultimate reward for any creator. ISBN 978-1-891824-01-2 • Softcover • 480 PP. • $19.95

❺ EXPLORER RACE: PARTICLE PERSONALITIES
All around you in every moment, you are surrounded by the most magical and mystical beings. They are too small for you to see individually, but in groups, you know them as the physical matter of your daily life. These particles might be considered either atoms or portions of atoms who consciously view the vast spectrum of reality yet also have a sense of personal memory like your own linear memory. Some of the particles we hear from are Gold, Mountain Lion, Liquid Light, Uranium, the Great Pyramid's Capstone, This Orb's Boundary, Ice, and Ninth-Dimensional Fire.
ISBN 978-0-929385-97-6 • Softcover • 256 PP. • $14.95

❻ EXPLORER RACE and BEYOND
With a better idea of how creation works, we go back to the Creator's advisors and receive deeper and more profound explanations of the roots of the Explorer Race. The Liquid Domain and the Double Diamond Portal share lessons given to the roots on their way to meet the Creator of this universe, and the roots speak of their origins and their incomprehensibly long journey here.
ISBN 978-1-891824-06-7 • Softcover • 384 PP. • $14.95

$\mathscr{Y}$ Light Technology PUBLISHING Presents

THE EXPLORER RACE SERIES

ZOOSH AND HIS FRIENDS THROUGH ROBERT SHAPIRO

⑦ EXPLORER RACE: COUNCIL of CREATORS

The thirteen core members of the Council of Creators discuss their adventures in coming to awareness of themselves and their journeys on the way to the council on this level. They discuss the advice and oversight they offer to all creators, including the Creator of this local universe. These beings are wise, witty, and joyous, and their stories of love's creation create an expansion of our concepts as we realize that we live in an expanded, multiple-level reality.
ISBN 978-1-891824-13-5 • Softcover • 288 PP. • $14.95

⑧ EXPLORER RACE and ISIS

This is an amazing book! It has priestess training, shamanic training, Isis's adventures with Explorer Race beings — before Earth and on Earth — and an incredibly expanded explanation of the dynamics of the Explorer Race. Isis is the prototypal loving, nurturing, guiding feminine being, the focus of feminine energy. She has the ability to expand limited thinking without making people with limited beliefs feel uncomfortable. She is a fantastic storyteller, and all of her stories are teaching stories. If you care about who you are, why you are here, where you are going, and what life is all about, pick up this book. You won't put it down until you are through, and then you will want more.
ISBN 978-1-891824-11-1 • Softcover • 352 PP. • $14.95

⑨ EXPLORER RACE and JESUS

The core personality of that being known on Earth as Jesus, along with his students and friends, describes with clarity and love his life and teaching 2,000 years ago. He states that his teaching is for all people of all races in all countries. Jesus announces here for the first time that he and two others, Buddha and Mohammed, will return to Earth from their place of being in the near future, and a fourth being, a child already born now on Earth, will become a teacher and prepare humanity for their return. This text is so heartwarming and interesting, you won't want to put it down.
ISBN 978-1-891824-14-2 • Softcover • 352 PP. • $16.95

⑩ EXPLORER RACE: EARTH HISTORY and LOST CIVILIZATIONS

Speaks of Many Truths and Zoosh, through Robert Shapiro, explain that planet Earth, the only water planet in this solar system, is on loan from Sirius as a home and school for humanity, the Explorer Race. Earth's recorded history goes back only a few thousand years, its archaeological history a few thousand more. This book opens up as if a light is on in the darkness, and we see the incredible panorama of brave souls coming from other planets to settle on different parts of Earth. We watch the origins of tribal groups and the rise and fall of civilizations, and we can begin to understand the source of the wondrous diversity of plants, animals, and humans that we enjoy here on beautiful Mother Earth.
ISBN 978-1-891824-20-3 • Softcover • 320 PP. • $14.95

⑪ EXPLORER RACE: ET VISITORS SPEAK

Even as you are searching the sky for extraterrestrials and their spaceships, ETs are here on planet Earth — they are stranded, visiting, exploring, studying the culture, healing Earth of trauma brought on by irresponsible mining, or researching the history of Christianity over the past 2,000 years. Some are in human guise, and some are in spirit form. Some look like what we call animals as they come from the species' home planet and interact with their fellow beings — those beings who we have labeled cats or cows or elephants. Some are brilliant cosmic mathematicians with a sense of humor who are presently living here as penguins. Some are fledgling diplomats training for future postings on Earth when we have ET embassies here. In this book, these fascinating beings share their thoughts, origins, and purposes for being here.
ISBN 978-1-891824-28-9 • Softcover • 352 PP. • $14.95

⑫ EXPLORER RACE: TECHNIQUES for GENERATING SAFETY

Wouldn't you like to generate safety so you could go wherever you need to go and do whatever you need to do in a benevolent, safe, and loving way for yourself? Learn safety as a radiated environment that will allow you to gently take the step into the new timeline, into a benevolent future, and away from a negative past.
ISBN 978-1-891824-26-5 • Softcover • 208 PP. • $9.95